D1279977

INSTRUCTIONAL PRODUCT RESEARCH

INSTRUCTIONAL PRODUCT RESEARCH

ROBERT L. BAKER
RICHARD E. SCHUTZ
editors

Southwest Regional Laboratory
for Educational Research
and Development

American Book Company
Van Nostrand Company
NewYork Cincinnati Toronto London Melbourne

American Book Company Regional Offices:
New York Cincinnati Atlanta Dallas Millbrae

D. Van Nostrand Company Regional Offices:
New York Cincinnati Millbrae

D. Van Nostrand Company International Offices:
London Toronto Melbourne

Library of Congress Catalog Card Number 70-160066

ISBN : 0-442-27862-4

The Southwest Regional Laboratory for Educational Research and Development is a public agency supported as a regional educational laboratory by funds from the United States Office of Education, Department of Health, Education, and Welfare. The opinions expressed in this publication do not necessarily reflect the position or policy of the Office of Education, and no official endorsement by the Office of Education should be inferred.

Designed by Gerald Levine

Printed in the United States of America. Published simultaneously in Canada by Van Nostrand Reinhold Ltd.

15   14   13   12   11   10   9   8   7   6   5   4   3   2

PREFACE

The materials contained in this book are intended for the novice in educational research and development. However, because the boundaries between master and novice in this rapidly growing field are often blurred, some elaboration of what the reader legitimately may and may not expect to derive from the materials is in order.

The seven instructional sequences unashamedly represent a simplification of the scholarship and research of the disciplines from which they were derived. The reader should not expect to acquire through the sequences the expertise of a highly qualified specialist in the behavioral sciences, information sciences, or analytic sciences. Moreover, he should still expect to be "put down" regularly for lack of sophistication by persons from these fields who take pleasure in such acts. But, assuming the reader can find a way to handle the interpersonal professional relationships involved, he will find that he can coexist cooperatively and often interchangeably with the discipline specialists and scholars. If the reader seeks a *user* rather than a *contributor* role with respect to the disciplines from which the sequences were derived, he will find these materials consonant with his intent.

In the language of the classroom, the sequences are "practical," not "theoretical." However, they do not have the practicality of a cookbook: the matters treated are simply too complex to be reduced to a set of operations expressed in common conversational terminology. The reader can thus expect to acquire proficiency with respect to *how* and *when* aspects of the sequences, but *what*, *where*, and *who* aspects are left to his own invention.

The sequences are directed to aspiring activists rather than kibitzers in research and development. Observable translation of proficiency into performance, however, lies, in the final analysis, above and beyond the scope of these materials. Previous use of the sequences has demonstrated satisfactorily that serious readers reliably acquire proficiency with respect to the instructional outcomes specified. However, we have found that what an individual does with his proficiency is a function of subsequent situational complexities which transcend the present materials.

All the instructional sequences reflect a common goal: to provide one alternative means for acquiring specified proficiency without encountering unforeseen gaps which circumvent attainment or irrelevancies which encumber progress. The materials reflect research and development which followed from this general proposition, but they should be viewed as dependable, not definitive. The research and development which resulted in their production will in the future render them obsolete. By that time, however, the novices of today can certainly be more proficient than they now are; with some luck and hard work they can be more proficient than the experts of today. These materials do not aspire single-handedly to effect this enhanced proficiency. They do aspire to provide dependable assistance to persons interested in effecting it.

R.L.B.
R.E.S.

ACKNOWLEDGMENTS

Special acknowledgment is extended to the following individuals who contributed generously of their time and talent in serving as consulting reviewers to the authors during final preparation of the instructional sequences in this volume:

Fred C. Niedermeyer   *Classifying and Interpreting Educational Research Studies*

Roger O. Scott   *Selecting Variables for Educational Research*

John F. McManus   *Choosing An Appropriate Statistical Procedure*

Gordon L. Gibbs   *The Use of Library Computer Programs for Statistical Analysis*

and
Victor Berzins, editorial review of all sequences

CONTENTS

THE USE OF LIBRARY COMPUTER PROGRAMS FOR STATISTICAL ANALYSES   193
Richard M. Wolf

Paul E. Resta

How to use this book

Despite its appearance this is not a conventional textbook. Field tryouts of the seven instructional sequences contained here suggest that its reader will adopt dramatically new reading and study approaches and that he will achieve a significantly higher operational understanding of the material than is likely with conventional texts.

All sequences allow you to monitor your own acquisition rate. Each contains expository material that will direct your effort, plus a series of exercises designed to assess your proficiency in various aspects of the objective being considered. Every effort has been made in these exercises to minimize "busy work," irrelevancies, and unnecessary mechanical aspects, and at the same time to ensure the relevance of the exercises to the natural instructional situation.

For best results, we therefore recommend the following procedures:

1. Read slowly.

2. Complete each en-route exercise with a minimum of looking back at the expository material or ahead at the answers.

3. Review all of your answers by pairing the answers given with the original questions.

4. Note any error you have made, as well as any questions or disagreements you may have with the answers provided.

5. Review the exposition preceding the exercise for clarification of either your error or specific disagreements you have with the interpretation presented.

6. Move into the next expository section and start the cycle again.

Such a procedure will require a slower pace than reading the same number of pages in a conventional textbook. For your information, the average time spent on each sequence during the tryouts ranged from one to three and one-half hours, depending upon the length of the sequence and the degree of the reader's previous familiarity with the concepts.

The field tryouts suggested a "best order" for working through the sequences; their order of presentation in this book is the most popular and the most frequently productive.

Depending upon your own requirements and background, however, the sequences can also be viewed as constituting three clusters, as follows:

I. Problem Formulation
1. *Classifying and Interpreting Educational Research Studies*
2. *Selecting Variables for Educational Research*

II. Planning and Reporting
3. *Components of the Educational Research Proposal*
4. *The Research Report*

III. Design and Data Analysis
5. *Simplified Designs for School Research*
6. *Choosing an Appropriate Statistical Procedure*
7. *The Use of Library Computer Programs for Statistical Analysis*

It is possible to start with any of the three clusters, but, by and large, you should have a high degree of familiarity with all concepts represented in every instructional sequence listed prior to your particular point of entry.

No matter what strategy you choose, the "Overview of Instructional Product Research" (pages xix-xxviii) is an effective place to begin — and to return to from time to time as you proceed through the instructional sequences. Its purpose is to help you understand the development framework in which directed research activities take place. Because the sequence topics, skills, and some operations are in themselves conventional, it *is* important that you be able to place them in their appropriate contexts as parts of a programmatic set of planned and sequenced activities yielding useful research on instructional products.

INSTRUCTIONAL PRODUCT RESEARCH

AN OVERVIEW OF INSTRUCTIONAL PRODUCT RESEARCH

All research endeavors, like all men, share certain characteristics and differ in others. The seven instructional sequences in this book, reflecting this concept, present key tools that researchers have found indispensable in the context of instructional product development. However, many a researcher will find some of the tools applicable to inquiry concerned with phenomena other than instructional products. Others will discover that they need additional tools beyond those presented here to effectively pursue inquiry into instructional product development. Such is the nature of research and its tools.

The utility of the seven instructional sequences lies, ultimately, in their application to all appropriate contexts. However, all the sequences were specifically generated out of and designed to forward instructional product research. This *Overview* describes, therefore, the conceptual framework for instructional product research from which the sequences were derived. As with most research reports, the framework is a "cleaned up" version, our initial framework having grown more differentiated and comprehensive as a result of our experience. Such is the nature of research and the application of its tools.

ANTECEDENTS OF INSTRUCTIONAL PRODUCT RESEARCH

While "instructional research" has a long history, "instructional product research" has only recently been recognized as a legitimate arena for disciplined inquiry. Instructional "products" are viewed here not as persons but as organized materials and procedures that can be used to reliably accomplish prespecified outcomes.

Interest in instructional products arose concurrently with a recognition that prevailing paradigms for educational improvement couched in terms of antecedent variables and consequent variables were simplistic. Educational researchers had traditionally viewed defined pupil performance (consequent variable) as a direct function of defined instruction (antecedent variable). And educational practice was similarly viewed — as directly influenced by research.

Though neat and tidy, these relationships proved spuriously simple. Despite fifty years of educational research, it was still impossible to identify any reliable relationships between pupil performance and conditions of instruction or to show any observable improvement in educational practice based upon research. This is not to say that pupil performance is immune to conditions of instruction or that educational practice is impervious to change. Neither is it to apologize for this state of affairs. Just as humanity has yet to learn how to cure all diseases or provide optimal transportation systems or accomplish many other humanitarian aims, so it has yet to arrive at totally adequate means of education. It does suggest, however, that further pursuit of earlier conceptual paradigms appears unnecessary. It suggests that our simplistic paradigms must be complexified before our operational practice can be simplified. And it suggests that our concern with research must be accompanied by a concern with development in education. Our valuation of science and its "why" utility must be accompanied today by construction of a technology in education that contains "how" utility as well.

Let us summarize the current dilemma of educational researchers before considering reasonable means for resolving it.

- Public support for research is directly proprotionate to the "improvements" that research can be said to generate.
- Improvements are outcomes of a development enterprise based on defined sets of procedures (technology).
- Both basic and directed (mission-oriented) research are required for adequate development of an educational technology.
- Educational researchers have historically resisted the personal constraints imposed by a mission orientation or by a requirement to lay their empirical foundation in the natural setting.
- Without a commitment to the development enterprise and to the building of supporting technologies, research findings have limited social utility outside the academic environment.
- With no visible effects stemming from research efforts, the public will cease to support that dimension of the academic and research environment.
- Yet, those educational researchers who most need viable, tested technologies for their professional survival are often the very people who ask, "Who needs them?"

RESEARCH, DEVELOPMENT, AND PRACTICE

The differential characteristics of research, development, and practice can be clarified as follows:

	Enterprise	Knowledge Base	Outcome Sought
1.	Research	Science	Literature
2.	Development	Technology	Products
3.	Practice	Lore	Service

The first and third lines are familiar in education. The second is sufficiently new to warrant elaboration, particularly in the present book which addresses itself to a new view of instructional product research. Technology should not be equated with practice nor should it be equated with science. Whereas *science* can be regarded as the search for more or less abstract knowledge, *technology* has been defined as the application of organized knowledge to help solve problems in our society (Wiesner, 1966). Nelson, Peck, and Kalachek (1967) have defined technology consistent with the above usage: "Technological knowledge is a set of techniques, each defined as a set of actions and decision rules guiding their sequential application, that man has learned which will

INSTRUCTIONAL PRODUCT RESEARCH

generally lead to a predictable and sometimes desirable outcome under certain specified circumstances." All activity resulting from the application of such decision rules constitutes *development* — constitutes the "systematic use of scientific knowledge directed toward the production of useful materials, devices, systems, or methods, including design and development of prototype and processes" (National Science Foundation, 1965). It is clear that we should not automatically expect the research enterprise to yield products; nor should we' fall prey to the notion that "it is just a simple translation of the literature to create a product." But neither can we accept a mere change in rhetoric and continued parallel-play by enterprisers. Products are truly the "useful" outcomes which result from the development effort.

What are the alternatives? Several possibilities have been suggested (Schutz, 1968). We might adopt the "stop the music" approach; we might conclude that the analytical-empiricist approach labeled "research" is worthless, in which case we would probably adopt what might be called a comprehensive existentialist position — "anything I don't agree with is bad." Amazingly, sectors of the educational community seem to be gravitating to this position: a position which, while it may be unassailable logically, is completely vulnerable practically. In other areas, scientific advances have rapidly bypassed holders of such views.

At the other extreme, one might adopt a "turn up the volume" position: "Research is fine; the problem is that it is simply not readily accessible." Effective use of modern communication technology will serve to increase the volume to an adequate level, but, as usual in education, we are using a powerful medium to transmit a weak message. It is doubtful that "fugitive literature" can do much to effect educational improvement. In fact, it is not the literature, but rather the means for translating research into a practically usable form that is fugitive. And this is a development function, not a communication function.

We should like to endorse a third alternative: a "change the tune" position in which we shift from viewing research as a means of generating abstract interrelationships termed theories to viewing research as a means of reducing uncertainty about natural phenomena. The two tunes utilize the same instruments and may be considered flip sides of the same record, but the "uncertainty reduction" tune is still foreign to the majority of pedagogical and research and development communities in education.

RESEARCH AND DEVELOPMENT AS UNCERTAINTY REDUCTION

R&D activities can be viewed as being directed toward obtaining new knowledge which, when combined with existing knowledge, will permit the creation of new and useful instructional products. Thus, research and development can be seen as a process of reducing uncertainty regarding the nature of new products and the efforts required to achieve prespecified outcomes; development proceeds by allocating and reallocating efforts among different uncertainty-reducing possibilities while activities are completed and knowledge accumulates.

Though development is ultimately concerned with production, it cannot be equated with production: production is the result of development; it is not synonymous with it. Production which takes advantage of "the present state-of-the-art" is always possible. Educational publishers, for example, have been and are now producing educational products. As noted in Figure 1 (Figures 1, 2 and 3 adapted from Glennan, 1967), the user is necessarily interested in "what comes off the production line," but in his interest he ignores prior research and development efforts which made the production feasible.

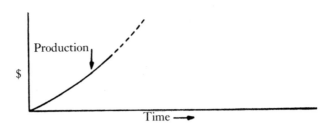

FIG. 1.   THE CONSUMER VIEW OF DEVELOPMENT

A development effort may be viewed as a combination of uncertainty-reducing, routine-engineering and production activities. The classical treatment of development as a linear sequence of research and development practice is reflected in Figure 2. Superficially, the classical view appears

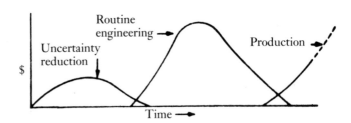

FIG. 2.   THE CLASSICAL VIEW OF DISTRIBUTION OF DEVELOPMENT EFFORTS

cautious and prudent. In actuality, however, it is risky and expensive in terms of both total cost and time generated in completing the linear sequence. This is not to say that development does not require time; even the most intelligent, well organized, and well motivated approach will not lead to instant solution of a significant problem, regardless of the extent of financial support available

INSTRUCTIONAL PRODUCT RESEARCH

or the degree of personal commitment on the part of those involved. As noted in Figure 3, a development effort that wishfully attempts to collapse uncertainty reduction, routine engineering, and production will inevitably be abortive.

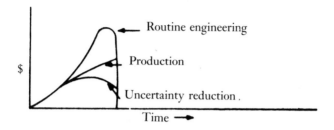

FIG. 3. UNREASONABLE OVERLAP OF EFFORTS AND DEVELOPMENT FAILURE

Figure 4 shows a reasonable overlap of development efforts calculated to produce a product as rapidly as possible with reasonable control of failure risk.

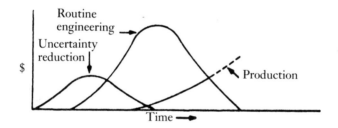

FIG. 4. REASONABLE OVERLAP OF EFFORTS

Adapted from T. K. Glennan, Jr. "Issues in the choice of development policies," in T. Marschak, T. K. Glennan, Jr., and R. Summers *Strategies for R & D*. New York: Springer-Verlag, 1967, Chapter 2.

To obtain a full perspective of the time and cost aspects of research and development in instructional improvement, the relationship depicted in Figure 4 should be viewed in the broader context of total time and total cost measured from initiation of a development effort to expiration of the product's usefulness.

This distribution of instructional improvement efforts is illustrated in Figure 5 (McCullough, 1966). By identifying the temporal relationships involved in development, installation, and use of a product, one can both describe the outcomes being produced at any given time and also obtain asymptotic cost curves.

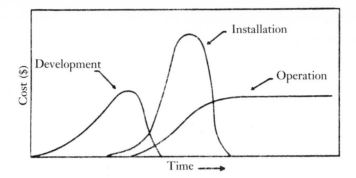

1. DEVELOPMENT: The production of research-based systems to accomplish specified instructional outcomes under natural conditions

2. INSTALLATION: The operational use of a program, without further direct assistance from the developer.

3. OPERATION: The continued use of a product to consistently obtain outcomes at or above a specified level of effectiveness

FIG. 5. MEASUREMENT OF TOTAL TIME AND TOTAL COST

Figure adapted from J. D. McCullough. *Cost Analysis for Planning—Programming—Budgeting Cost—Benefit Studies*. RAND Corporation Paper, P-3479, 1966, p. 18.

Properly conceived development efforts, with accompanying time-cost planning to ensure appropriate installation and operation of the resulting products, create a symbiotic relationship between those interested in improving and those responsible for operating schools. From this development perspective, present practices are inevitably seen as less than perfect. Similarly, from a practitioner's viewpoint, development efforts are seen as unworkable. But this is simply the recognition that development is not practice. It is unethical and unreasonable to imply that an undeveloped system is immediately usable. It is also unethical and unreasonable to oppose development efforts simply because they cannot be performed instantaneously.

INSTRUCTIONAL PRODUCT RESEARCH

RESEARCH AND DEVELOPMENT STAGES

R&D activities are essentially a sequence of trial revision interactions, with modifications after each test to successively approximate the consequence being sought (Schutz, 1970). The cyclical nature of the process within each stage of development may be diagrammed as in Figure 6.

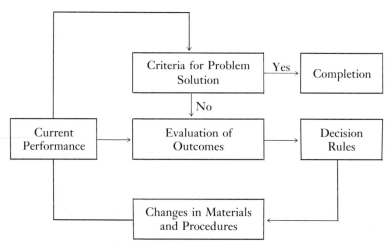

FIG. 6.   RESEARCH AND DEVELOPMENT STAGES

The overall development process at SWRL has included those stages and activities shown in Table 1. The stages of instructional product development charted there are consistent with but extensions of those reported in *Rules for the Development of Instructional Products* (Popham and Baker, 1971). The column labeled "Uncertainty Focus" generally defines or bounds the research objectives for each stage of product development. This serves to guard against confoundment of research questions at each successive stage and provides the basis for systematic application of a self-corrective mechanism.

Using SWRL's beginning reading program as the base, we can cite examples of the kinds of studies conducted to reduce specified uncertainty at each stage of product development (these are only examples, not a total blueprint of activity):

Formulation

- UNCERTAINTY FOCUS: Specification parameters
- PURPOSE: To improve letter string discrimination and to assess the effects of contextual cues on sight word learning and retention in beginning readers

TABLE 1
INSTRUCTIONAL PRODUCT DEVELOPMENT STAGES

Stage	Activity	Uncertainty Focus	Typical Duration of Tryout
Formulation	Specifying the desired instructional outcomes, identifying the skills required to achieve the outcomes, and designing strategies for teaching the skills	Specification parameters	One to several experimental sessions
Prototype	Testing instructional strategies by empirically investigating variations of materials and methods and by assessing the impact of each variation	Product specifications	One day to a few weeks
Component	Producing a segment of instruction and trying it out with a single learner or groups of learners in a natural setting to determine whether the instruction accomplishes its objectives	Instruction parameters	One week to a few months
Product	Successively trying out and revising a combination of components in a natural setting until acceptable levels of performance have been attained	Instructional effectiveness	One to several "semester" units
Installation	Integrating a product into programs combined with existing school instruction in order to determine procedures for operational use of a program without direct assistance of the developing agency	User training and program management	One to several "semester" units
Manufacturing	Involving the agency which will assume direct editorial and production responsibility for a commercially manufactured program	Program integrity and list cost	One editorial cycle
Marketing	Integrating a program into a licensee's extant portfolio and involving its sales force in the operational use of the training systems without direct assistance of the developing agency	Communication and distribution	One to several years

- REPORTING DOCUMENTS:
    "Transfer of Mixed Word Identification Training to a Reading Context"
    "Preschool Children's Recognition of Phonemes in a Word Context"
    "Kindergarten Children's Discrimination and Production of Phonemes in Isolation and in Words"

Prototype

- UNCERTAINTY FOCUS: Product specifications
- PURPOSE: To identify criterion exercise testing procedures and mechanical requirements which would be most effective for use with kindergarten pupils
- REPORTING DOCUMENT:
    "Specifications of Teacher-Administered Tests for the SWRL Beginning Reading Program"

Component

- UNCERTAINTY FOCUS: Instruction parameters
- PURPOSE: To test the differential effectiveness of two word-attack instructional procedures for use in the beginning reading program
- REPORTING DOCUMENT:
    "Learning and Transfer Effects of Systematic Variations in Word-Decoding Instruction"

Product

- UNCERTAINTY FOCUS: Instructional effectiveness
- PURPOSE: To determine the effectiveness of the First-Year Communication Skills Program in attaining prespecified instructional outcomes
- REPORTING DOCUMENT:
    "Evaluation of the First-Year Communications Skills Program: A Report of the 1970-1971 Year-Long Tryout"

Installation

- UNCERTAINTY FOCUS: User training and program management
- PURPOSE: To test the effectiveness of teacher training procedures for the instructional support systems and to monitor classroom activities relevant to the maintenance of reading skills acquired
- REPORTING DOCUMENTS:
    "Relevance of Teacher Management of Pacing Requirements to Maintenance of Reading Skills through the Summer"
    "Parent Evaluation Summary: Summer Reading Program"
    "Tryout of Trainer and Parent Training Components of the Parent-Assisted Learning Program"

Manufacturing

- UNCERTAINTY FOCUS: Program integrity and list cost
- PURPOSE: To evaluate the differential ability of commercial publishers to successfully produce the *Kindergarten Program*
- REPORTING DOCUMENT:
  "Analysis of Publisher Proposals for Format Design and Mechanical Requirements of the *Kindergarten Program* as Reflected Against Pricing and Instructional Requirements"

Marketing

- UNCERTAINTY FOCUS: Communication and distribution
- PURPOSE: To assess extant marketing and distribution capabilities of prequalified publishers as they relate to the unique requirements of the *Kindergarten Program*
- REPORTING DOCUMENT:
  "Evaluation of Publishers' Promotion, Sales, and Service Plans and Capabilities to Maximally Saturate Educational Markets"

While the foci of uncertainty reduction are on aspects of educational systems clarification at several stages (Baker and Schutz, 1971), the ultimate utility of such activities rests with the researcher's ability to develop increasingly more effective educational products reflective of state-of-the-art programmatic R&D outcomes. At present, a product is not licensed for commercial distribution until the "marketing" stage of development has been completed for all of the applicable component systems. For example, the commercial edition of SWRL's *Kindergarten Program* includes all materials and procedures for (1) two instructional systems, the Instructional Concepts and the Beginning Reading programs; (2) three instructional support systems, the Tutorial, Parent-Assisted Learning, and Summer Reading programs; (3) accompanying formal teacher training programs; (4) written installation procedures; and (5) quality-assurance materials and procedures. These reflect the Laboratory's best efforts to utilize current state-of-the-art educational development technology and to meet the program systems' requirements described by Baker and Schutz (1971, pp. xvi-xxii).

Continuous directed research in a programmatic educational R&D effort helps to ensure that the next product generation is reflective of what is not presently within the state-of-the-art. Instructional product research thus converts an illusive vision of the future into matter-of-fact form. In addition to contributing to the effectiveness of "in-use" instructional products, such planned and sequenced research also builds an increasingly sophisticated scientific and technological base upon which to conduct future inquiry into products for instruction.

—Robert L. Baker and Richard E. Schutz

CLASSIFYING AND INTERPRETING EDUCATIONAL RESEARCH STUDIES

Howard J. Sullivan

CONTENTS

Carefully planned educational research studies are a vital source for identifying methods of improving school programs. Yet research is often conducted in such a way that its potential contribution is minimized. Frequently, better initial planning of a study can markedly increase the amount of useful information that it will yield.

Research studies can be classified into common types, each of which has its own distinguishing characteristics. The type of study determines its potential contribution in helping researchers and educators identify better educational programs. The researcher who wishes to derive a certain kind of information from a study must be careful to plan the type of study that will, in fact, yield that kind of information. Thus, skill in classifying studies and in interpreting their results is essential to planning the most useful types of educational experiments.

This sequence deals with skills essential to proper planning and interpretation of educational research studies. Upon completing this sequence, the learner should be able to perform the following tasks when given brief descriptions of educational research studies:

1. To identify the types of variables in the study

2. To name the type of study

3. To identify permissible statements of conclusion that may be derived from the study

No attempt is made in the sequence to describe refinements that may reduce threats to the validity of various research findings, although this is indeed another important issue.

Classifying Variables

Research studies are classified into types on the basis of the variables being studied. To classify research studies he encounters, an individual must therefore be able to identify different kinds of variables. A variable is any factor having two or more distinguishably different properties or values. For example, sex is a variable because it has two properties, maleness and femaleness, that are distinguishably different. Reading achievement, as indicated by test scores, is also a variable because the various test scores obtained by students are distinguishably different from one another; that is, a score of 18 is distinguishable from a score of 19 or 20.

EXERCISE 1
IDENTIFYING VARIABLES

Place a check beside the number of each factor which is a variable.

1. ____ Age of students

2. ____ Class size

3. ____ Amount of assigned homework

All three may have a number of different properties. Thus all three are variables. Remember that a variable is any factor having two or more distinguishably different properties or values. Age of students is a variable because any group of students may contain students of different ages; class size is a variable because the size of different classes varies; and amount of assigned homework is a variable because different amounts of homework may be assigned to various students or classes.

CRITERION VARIABLES

The researcher in an educational research study is typically concerned with the relationship between an instructional treatment or learner characteristic and a criterion variable. The criterion variable represents a desired instructional outcome or objective. For example, student achievement is often a criterion variable in educational research because it represents a highly desired instructional outcome. Similarly, college attendance has been employed as a criterion variable by researchers who have hoped to identify procedures for increasing student attendance at college.

CLASSIFYING CRITERION VARIABLES

Place a check beside the number of each item which would be a plausible criterion variable in an educational research study.

1. ____ Sex of student

2. ____ Dropout rate

3. ____ Student reading rate

4. ____ Student participation in extracurricular activities

The plausible criterion variables are 2, 3, and 4. Consider each item. Sex of student is a fixed characteristic of the individual, one whose attempted change would be totally unrealistic. Dropout rate has frequently served as a criterion variable in educational research studies, because a decrease in dropout rate is considered by many to be a desirable educational outcome. Reading rate is also a potential criterion variable because of the desirability of an increase in the reading speed of students. Student participation in extracurricular activities is another variable that has received the attention of many educators. Because an increase in student participation can be considered to be a desirable and attainable educational outcome, item 4 in the exercise is also a plausible criterion variable.

Normally, the criterion variable is some aspect or product of learner behavior, such as achievement or dropout rate. Naturally, there may be more than one criterion variable in a single research study. Various teacher or parent behaviors may also serve as criteria in a study in which a specified student behavior is the criterion variable of utmost concern.

VARIATES

A second important type of variable in an educational research study may be called, simply, the "variate." The variate is the characteristic or student experience whose relationship to the criterion variable is being studied. As an example, consider a study of the relationship between sex and reading achievement. Reading achievement is the criterion variable because it represents the desired outcome. Sex, on the other hand, is the variate because it is the characteristic whose relationship to the criterion is being studied. Similarly, in a study of the relationship between type of classroom organization and student achievement, type of classroom organization is the variate because its relationship to the criterion variable (student achievement) is being investigated.

Classification of any variable as either a variate or a criterion variable is always determined by its use in the research study at hand, rather than by the nature of the variable itself. Whereas student achievement is the criterion variable in the study cited immediately above, under certain conditions it could be the variate. This would be the case, for example, in a study of the relationship between student achievement in high school and graduation from college. Remember that the criterion variable indicates the desired educational outcome. The variate is the characteristic or student experience whose relationship to the criterion variable is being studied.

CLASSIFYING VARIATES AND CRITERION VARIABLES

Write "V" beside each *variate* and "C" beside each *criterion variable.*

Is

1. ____ inquiry training
related to
2. ____ measured problem-solving ability?

How is

3. ____ Grade 1 absence rate
affected by
4. ____ Head-Start training?

What is the relationship between

5. ____ student grades
6. ____ and car ownership?

The variates are items 1, 4, and 6. These are the student experiences or characteristics whose relationship to the criterion variable is being investigated. The criterion variables are 2, 3 and 5. These represent the desired educational outcomes or objectives.

CLASSIFYING VARIATES AND CRITERION VARIABLES

Write "V" beside each *variate* and "C" beside each *criterion variable* in the spaces provided.

How does

1. ____ type of mathematics curriculum
affect
2. ____ mathematics achievement?

Is there a relationship between

3. ____ length of school year
4. ____ and pupil absence rate?

Is

5. ____ student attitude toward school
related to
6. ____ amount of assigned homework?

The variates are 1, 3, and 6; the criterion variables are 2, 4, and 5.

MANIPULABLE VARIATES

The examples of variates above have included two types. It is important to discriminate between types of variates because the variate in a study determines both the type of research study and the kind of information the study will yield.

One type of variate consists of those factors related to the student and his education which can be changed or controlled by the investigator through administrative fiat. Examples of this group of variates would include the type of instructional materials used by students, the type of classroom organization in a school or school district, and such instructional practices as use of grades and assignment of homework. Variates such as these are said to be manipulable. A manipulable variate is any variable having different properties or values to which subjects of research studies can be randomly assigned. Consider type of classroom organization again. It is an example of a manipulable variate because an experimenter can randomly assign subjects to different properties of this variable, such as non-graded classes and graded classes.

NON-MANIPULABLE VARIATES

A non-manipulable variate, on the other hand, is a variable having properties or values to which subjects cannot be randomly assigned. Socioeconomic status is an example of a non-manipulable variate because the experimenter cannot randomly assign subjects to different levels of socioeconomic status. That is, the experimenter cannot randomly assign one subject to low socioeconomic status (SES), a second subject to middle SES, and a third to high SES. The experimenter cannot control a non-manipulable variate sufficiently to assign subjects to different properties or values of the variate.

EXERCISE 5
IDENTIFYING MANIPULABLE AND NON-MANIPULABLE VARIATES

Write "M" beside each *manipulable* variate and "N" beside each *non-manipulable* variate.

1. _____ Type of reading program

2. _____ IQ

3. _____ Car ownership

4. _____ Number of school-counseling sessions

5. _____ Use of educational film

Items 1, 4, and 5 are manipulable. That is, the experimenter can control these variates to the extent that he can assign subjects at random to different types of reading programs, a different number of counseling sessions, and educational films. Items 2 and 3, IQ and car ownership, are non-manipulable. While IQ scores may be altered over a prolonged period or through a concentrated training program, it is not possible for the experimenter to control IQ to the extent that he can simply assign different individuals to various levels of IQ. Neither, of course, can an experimenter assign some individuals to car ownership while withholding the same variate from others.

IDENTIFYING MANIPULABLE AND
NON-MANIPULABLE VARIATES

Write "M" *(manipulable)* or "N" *(non-manipulable)* for each of the following variates, so that each variate is judged to be manipulable or non-manipulable on the basis of whether students can be randomly assigned to groups having different properties of the variate.

1. _____ amount of parental income

2. _____ age of student

3. _____ amount of oral reading practice in class

4. _____ age of teacher

5. _____ frequency of scheduled classroom discussions

Amount of parental income and age of student, items 1 and 2, are clearly non-manipulable. Items 3, 4, and 5 *are* manipulable. To be sure, the experimenter cannot manipulate the age of a given teacher, but recall that students, not teachers, are the subjects. The experimenter can randomly assign students to teachers of different age levels by assigning, say, Student A to 20- to 29-year-old teachers, Student B to 30- to 39-year-old teachers, and so forth. Therefore, age of teacher is a manipulable variate in this case. If teachers were the subjects in the experiment, however, teacher age would be non-manipulable.

Three Classes of Research Studies

Research studies can be identified as belonging to one of three classes based upon the nature of the variate in each study. Therefore, one must be able to distinguish between manipulable and non-manipulable variates in order to classify research studies correctly. In turn, the type of study determines the kind of information that can be derived from it. The three types of research studies to be described here are *status*, *associational*, and *experimental* studies.

STATUS STUDIES

One type of study common to educational research is the status study. *A status study is any study in which the variate is non-manipulable.* Consider research designed to investigate the following question: Is there a relationship between socioeconomic status and student grades in high school? Socioeconomic status, the variate in the study, is non-manipulable, making this a status study.

EXERCISE 7

IDENTIFYING STATUS STUDIES

Place a check beside the number of each item which indicates a status study.

1. ____ Is car ownership related to high school grades?

2. ____ What is the relationship between the amount of physical education required in high school and senior year performance in the AAHPER Physical Fitness Tests?

3. ____ Does the number of book reports assigned in English I and II affect student attitudes toward reading?

4. ____ Is college attendance related to parental educational level?

Items 1 and 4 are status studies. Item 1 is a status study because the variate, car ownership, is non-manipulable. Items 2 and 3 have manipulable variates, amount of required physical education and number of assigned book reports, so 2 and 3 are not status studies. Parental education level is a non-manipulable variate, so item 4 is a status study.

ASSOCIATIONAL STUDIES

Associational studies constitute a second type of educational research study. Associational studies differ from status studies in that the variate in an associational study is manipulable, although it is not actually manipulated in the study. That is, the experimenter can randomly assign subjects to different properties or values of the variate, but he does not do so in the study. *An associational study is, therefore, a study in which the variate is manipulable, but is not manipulated.* The variate could potentially be manipulated, but for some reason it is not.

The procedure in associational studies frequently involves the comparison of two or more groups of individuals who already possess different properties of a manipulable variate. For example, a study of the relationship between type of classroom organization in high school and standardized achievement test performance could be conducted by selecting a sample of graduating high school seniors who had been in ability-grouped classes throughout high school and a second sample from non-ability-grouped classes. No matter what procedure the experimenter used to select his sample from among each of the two groups, the fact remains that he chose subjects who already differed on the classroom-organization dimension. This is not the same as randomly assigning subjects to ability-grouped and homogeneous classrooms prior to high school. Type of classroom organization is a manipulable variate, but it was not manipulated by the experimenter. Therefore, the study is an associational study.

The variate in the study described above was, in fact, no longer manipulable for the subjects being studied, since they had already completed high school. Nevertheless, the variate must be classified as manipulable, strictly on the basis of its potential manipulability for future groups of subjects, irrespective of its manipulability for the current sample.

When the variate in a study is potentially manipulable, the procedures employed in the study determine whether the variate was actually manipulated. The variate is not manipulated if subjects are selected because they possess different properties of it prior to the study, or if two or more properties of the variate are made available to them on a voluntary basis rather than by random assignment. An example of the latter situation would be the comparison on some criterion of, say, Head Start children and non-Head Start children from deprived backgrounds, when enrollment in the Head Start program had been voluntary for the children from both groups.

EXERCISE 8

CLASSIFYING TYPES OF STUDIES

Write "S" if the following is a *status study*, "A" if it is an *associational study*, and "N" if it is *neither*.

RESEARCH QUESTION: Is amount of classroom discussion related to student achievement?

PROCEDURES: Several sixth-grade classes in a school district are observed during the school year and then divided into two groups based on the amount of discussion time daily. Fifty subjects (S's) are randomly selected from the classes that had more than thirty minutes' daily discussion. Their achievement gain during the year is compared to that of fifty randomly selected S's from classes that had less than thirty minutes' daily discussion.

_____ Type of study.

This describes an associational study. Amount of classroom discussion is a manipulable variate, but it was not manipulated in this instance. Instead, each of the two groups was formed by selecting only subjects who already possessed an amount of classroom discussion different from subjects in the group.

EXERCISE 9
CLASSIFYING TYPES OF STUDIES

Write "S" if this is a *status study*, "A" if it is an *associational study*, or "N" if it is *neither*.

RESEARCH QUESTION: Is student achievement in English affected by class size?

PROCEDURES: At the beginning of the school year, the students at Overbrook High School are randomly assigned to one of two types of English classes: classes with 18-22 students, or classes of 38-42 students. The two groups are compared at the end of the school year on several aspects of English achievement.

_____ Type of study.

This is neither a status nor an associational study. Subjects are randomly assigned to different levels of the variate (class size) prior to the start of the study. Therefore, the variate is manipulated, so the study cannot be either status or associational.

EXERCISE 10
CLASSIFYING TYPES OF STUDIES

Write "S," "A," or "N" to indicate the type of study this is.

RESEARCH QUESTION: Is there a relationship between IQ and performance on the Minnesota Creativity Tests?

PROCEDURES: Fourth- and fifth-grade students are divided into high IQ (100 and above) and low IQ groups (99 and below), based upon their IQ's at the beginning of the school year. The end-of-year creativity scores of the two groups are compared.

_____ Type of study.

The study described is a status study because the variate, IQ, is not manipulable.

EXERCISE 11
CLASSIFYING TYPES OF STUDIES

What type of study is this?

RESEARCH QUESTION: Is pupil absence rate related to age of teacher?

PROCEDURES: At the end of the 1970-71 school year, the absence rate for that year of all elementary pupils in the New York City District who had teachers under age 35 is compared with that of all pupils who had teachers aged 35 and older.

_____ Type of study.

Although age of teacher (the variate) is manipulable, it is not manipulated in the study. That is, students were not randomly assigned to teachers of each age group at the beginning of the year. Thus, this is an associational study.

EXPERIMENTAL STUDIES

By this time, you may have determined the defining characteristics of the third type of study, the experimental study. In an experimental study, subjects are randomly assigned to different properties or levels of the variate. *Thus, an experimental study is a study in which a manipulable variate is actually manipulated.*

Frequently, the terms "independent variable" and "dependent variable" are used rather loosely in educational research literature to refer to the variate and criterion variable in any type of research study. However, these two terms are used correctly to indicate the variate and criterion variable in *experimental studies only*. They should not be used in reference to nonexperimental studies. Variate and criterion variable are used in referring to nonexperimental studies, whereas independent variable and dependent variable are the preferred terms when referring to an experimental study.

The independent variable is so called because it is the variable that the experimenter manipulates *independently*. That is, he assigns subjects at random to different properties or values of the variable, and the subjects' possession of these properties or values is not dependent on other factors. The term "independent variable" is used properly only in reference to experimental studies because independent manipulation of a variable (the variate) occurs only in experimental studies.

The dependent variable is the variable that the experimenter examines to determine whether it is affected by manipulation of the independent variable. The experimenter attempts to determine whether or not the criterion variable is dependent upon a change in the independent variable.

An experimental study of the effect of class size on English achievement can serve to illustrate independent variables and dependent variables. Class size was manipulated by the experimenter and was the independent variable. The experimenter studied English achievement to determine if it was affected by manipulation of class size. The dependent variable, therefore, was English achievement.

EXERCISE 12

CLASSIFYING INDEPENDENT AND DEPENDENT VARIABLES

Write "IV" beside each *independent variable* and "DV" beside each *dependent variable*, assuming that each refers to an experimental study.

Is

1. ____ student achievement, as measured by test performance, related to
2. ____ amount of homework assigned by the teacher?

Is there a relationship between

3. ____ sex of teacher
4. ____ and attitude toward school as measured on an attitude scale?

Does

5. ____ type of student dormitory (coeducational or non-coeducational) affect
6. ____ college grades?

The independent variables are 2, 3, and 5, because they are the manipulated variates. The dependent variables, which may be affected by the manipulation of the independent variables, are 1, 4, and 6.

CLASSIFYING INDEPENDENT AND DEPENDENT VARIABLES

Write "IV" beside each *independent variable* and "DV" beside each *dependent variable*, assuming that each refers to an experimental study.

What is the relationship of

1. ____ student attitudes toward mathematics
to
2. ____ teacher knowledge of mathematics?

Is

3. ____ voluntary enrollment in a second-year foreign language course (French II, or Spanish II, for example) affected by
4. ____ instructional method in the first-year course?

Does

5. ____ frequency of verbal praise given by the teacher to students influence
6. ____ scores on course examinations?

The independent variables are 2, 4, and 5. The dependent variables are 1, 3, and 6.

Although independent variable and dependent variable are the preferred terms of experimental studies, variate and criterion variable are the terms used throughout this sequence in referring to research studies in general, since they are comprehensive terms that can legitimately be used in reference to all three types of studies.

Now that the three types of educational research studies have been described, review their distinguishing characteristics:

Type of Study	Distinguishing Characteristic
Status	Non-Manipulable Variate
Associational	Manipulable Variate That Is *Not* Manipulated
Experimental	Manipulable Variate That Is Manipulated

EXERCISE 14

CLASSIFYING TYPES OF STUDIES

Write "S" if this is a *status study*, "A" if it is an *associational study*, or an "E" if it is an *experimental study*.

RESEARCH QUESTION: Is achievement at the end of Grade 1 related to Head Start Training?

PROCEDURES: The initial population is all first-grade children in Mountain Vale Unified School District whose parents have an income of less than $3,000 annually. One hundred are randomly selected from among those who received Head Start Training before entering school, and 100 are randomly selected from among those who did not. The standardized achievement scores of the two groups at the end of Grade 1 are compared.

_____ Type of study.

This is an associational study because the two groups of children were selected after one group had been exposed to Head Start Training. Thus, although Head Start Training is potentially manipulable, it was not manipulated in the study.

EXERCISE 15

CLASSIFYING TYPES OF STUDIES

What type of study is this?

RESEARCH QUESTION: Does a five-minute orally-administered speed drill during arithmetic period affect arithmetic computation speed and accuracy?

PROCEDURES: The inclusion of a five-minute orally administered speed drill in each arithmetic lesson during the school year is assigned at random to one-half the teachers in Pottsdale Elementary District. A "no drill" condition is assigned to the remaining teachers. Pupils are randomly assigned to teachers at the beginning of the year and tests are administered to determine computation speed and accuracy at the end of the year. The "drill" and "no drill" groups are compared.

_____ Type of study.

The variate, the orally administered speed drill, was manipulated in the study. Consequently, the study is an experimental study.

EXERCISE 16

CLASSIFYING TYPES OF STUDIES

What type of study is this?

RESEARCH QUESTION: Is inquiry training related to student achievement in science?

PROCEDURES: Half the students in Oswego Junior High School are randomly assigned to a two-year Inquiry Training Program involving specified instructional procedures in science. The remaining students are assigned to an expository program involving a different set of specified procedures. Science achievement of the two groups is measured and compared at the end of the two-year program.

_____ Type of study.

This is an experimental study because the amount of inquiry training was manipulated.

EXERCISE 17

CLASSIFYING TYPES OF STUDIES

What type of study is this?

RESEARCH QUESTION: Is there a relationship between high school achievement and level of occupational aspiration (LOA)?

PROCEDURES: All entering freshmen at Guadalupe High School are administered a Vocational Guidance Inventory on which they indicate the adult occupation that they wish to enter. On the basis of their responses to the Inventory, the students are classified into a High LOA group and a Low LOA group, depending on whether or not they chose one of the professions. Fifty students are selected at random from each LOA group, and at the end of their senior years the cumulative high-school grade-point averages of the two groups are compared.

_____ Type of study.

This is a status study because occupational goal level, as assessed in this item, is non-manipulable.

This completes the section on classifying research studies. You should now be able to identify several classes of research variables and to classify examples of the three types of studies described. Your skill at classification will now assist you in interpreting the results of educational research studies.

Interpreting the Results of Educational Research Studies

Many studies reported in educational research journals contain statements of conclusion that are not warranted on the basis of the procedures employed. Conclusions that can be drawn from research vary with the types of studies conducted. Positive findings from non-experimental studies, for example, imply that a certain type of relationship exists between the variate and criterion, while positive findings from an experimental study indicate a different kind of relationship. Often, conclusions drawn from nonexperimental studies reported in the educational literature would justifiably be derived only from experimental studies. Such improper conclusions may mislead educators who base certain of their opinions and school practices on information presented in research-based articles.

DERIVING STATEMENTS OF RELATIONSHIPS BETWEEN VARIABLES

The skilled researcher plans studies that yield information of the greatest importance for educational practice, and he presents conclusions that are justified by the procedures and results of his study. To plan a study that will yield the type of information he is seeking, he must be able to determine in advance the kinds of inferences that can be derived from particular procedures and results. In conducting the study, he attempts to determine whether or not a certain relationship exists between the variables being investigated. How can this relationship be stated at the conclusion of the investigation?

There are two basic types of statements that can be made about the relationship between a variate and criterion variable (used comprehensively to refer to all three types of studies) when the results of a study indicate that a statistically significant relationship exists between these two variables. One such statement is called a statement of association. A statement of association indicates that a relationship exists between the variate and the criterion variable.

It is important to note that a statement of association does *not* indicate that a change in the variate (i.e., manipulation of the variate) will produce a change in the criterion variable. For example, consider these frequently used statements of association.

1. *There is a relationship* between the variate and the criterion variable.

2. The criterion variable *is related to* (or associated with) the variate.

3. A positive (or negative) *relationship exists* between the variate and criterion variable.

Note that each statement indicates only an association or relationship. It does not state that one condition causes the other or that a change in one variable will produce a change in the other. Such phrases as "is associated with," "is related to," and "there is a relationship between" are key phrases in statements of association.

The second type of statement used to describe a relationship between variables is the statement of causality. Unlike statements of association, statements of causality indicate that an induced change in the variate will produce or cause a change in the criterion. Thus, a statement of causality indicates that manipulation of the variate produces a change in the criterion variable. Statements of association, on the other hand, do not indicate causation.

Statements of causality always contain a key word or phrase indicating that the change in the variate leads to the change in the criterion variable. The list below provides some examples of statements of causality.

1. Achievement *is improved as a result of* an increase in amount of homework.

2. Children's attitudes toward school *will improve* if they receive more praise.

3. Some students attended college *because* they received more school counseling than others.

4. Reducing class size *increases* student achievement.

Commonly found in statements of causality are words or phrases such as "because," "will produce," "will increase if," "results in," and "affects."

EXERCISE 18

CLASSIFYING STATEMENTS OF RELATIONSHIP

Write "A" beside each statement of *association* and "C" beside each statement of *causality.*

1. _____ Shorter lunch periods result in reduced damage to school property.

2. _____ Children's social adjustment in Grade 1 is enhanced by increased dramatic play in kindergarten.

3. _____ A negative relationship exists between amount of class discussion and standardized achievement test performance.

4. _____ Student achievement is positively related to the size of the school library.

Statements 1 and 2 are statements of causality. Each indicates that the change in the criterion variable is produced by a change in the variate. Statements 3 and 4 are statements of association. They simply indicate that a relationship exists between the variate and the criterion variable.

CLASSIFYING STATEMENTS OF RELATIONSHIP

Write "A" beside each statement of *association* and "C" beside each statement of *causality*.

1. ＿＿ Reading achievement will increase if more time is spent on silent reading in class.

2. ＿＿ There is a negative relationship between amount of assigned homework and student attitude toward school.

3. ＿＿ A lower student dropout rate is associated with a higher percentage of women teachers under age 30.

4. ＿＿ A longer school day produces a decrease in student participation in extra-curricular activities.

Statements 1 and 4 are statements of causality, while 2 and 3 are statements of association.

Classifying Statements of Conclusions

The type of statement that can be made about the relationship between the variables in a study depends upon the type of study conducted. Suppose that a study reveals a significant relationship between the variate and the criterion variable. Given this relationship, *statements of association can be made from all three types of studies: status, associational, and experimental.* Thus, when a reliable relationship exists between the variate and criterion variable in a study, statements of association may be made about these two variables irrespective of the type of study. However, *statements of causality are permissible only from the findings of an experimental study.*

Unfortunately, educational research literature contains many instances in which statements of causality are made on the basis of data from nonexperimental studies. It is extremely important to avoid this type of error in writing research reports and to be able to identify invalid conclusions appearing in research reports written by others. Remember, statements of causality are permissible only from experimental studies. Statements of association, on the other hand, are permissible from all three types of studies.

CLASSIFYING STATEMENTS OF CONCLUSION

Write "E" beside each statement which can be made only on the basis of an *experimental study*. Write "A" beside each statement which can be made for all studies.

1. ____ Team teaching will produce increased student achievement.

2. ____ A relationship exists between type of course (elective or required) and student absence rate.

3. ____ Merit pay affects teacher morale.

4. ____ Individual assessment leads to improved learner achievement in reading and math.

Statements 1, 3, and 4 are statements of causality. They should be marked with an E because they can be made only on the basis of experimental studies. Statement 2 is a statement of association and may be made about both nonexperimental and experimental studies.

CLASSIFYING STATEMENTS OF CONCLUSION

Write "E" beside each statement that can be made only on the basis of an *experimental study*. Write "N", beside each statement which can be made from both *nonexperimental and experimental studies*.

1. ____ Students will achieve better in mathematics if they use textbook X than they will if they use textbook Y.

2. ____ Reading achievement will be increased if reading class is held during the first period of the day.

3. ____ There is a relationship between boys' reading achievement and type of plots found in the basic reading textbooks.

4. ____ Voluntary student enrollment in physics is associated with type of physics program.

Statements 1 and 2 can be made only on the basis of experimental studies. Statements 3 and 4 could be made from both nonexperimental and experimental studies.

IDENTIFYING PERMISSIBLE CONCLUSIONS

The final tasks in this sequence involve application of all the skills treated above. You will be asked to identify the type of study described and to indicate whether given statements of conclusion are permissible, based upon the findings of the study. Permissible types of statements from each type of study are reviewed below.

Type of Study	*Permissible Conclusions*
Nonexperimental	Statements of Association
(Status and Associational)	
Experimental	Statements of Association *and* Statements of Causality

---

EXERCISE 22

CLASSIFYING TYPES OF STUDIES

Write "S" *(status)*, "A" *(associational)*, or "E" *(experimental)* to indicate the type of study.

RESEARCH QUESTION: Is type of school program (work-study or regular program) related to dropout rate?

PROCEDURES: One hundred potential dropouts were identified from among beginning high school juniors. Fifty of the 100 were assigned at random to a work-study program during their junior and senior years that involved class attendance in the morning and four hours of paid work in local businesses and industries in the afternoon. The remaining fifty were assigned to the regular school program and were not offered the special program.

RESULTS: Forty-two of those in the vocational program completed school. Twenty-seven of those not in the vocational program completed school.

_____ Type of study.

The variate, type of school program, was manipulated. The study is experimental.

Items in the following exercise are statements of relationship based on the study just described. Assume that the relationship between the variate and criterion variable reported under *Results* in the above description of the study is statistically significant. Also assume that each statement of conclusion below applies to a population identical to the sample in the study. Consider each of the statements to determine whether it is permissible or not permissible based upon the study.

EXERCISE 23

IDENTIFYING PERMISSIBLE CONCLUSIONS

Write "P" beside the number of each statement which is *permissible* based upon the study described in Exercise 22. Write "NP" beside the number of each statement which is *not permissible* based upon the study.

1. _____ Participation in the special work-study program will increase the number of potential dropouts who complete high school.

2. _____ Completion of high school by beginning juniors identified as potential dropouts is related to type of program offered by the school.

3. _____ The dropout rate will be lower if juniors who are potential dropouts participate in the special work-study program.

4. _____ More juniors identified as potential dropouts complete high school as a result of participating in the special two-year vocational-training program than would otherwise do so.

All four statements are permissible. Statements 1, 3, and 4 are statements of causality. Statement 2 is a statement of association. Both types of statements are permissible from an experimental study.

EXERCISE 24

CLASSIFYING TYPES OF STUDIES

What type of study is this: "S", "A", or "E"?

RESEARCH QUESTION: Is first-grade reading achievement related to type of reading instruction?

PROCEDURES: Some first-grade teachers in Carver Elementary District teach reading using the Initial Teaching Alphabet (ITA); others use traditional orthography (TO). End-of-year standardized achievement test scores are obtained for 100 first-grade students randomly selected from among all students in the district who were taught with ITA and for 100 first graders randomly selected from those taught with TO.

RESULTS: TO mean score = 2.0 (grade-placement norms)
ITA mean score = 2.5

_____ Type of study.

The study is associational. The subjects were selected after they had been assigned to their respective groups, rather than being assigned at random to the different types of reading instruction. Therefore, the variate was not manipulated.

The exercise following contains a number of statements about the variables investigated in the study described above. When considering this exercise, again assume that the results indicate a significant difference in performance between the two groups and that each statement of conclusion below applies to a population identical to the subjects from the study.

EXERCISE 25

IDENTIFYING PERMISSIBLE CONCLUSIONS

Write "P" beside the number of each statement which is *permissible* based upon the study described in Exercise 24. Write "NP" beside the number of each statement which is *not permissible* based upon the study.

1. _____ First-grade students taught with ITA will achieve better than those taught with TO.

2. _____ ITA is a more effective method for teaching reading than TO.

3. _____ Use of ITA is associated with better reading achievement by first graders than is use of TO.

4. _____ Teaching with ITA materials results in better reading achievement than teaching with TO materials.

Statements 1, 2 and 4 indicate causality. They are not permissible from an associational study. Item 3 is permissible because it is a statement of association.

Uses of Status, Associational, and Experimental Studies

Successful completion of the exercises in this program will enable the learner to identify several types of research variables, to classify examples of research studies, and to identify permissible statements of conclusion based upon the procedures and results of educational research studies. The program content relevant to these skills is summarized below.

Type of Study	Distinguishing Characteristic
Status	Nonmanipulable Variate
Associational	Manipulable Variate That Is *Not* Manipulated
Experimental	Manipulable Variate That Is Manipulated

Preferred Name for Variables	Permissible Statements
Variate and Criterion Variable	Association
Variate and Criterion Variable	Association
Independent Variable and Dependent Variable	Causality and Association

Information yielded by each type of study described in this sequence is potentially useful in various situations, although the degree of usefulness varies considerably according to the type of study. It is not an explicit purpose of the sequence to cover in detail the uses of the three types. However, in planning and developing an educational program, it is important for the educator to be able to identify the potential contribution of each type of study. Therefore, this final section briefly describes a major use of each type.

Nonexperimental studies are sometimes most practical because they typically involve much less expense than experimental studies. They may also provide useful data for planning an experimental study of particular variables or for determining whether such a study is warranted. Status studies are normally the least useful type, although their results may occasionally be helpful in planning educational programs or further research. For example, one study mentioned above involved an investigation of the relationship between sex of student and reading achievement. It is well know from studies of this type that girls read better than boys in the primary grades. Although sex of student cannot be manipulated in an effort to increase reading achievement, a researcher may seek to identify manipulable variables related to "girlness" that could be responsible for the better reading performance. He might suspect that girls read better because they may be receiving differential treatment from primary teachers, such as being praised more or called upon to read more than boys, or because the types of plots in primary reading books may be more appealing to girls. He could then plan one or more studies to determine whether such manipulable variates, rather than girlness per se, are the critical factors in the better performance of girls and whether manipulation of these variates improves the reading performance of boys. Thus, the results of status studies can sometimes be used by the researcher or educator to identify manipulable variates that are related to the status factor and can be manipulated experimentally to produce a change in the criterion variable. However, potentially important manipulable variates normally can be identified more efficiently from a direct analysis of factors contributing to the criterion behavior than from data yielded by status studies.

Because of their low cost in comparison to experimental investigations, associational studies are often useful as pilot studies. For example, a district superintendent may wish to increase class sizes in the district if the increased size will not have an adverse effect on student achievement. If appropriate records on class enrollments and student attainment are available from recent years, he can study the recorded achievement of students from classes of various sizes to determine the relationship between class size and achievement under normal conditions. A finding of "no relationship" between the two variables would indicate a low probability that class size would influence achievement in an experimental investigation. The superintendent might, therefore, decide to increase class sizes without undertaking the cost and time expenditures required for an experimental study.

On the other hand, what if the associational study described above yielded a significant relationship between class size and student achievement? There are several reasons why the superintendent could not be sure that the better achievement was due to smaller class size instead of some related factor, but the probability of an experimental study revealing a significant relationship would be much greater when an associational study of the same variables had yielded a significant relationship. In this case, the superintendent might decide that an experimental study should be conducted in a limited number of schools to determine whether a district-wide change in class size would actually affect achievement in the district.

Experimental studies are the most useful for educational research because they can be used to predict the effect that an induced change in a school program will have on performance in situations comparable to the research setting. It is generally agreed that educational experimentation should be concerned primarily with the identification of procedures and programs that are or could be effective in the schools. Carefully planned manipulation of variables that can be controlled by school personnel is the research strategy with the greatest potential for identifying such procedures and programs. Thus, experimental research studies are the researcher's most useful source of information leading to improved school programs.

REFERENCES

Barg, W. R. *Educational Research: An Introduction.* New York: David McKay Company, Inc., 1963.

Davitz, R., and Davitz, L. J. *Guide for Evaluating Research Plans in Education and Psychology.* New York: Columbia University, Teachers College, 1967.

Fellin, P., Tripodi, T., and Meyer, H. J. *Exemplars of Social Research.* Itasca, Ill.: F. E. Peacock Publishers, Inc., 1969.

Gage, N. T. *Handbook of Research on Teaching.* Chicago: Rand McNally & Company, 1963.

Good, C. V. *Introduction to Educational Research.* New York: Appleton-Century-Crofts, Inc., 1954.

Kerlinger, F. N. *Foundations of Behavioral Research.* New York: Holt, Rinehart and Winston, Inc., 1964.

Tripodi, T., Fellin, P., and Meyer, H. J. *The Assessment of Social Research.* Itasca, Ill.: F. E. Peacock Publishers, Inc., 1969.

Van Dalen, D. B., and Meyer, W. J. *Understanding Educational Research.* New York: McGraw-Hill Book Company, 1966.

Wiersma, W. *Research Methods in Education: An Introduction.* Philadelphia: J. B. Lippincott Company, 1969.

NOTES

NOTES

SELECTING VARIABLES FOR EDUCATIONAL RESEARCH

Paul E. Resta

Robert L. Baker

CONTENTS

This sequence describes approaches to identifying and selecting variables for formulating a research problem (commonly referred to as the problem formulation task) and delineates the pitfalls to avoid in selecting these variables. Also included is a brief discussion of the actual statement of the research problem, as well as initial information sources to be used in the pursuit of solutions to the problem.

Specific objectives of this sequence are to enable you:

1. To identify factors which are variables in educational research, given exemplars and non-exemplars

2. To develop a list of variables in a specific problem area

3. To construct a comprehensive analysis of variables related to a specific problem area

4. To select variables on the basis of potential relevance

Types of Educational Variables

The statement of the problem is the nucleus of any educational research endeavor. If it is well formulated, sound strategies and techniques for solving the problem will follow. But formulating a sound problem statement is itself contingent upon a preceding operation—

namely, the identification and selection of the variables to be investigated.

Once the educational variables have been identified and selected, the research problem statement usually assumes one of two forms, depending on whether the study is experimental, associational, or status. In an experimental study, for example, the statement of the problem is likely to be:

What is the effect of variable X on variable Y?

In both the associational and status studies, the problem statement will probably be of the form:

What is the relationship between variable U and variable V?

In all cases, what is being sought is knowledge regarding the nature of relationships between the variables.

In experimental studies the researcher is interested in two types of variables: dependent and independent. Dependent variables will include items such as student performance, staff turnover, per pupil cost — variables that can be termed "dependent" because they vary with and may be dependent upon certain environmental manipulations. Independent or manipulable variables, in contrast, are those aspects of the environment over which the researcher exercises direct control. Examples of independent variables are practice strategies, types of textbooks, and methods of feedback.

In the statement of an experimental research problem, the researcher must clearly specify the independent and dependent variables. Consider an example of a simple problem statement:

What are the effects of immediate knowledge of results on mathematics achievement?

The independent variable in this statement is "knowledge of results." It can be manipulated by three different strategies:

1. telling the student how many problems he answered correctly

2. making available acceptable answers to the problems

3. providing an explanation as to why a given answer is right or wrong

The dependent variable in the statement is "mathematics achievement," which can be measured by using a teacher-constructed achievement test.

Another possible relationship between the variables is implied by the statement of the research problem. By asking, "What are the effects of immediate knowledge of results on mathematics achievement?" the researcher also describes a hypothesized relationship between the dependent and independent variables such as, "If knowledge of results were varied systematically in some predetermined way, what subsequent influence would this have on mathematics criterion performance?"

IDENTIFICATION OF INDEPENDENT AND DEPENDENT VARIABLES IN PROBLEM STATEMENTS

Write "I" beside the number of each *independent variable* and "D" beside the number of each *dependent variable* in the following experimental research statements.

What are the effects of

1. _____ test score presentation
   on
2. _____ student mathematics achievement?

What are the effects of

3. _____ subject matter organization
   on
4. _____ student concept acquisition in biology?

Items 1 and 3 are the independent variables. Both "test score presentation" and "subject matter organization" are variables which can be manipulated by the experimenter. For example, he might present the test scores immediately after the test, or after one day, or after one week. Subject matter organization might be manipulated by organizing the subject matter chronologically or by natural units. Both these variables are manipulable by the experimenter and are, therefore, independent variables. Items 2 and 4 are behaviors which the experimenter hopes will vary as a result of his manipulation; thus, they are the dependent variables.

Identification and Selection of Dependent Variables

Formulation of the research problem usually begins with identification and selection of the dependent variables. Experimental research consists, essentially, of determining the effect of independent variables on other factors (dependent variables) in the study.

THREE TYPES OF DEPENDENT VARIABLES

The most common types of dependent variables employed in educational research can be classified into three categories: learner-related, school-related, and home- and community-related. As one might expect, the learner-related category receives the most research attention. As an example, a researcher may want to know what can be done to change students' attitudes toward school. Or, he will investigate ways to improve spelling performance. Research focusing upon school-related variables, on the other hand, concerns itself with matters such as the amount of annual teacher turnover. Home- and community-related variables might include the number and types of books in the pupil's home. Other dependent variables within these three categories are:

   1. *Learner-Related Dependent Variables*
      subject matter achievement
      reading performance
      oral communication performance
      written communication performance
      class attendance, tardiness
      attitudes (toward subject matter, teacher, school, property, and the like)
      library usage

participation in extracurricular activities
incidence of classroom disruptive behavior
drop-out rate
homework completion

2. *School-Related Dependent Variables*
staff turnover
staff attitudes
logistical indexes

3. *Home- and Community-Related Dependent Variables*
parental attitudes
participation in community activities
number and types of books in homes
parent involvement in school activities
homework assistance
family transiency rate
family income levels
parental response to report cards and teacher letters

This is only a small sample of the dependent variables frequently used in educational research. Of the three types of variables, the learner-related variables are of primary concern in most experimental education studies, while the home- and community-related variables are the most inaccessible and difficult to observe.

In formulating a research problem, the researcher typically selects learner-related variables. They may be the average scores on a standardized achievement test, the number of high school graduates who go on to college, or the average number of errors on a first-grade reading test. Although the researcher usually has an idea of the type of learner behavior he wishes to modify, his initial conception is often broad and vague. He must refine his initial concept until the desired learner behavior is specified precisely. Therefore, identification and selection of the dependent variable usually involves the following steps:

1. Identifying the learner behavior to be changed (reading performance, mathematics achievement, or spelling, for example)

2. Analyzing the learner behavior (as an example, mathematics achievement which might be divided into addition, subtraction, multiplication, and/or division skills)

3. Selecting the most important specific learner behavior(s) (The researcher interested in mathematics performance

might be particularly interested in certain addition and subtraction skills.)

4. Specifying how the specific behaviors will be measured (that is, defining the dependent variable operationally)

An example of the application of this strategy for identifying and selecting the dependent variable would be an educational researcher's concern with improving the reading performance of first-grade students in his district. Reading performance can be applied to a number of specific behaviors, such as word recognition and recall of facts. It can also be applied to a wide variety of reading tasks, such as reading for information and reading to follow directions. Therefore, the researcher must analyze what he means by reading performance by answering questions such as:

1. How is reading defined?

2. What properties are necessary and sufficient to describe reading behavior?

3. What are the different kinds of reading performances?

4. What are the different kinds of reading situations, and how are they related to performance?

5. How is reading measured?

While not all-inclusive, such questions assist the researcher in focusing on the precise behavior he wishes to change, without his having ignored other important related behaviors.

Suppose that, in analyzing first-grade reading behavior, the researcher identifies word recognition as a critical point in learning to read. In reviewing previous reading literature and research, he finds corroboration that word recognition is a critical aspect of learning to read. He therefore selects word recognition as the specific dependent variable for this study.

Although the label "word recognition" for the dependent variable is relatively clear, it nevertheless leaves unanswered certain questions regarding the nature of the specific learner behavior and the types of stimuli to which the learner must respond. A more specific label, "single word recognition," tells us that the learner is to respond to single words, but it does not tell us what types of single words are to be presented. Are they to be among the 1,000 most common English words in American usage? Are the words to be restricted in length? If so, what is to be the longest word?

Further, what is meant by "recognition" and how will it be measured? Should the subject be able only to pronounce the word correctly when it is presented, or should he be able to indicate in some way what the word means? Should the subject say aloud specific words which are embedded in short passages of reading material, or should single words on individual cards be read aloud? Should the subject select certain words out of four alternative words presented on a page, or should he be asked to locate, out of several alternatives, a picture depicting the word? These are but a few of the choices the researcher must consider carefully before selecting a specific behavior-measurement arrangement to be used in the study.

After the researcher has chosen the dependent variable and the specific way it is to be measured, it then becomes necessary to operationally describe the dependent variable, precisely and unambiguously, so that it can be recognized by other researchers. Two adequate descriptions of dependent variables are:

1. The dependent variable in this study is word fluency, which is defined as the extent to which a subject can produce particular types of words within specified time limits. Word fluency will be measured by a group test administered to all subjects. The instructions in the test are to write as quickly as possible a list of words which contain the letter *s*. This is followed by a word list for the letters *j*, *t*, and *k*. Three minutes will be allotted to each letter. The score on this measure will be the number of complete words written after repetitions have been excluded.

2. The dependent variable in this study will be the percentage of students in the experimental and control groups who: (a) graduate from high school, and (b) enroll in a two- or four-year college. High school graduation information will be obtained from high school records, and college attendance information will be obtained from the college or university.

Both examples are adequate descriptions of the dependent variable because they clearly specify not only the behavior or outcome constituting the dependent variable, but the way in which the dependent variable will be measured.

Two inadequate descriptions of dependent variables are:

1. The dependent variable will be discrimination of punctua-

tion errors in selected passages. The test will be administered and graded by each fifth-grade teacher.

2. Scholastic achievement is designated as the dependent variable and will include every aspect of the student's response to the total school environment.

Both are inadequate operational definitions of the dependent variables. The first specifies the behavior but does not adequately specify how it will be measured. The second does not specify either the types of learner behaviors or outcomes desired, or how they will be measured.

IDENTIFICATION OF OPERATIONALLY DESCRIBED DEPENDENT VARIABLES

Write "A" if only the *behavior* (or the outcome) is specified in the following descriptions of dependent variables, "B" if only the *measurement procedure* is specified; "C" if *both* the behavior (or outcome) and measurement procedure are specified; and "D" if *neither* is specified.

1. ＿＿ The dependent variable will be essay writing on the history of the French Revolution.

2. ＿＿ The dependent variable will be the social adjustment of the first-grade pupils as judged by teachers and parents.

3. ＿＿ The dependent variable will be the reading performance of second-grade students. This will be measured by having students read four passages aloud. The score will be the percentage of errors per 100 running words. Errors will consist either of a mispronunciation, omission or substitution of a word, or a hesitation of over three seconds. Mistakes in proper names will not constitute errors.

Item 1 should have been marked *A* because, although it specifies the type of behavior (essay writing), it does not indicate how the product (the essay) will be measured. Item 2 is too ambiguous in its present form to constitute an operational definition of the dependent variable. "Social adjustment" has to be more precisely defined, and the specific criteria for its measurement have to be spelled out. This item, therefore, should have been marked *D*. The last item should have been marked *C* because it specifies both the behavior and the manner in which it will be measured.

IDENTIFICATION OF STEPS IN THE SELECTION
OF THE DEPENDENT VARIABLE

Number any or all of the following steps you would recommend that a researcher follow if he wishes to conduct a study investigating ways of improving the mathematics performance of fourth-grade pupils in his district. In what order should he use the steps to *select the dependent variable?*

A. ____ Identify the learner behaviors he is interested in changing.

B. ____ Identify the most important independent variables.

C. ____ Analyze the learner behaviors and select the most important specific learner behaviors.

D. ____ Specify how the specific behaviors will be measured (i.e., operationally define the dependent variable).

E. ____ Compare his list of independent variables with lists of exemplar dependent variables.

Steps A, C, and D are the most efficient steps to follow, respectively, in the identification and selection of the dependent variable. Step B concerns the independent variable and should be dealt with after the dependent variable is specified. Step E might be an interesting activity, but it isn't a step to be taken in selecting the dependent variable.

To formulate the research problem, the researcher must first identify and select the dependent variable. After carefully analyzing it, he must define it well and describe the specific way it will be measured.

Identification and Selection of Independent Variables

After the dependent variable has been selected and clearly defined, the next step in the formulation of the research problem is to identify and select the independent variables. Recall that the educational researcher interested in improving the reading performance of the first-grade pupils in his district ultimately selected word recognition as his dependent variable. His selection was based on a systematic analysis of the gross behavior (reading performance) and its specific behavioral components, as well as its empirical significance and interest. The researcher clearly defined what it is he would like to change: he wants to improve word recognition skills. His next task in the formulation of the problem is to identify those things that are likely to improve performance in word recognition tasks. In other words, he must define the independent variable(s).

The researcher can manipulate many things that might have an effect on word recognition performance. He can manipulate the type of textbook by supplying his subjects with textbooks having different organization or subject matter. Or, he can manipulate the amount of practice pupils receive by arranging them into groups, each of which receives different amounts of practice.

The experience or training of the teacher might have an effect on word recognition performance. This could be investigated by assigning pupils to teachers with distinct types of training or experience. The researcher might also investigate whether the type of classroom arrangement affects word recognition performance, in which case he could manipulate this by randomly assigning students to rooms with different physical arrangements. These are but a few of the variables that might be considered. All, however, have one property in common: they are all manipulable variables—as the independent variable in an educational experimental study must always be.

FOUR TYPES OF INDEPENDENT VARIABLES

Not all educational studies, however, are experimental, nor are all of the educational variables that are studied manipulable. Non-manipulable variables (termed "variates") can be investigated in status studies, and the manipulable variables which the researcher chooses not to manipulate can be the focus for associational studies. Following is a listing of some of the independent variables and variates commonly used in educational research. The list is not complete enough to cover all potentially relevant variables which must be considered in formulating a specific research problem. However, it can provide a starting point for the researcher in developing his own list of potentially relevant independent variables.

Remember that the researcher must keep in mind the distinction between manipulable and non-manipulable variables when considering potentially relevant variables for inclusion in a study. Some of the variables suggested on page 46, such as the age or intelligence of the learner, are undoubtedly related to specific dependent variables (e.g., word recognition) but are beyond the researcher's control. Although non-manipulable independent variables cannot conveniently be built into more powerful instructional techniques and strategies, they can be closely related to specific dependent variables. The knowledge of such relationships may even be necessary in order to gain an adequate picture of an instructional problem.

TABLE 1
FOUR TYPES OF INDEPENDENT VARIABLES

INSTRUCTIONAL VARIABLES	LEARNER VARIABLES	TEACHER VARIABLES	ENVIRONMENTAL VARIABLES

1. Textbook
  a. Textbook X
  b. Textbook Y
2. Classroom organization
  a. Number of students
  b. Teaching role (team teaching, lecture)
3. Mode of instruction
  a. Discovery
  b. Expository
  c. Programmed
4. Instructional content organization
  a. Hierarchical content sequence (sequence of principles and concepts are based on an analysis of subject matter hierarchy)
  b. Problem-referenced (content organized by categories of problems which
	1. Biological variables
	  a. physical condition and health of learner
	  b. maturational factors
	  c. sex differences
	  d. fatigue factors
	2. Learner aptitudes and abilities
	  a. general aptitude or intelligence
	  b. specific aptitudes (e.g., mathematics, computer programming, music)
	3. Social and educational history
	  a. record of previous academic successes and failures
	  b. case history recording previous critical inci-
		1. Intelligence
		  a. General intelligence (e.g., Binet IQ)
		  b. Simple factorial system (e.g., Wechsler Adult Intelligence Scale)
		  c. Complete factorial system (e.g., Guilford rating)
		2. Teacher training
		  a. Specific knowledge and skills
		  b. Performance in student teaching
		  c. Achievement in teaching methods course
		3. Personality characteristics
		4. Social history
			1. School
			  a. Location
			  b. Organization
			  c. Plant and equipment
			2. Socio-economic factors
			  a. Cultural values
			  b. Peer group values
			  c. Economic status
			3. Home
			  a. Location
			  b. Number of books available
			  c. Size
			  d. Family activities
			  e. Parental income
			4. Classroom
			  a. Temperature
			  b. Illumination
			  c. Ventilation
			  d. Noise

may be either practical or theoretical in nature)

5. Learner practice
   a. Amount (total amount of practice provided to attain specified instructional objective)
   b. Type of practice
      1) individual
      2) group (choral responses within the classroom)
6. Grouping of students
   a. Homogeneous
   b. Heterogeneous
7. Subject-matter characteristics
   a. Scientific
   b. Social science
   c. Aesthetic
8. Frequency of assessment
   a. Low frequency (e.g., assess only once or twice per course)
   b. High frequency (e.g., assess daily or weekly)
9. Type of pupil response
   a. Identifying
   b. Naming

dents (educational, emotional, family)

5. Biological factors
   a. Age-maturity
   b. Health
   c. Fatigue (initial and terminal)
   d. Sex differences
   e. Physical characteristics
6. Teaching experience
   a. Years
   b. Type of school system
   c. Grade levels
7. Educational background
   a. Years of college
   b. Type of degree
8. Subject-matter sophistication

e. Classroom layout
f. Hour

TABLE 1 (Continued)

INSTRUCTIONAL VARIABLES	LEARNER VARIABLES	TEACHER VARIABLES	ENVIRONMENTAL VARIABLES

c. Describing
d. Ordering
e. Constructing
 	
10. Feedback or knowledge of results
  a. Type of feedback
    1) indication that response is either correct or incorrect
    2) in addition to (1) above, indicate what is the correct answer or response
    3) in addition to (1) and (2) above, explain why the response is correct or incorrect
  b. Frequency
    1) after each response or task
    2) after each instructional unit
 	
11. Response consequences
  a. Type of consequence
    1) positive consequences
      a) confirmation (verbal,			

textual)
b) social approval (verbal, smile, tactile)
c) tangible reward (food, toys)
d) token reward (chips, coupons)
2) negative consequences
a) social disapproval (verbal, frown)
b) withdrawal of reward
c) physical punishment
3) no consequence
b. Amount of consequence
1) fixed amount per task or response
2) variable amount per task or response
c. Frequency of consequence
1) following every response or instructional task
2) ratio (variable or fixed ratio of consequences to responses)
3) interval (variable or fixed interval of consequence to responses)
d. Timing of consequence
1) immediate
2) delayed

Strategies for Selecting Independent Variables

Identification and selection of the independent variables may occur in any of several ways. In the example of the researcher interested in improving word recognition performance, the option of selecting the dependent and independent variables was the researcher's alone. In other instances the independent and dependent variables may already have been selected by an administration or curriculum committee. For example, a curriculum committee might observe that the current vocabulary repertoire of elementary school pupils is limited and decide that a change in vocabulary training is required. The committee might select two different vocabulary training programs and decide to compare their effectiveness in terms of student scores on a locally-developed vocabulary test. They then might consult an educational researcher and request his assistance in the formulation of the problem and the design of the experiment.

In this instance the researcher's contributions would be limited to (a) checking to be sure that other important variables have not been inadvertently overlooked or left uncontrolled, and (b) working out the procedures for implementing the study. In both cases he should start his problem formulation by making a comprehensive list of all known variables that could relate to the problem area. Too often, researchers formulate problems after considering only a few known variables, then discover later that an important variable has been overlooked. To prevent this, the researcher should develop a comprehensive list of all the potentially relevant variables.

Three alternative strategies are available to the researcher in developing a comprehensive list of potentially relevant variables from which to select the most promising ones. The first is the method of searching and analyzing reports of previous research. A second strategy is to analyze extant or "on-hand" data such as teacher logs, school records, the raw data of previous studies, or the data from pilot (i.e., exploratory) studies. A third strategy involves observation and analysis of a current instructional setting in order to determine those events or stimuli that appear to have an effect on the dependent variable. The three methods are often used in combination to develop a comprehensive list of variables.

After the researcher has developed his list of variables, he should:

1. Analyze each variable for potential relevance

2. Select the most relevant manipulable variables for inclusion in the experimental study

SEARCH AND ANALYSIS OF THE LITERATURE

To safeguard against inadvertently investing considerable time and effort "reinventing the wheel," the researcher first conducts a systematic search and analysis of related research. Review of the literature allows him to profit from the efforts and techniques of others who have performed similar or related studies using the same variables and enables him to start his research where others have left off.

In reviewing previous studies, the experimenter should seek answers to the following questions:

1. What variables are known to be related to the learner behavior in which I am interested?

2. How have these variables been defined and described by others?

3. How have the variables been manipulated in previous studies? Do these suggest other probable ways of manipulating them?

4. Is the previous research on the specific variables sound methodologically and is it comprehensive?

A thorough analysis of the literature for answers to these questions will minimize the risk of overlooking important variables or selecting inappropriate manipulations of the variables. The Appendix (p. 77) provides additional information on procedures to follow in a systematic search and analysis of related research.

In most cases, all of the important relevant independent variables will not have been identified in previous research. The researcher, therefore, should always give careful consideration to other as yet unstudied variables which may be significantly related to the dependent variable. One technique for doing so is to analyze carefully available extant data such as school records and teacher logs (or even unpublished raw data from earlier studies) relative to the learner behavior to be changed.

Consider an example of a researcher concerned with the problem of improving the reading performance of first-grade students. He has noted that the average number of errors is "high" when the reading test scores of first grades in the five schools of a suburban school district are combined. He also believes it should be possible to reduce the average number of errors considerably.

Supporting this speculation is the fact that the reading performance of the children in a few of the first-grade classes is much better than that of the other first-grade classes. As can be seen in Table 2, for example, Class 1 of School A and Classes 1 and 2 of School E have a much lower error rate than do equivalent classes in other schools in the district. Two out of three classes, in fact, are already performing at the desired criterion performance level (in this case an average of no more than two errors per page). The researcher would like to account for the observed differences between the classes.

He notices, for one thing, that School E has the largest class sizes (see Table 3) and also the highest reading performance (Table 2). School C, in contrast, has small average class sizes but the highest average number of errors. On the basis of this data, however, one should not be quick to hypothesize that larger class size means better reading performance. When examining a potentially relevant variable such as class size, it is vital to consider carefully what might account for apparent differences. It may be that the district deliberately reduced the size of classes in School C to provide more individual attention to the students in this area because they were performing at a low level.

TABLE 2
AVERAGE NUMBER OF READING ERRORS
IN THE FIRST GRADE BY SCHOOL
AND CLASS

School	Class	Class Average Number of Errors	School Average Number of Errors
A	1	2	3.5
	2	5	
B	1	6	6.7
	2	8	
	3	7	
	4	6	
C	1	8	8.5
	2	10	
	3	6	
	4	10	
D	1	6	6.0
	2	5	
	3	7	
E	1	3	2.0
	2	1	

TABLE 3
NUMBER OF FIRST-GRADE CLASSES AND
AVERAGE NUMBER OF STUDENTS PER
FIRST-GRADE CLASS IN DISTRICT
SCHOOLS

School	Number of First-Grade Classes	Number of Students in First Grade	Average Number of Students Per Class
A	2	52	26
B	4	105	26
C	4	96	24
D	3	72	24
E	2	58	29

In these instructional settings, it may be that size is a function of variables such as socioeconomic environment and district assignment of teachers to schools. As shown in Table 4, School C is situated in a lower-middle income area. This is not to say that there is no relationship between reading performance and class size, but rather that the only way this can be determined is through experimentation. Such experimentation would require that the researcher manipulate the variable of class size and randomly assign classes to the experimental treatment. The outcome of such a study, assuming it were well executed and carefully controlled, would indicate whether class size had an effect on reading performance. What is important, however, is the researcher's selection of independent variables that are most likely to have an effect on the dependent variable. To select class size as the independent variable solely on the basis of the data in Table 2 would not be justified. The data in Tables 2 and 3 provide "leads" only. The researcher must consider the potential relevance of each variable before making his selection. He must also be certain before making his selection that he has carefully identified and analyzed potentially relevant variables.

In completing his analysis of potentially relevant variables, the researcher should also examine data such as family size (Table 5), intelligence (Table 6), and teaching experience (Table 7).

TABLE 4
SMOOTHED DISTRIBUTION OF ANNUAL
PARENTAL INCOME IN DISTRICT
SCHOOLS

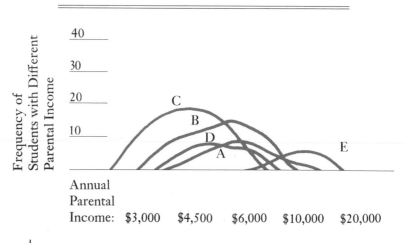

TABLE 5
AVERAGE NUMBER OF CHILDREN IN FAMILIES OF FIRST-GRADE PUPILS IN DISTRICT SCHOOLS

School	Average Number of Children in Family
A	3.5
B	5.2
C	5.8
D	3.6
E	2.8

TABLE 6
MEAN IQ SCORES FOR DISTRICT FIRST-GRADE CLASSES

School	First-Grade Class	Mean IQ Score
A	1	103
	2	101
B	1	98
	2	90
	3	91
	4	93
C	1	92
	2	91
	3	101
	4	93
D	1	103
	2	105
	3	107
E	1	108
	2	112

TABLE 7
TEACHING EXPERIENCE OF DISTRICT
FIRST-GRADE TEACHERS

School	First-Grade Class	Teaching Experience			
		1 yr.	2-3 yrs.	4-10 yrs.	11+ yrs.
A	1				X
	2			X	
B	1		X		
	2	X			
	3	X			
	4			X	
C	1		X		
	2	X			
	3	X			
	4	X			
D	1			X	
	2	X			
	3		X		
E	1				X
	2				X

After compiling all available data, as above, the researcher in this example began his analysis. In selecting the independent variable(s), he first identified and described the potentially relevant variables and then listed the status of each within the district's classes. As he analyzed each variable, he made comments regarding its potential relevance. Although oversimplified, Table 8 illustrates the approach that he used.

TABLE 8
LISTING AND DESCRIBING POTENTIALLY RELEVANT VARIABLES FOR THE READING EXAMPLE

Potentially Relevant Variable with Description	Variable Status in District Classes	Potential Relevance
1. Instructional Variables		
a. Textbook		
1) Primer X	Schools C, D, E: used in first grade classes	No obvious difference between classes
2) Primer Y	Schools A, B: used in first grade classes	
b. Grouping of students		
1) homogeneous	School A: Class 1 School B: Classes 1 and 2	Higher performance in homogeneously grouped classes
2) heterogeneous	Schools B, C, D, E	
c. Subject-matter organization	Identical for all classes	
d. Classroom organization		
1) 1 to 2 reading groups	Schools A, C: all classes have 1 to 2 reading groups	No obvious difference
2) 3 or more reading groups	Schools B, D, E: all classes have 3 or more reading groups	
e. Class size	School E: Classes 1 and 2 has largest class size	Higher reading performance in larger classes
f. Mode of instruction		
1) "Look and Say"	School A: Class 1 Schools B, C, D: used in all classes	Higher performance in phonics groups
2) phonics	School A: Class 2	

Potentially Relevant Variable with Description	Variable Status in District Classes	Potential Relevance
	School E: Classes 1 and 2	
g. Type of learner response demanded	Vocal response demanded of students in all classes	
h. Type of knowledge of results 1) correct answer	School A: Class 2 School B: Classes 2 and 3 Schools C, D: all classes School E: Class 1	Appears to be slightly higher performance in groups given explanation as to why answer is right or wrong
2) explanation as to why answer is right or wrong	School A: Class 1 School B: Classes 1 and 4 School E: Class 2	
i. Timing of knowledge of results	Tutorial method used in all classes	
j. Reinforcement 1) no reinforcement other than knowledge of results	Schools A, B, C, E	No apparent differences
2) fixed amount for every step	School D: gold stars given for each errorless page	
k. Amount of learner practice 1) 1 hour per day	School A: Class 2 School B: all classes School C: Class 4 School D: all classes	Possible difference in favor of groups having more practice
2) 1-1/2 hours per day	School A: Class 1 School C: Classes 1, 2, and 3 School E: Classes 1 and 2	

Potentially Relevant Variable with Description	Variable Status in District Classes	Potential Relevance
1. Length of practice period 1) 1/2 hour	School B: Classes 3 and 4 School C: Class 4 School D: all classes School E: both classes	No apparent differences between groups with varied practice period durations
2) 3/4 hour	School A: Class 1	
3) 1 hour	School A: Class 2 School B: Classes 1 and 2 School C: Classes 1, 2, and 3	
2. Learner Variables a. General intelligence	School E, Classes 1 and 2, and School D, Classes 1 to 3, have higher measured intelligence than classes in Schools A, B, or C	Classes having higher measured intelligence in general have higher reading performance than those with lower measured intelligence
3. Teacher Variables a. General intelligence	Teacher intelligence scores approximately the same among schools	
b. Teaching experience	Teachers in Schools A and E have greater teaching experience than those in Schools B, C, and D	Better reading performance in groups with longer teaching experience
4. Environmental Variables a. Size of family	School E has smallest average number of children in family Schools B and C have largest number	Better reading performance apparent in groups having smaller average number of children in family
b. Parental income	School E has highest parental income Schools B and C have lowest	Difference (although not consistent) in reading performance of parental income groups

The foregoing indentification of variables is certainly not complete; other variables may have occurred to you that were not included. The list points up, however, one of the major advantages of systematic identification and analysis of independent variables. After listing all the variables which have been considered, it is far easier to spot errors of omission — before a research project is started, not later. Another advantage of this approach is that it provides the researcher with a systematic method of considering each variable and making a decision regarding its potential relevance. The deletion of a variable from the list should be done only on the basis of evidence that there is little or no relationship between the listed variable and the criterion variable.

In the example we have been studying, the researcher was able ultimately to exclude variables such as type of reading text, subject matter organization, type of response demanded of student, reinforcement, timing of knowledge of results, teacher intelligence, and length of practice period as not being closely linked to the observed discrepancy in reading performance. He thus narrowed the list of potentially relevant variables to the following:

1. grouping of students

2. class size

3. mode of instruction

4. type of knowledge of results

5. amount of learner practice (reading)

6. general intelligence of students

7. parental income

8. family size

9. teaching experience

The researcher thus attempted to isolate those potentially relevant variables which he felt might be most strongly related to his previously specified dependent variable. If only non-manipulable variables had been isolated as potentially relevant in his analysis, he would not have been able to perform an experimental study. It would have been possible, however, to perform a status study in which he examined the relationship of the non-manipulable variables to the criterion variable. In this instance, the researcher identified both manipulable and non-manipulable variables as potentially relevant to the dependent variable.

IDENTIFYING MANIPULABLE AND
NON-MANIPULABLE VARIABLES

Write "M" beside the number of each *manipulable variable* and "N" beside the number of each *non-manipulable variable* for each of the following items isolated by a researcher in his analysis of on-hand data.

1. _____ grouping of students

2. _____ class size

3. _____ mode of instruction

4. _____ type of knowledge of results

5. _____ amount of learner practice (reading)

6. _____ general intelligence of students

7. _____ parental income

8. _____ family size

9. _____ teaching experience

There is little that a researcher can do to manipulate the general mental ability of students, parental income, or family size. Items 6, 7, and 8 are, therefore, all non-manipulable variables.

However, it is possible to manipulate the grouping of students, class size, instructional mode, type of knowledge of results, and amount of practice (items 1-5).

Item 9 can be considered a manipulable variable, although it is more difficult to classify. To be sure, the experimenter cannot directly control the type of teaching experience received by each teacher. He can, however, as part of an experimental treatment, randomly assign students to teachers with different levels of teaching experience, thereby manipulating this variable.

The researcher in the example above has now narrowed his analysis to only the manipulable variables list. Subsequently, in making a more detailed assessment of the variables, he identifies the following as being the most likely to be related to the observed discrepancy in reading performance:

1. grouping of students

2. instructional mode.

Having settled upon these two variables, his next step is to formulate a researchable question. He phrases this as:

What are the effects of mode of instruction (Phonics and "Look and Say") and student grouping (two grouping conditions) on the reading performance of first-grade pupils?

Potentially, answering such a significant question has an imposing payoff—which is one of the requisites of a good research question. But consider what the researcher has committed himself to. The real payoff will come as a function of his ability to:

1.   Specify precisely in operational terms the two treatment conditions related to instructional mode (Phonics and "Look and Say")

2.   Develop an adequate, direct measure of reading performance to be used as a criterion variable

3.   Design an experiment which yields valid outcomes

ANALYSIS OF AN INSTRUCTIONAL SETTING

Another method of identifying potentially relevant variables is the careful observation and precise description of an instructional situation. Using this approach, a researcher may observe and analyze an existing instructional situation to determine what types of events or stimuli appear to have an effect on the dependent variable. In pursuing this approach, the researcher should ask:

1.   What types of events or stimuli appear to have an effect on the dependent variable (usually, learner behavior)?

2.   What are the unique or distinguishing characteristics of these events or stimuli?

3.   In what ways, if any, do these events or stimuli appear related to each other or to other situations?

As an example, a researcher observes a high school French class recitation. The strategy of the teacher is to addresss a question to a given pupil, allow the pupil to answer the question, and then provide direct reinforcement. The observer notes that other pupils, not included in the interaction but proximate to the respondent, appear to learn to the same extent as the questioned pupil. In analyzing this situation the researcher further identifies the type of reinforcement (direct or vicarious) as a variable that is potentially relevant to the dependent variable of accuracy in pronouncing French words in sentences. Based on his analysis, the researcher continues his observation, talks to the teacher or other researchers, and reviews research related to this area before making a final selection of independent variables.

In practice, the three approaches to identifying potentially relevant variables (analysis of related research, extant or "on-hand" data, and the instructional setting) are often used in combination to provide a comprehensive list of variables. Much of the educational research that is done today utilizes each of these approaches in extending the knowledge gleaned from earlier phases of the program.

Consider another example to illustrate how the three approaches can be used in combination to identify and select potentially relevant variables. A simple evaluative study was completed comparing the effectiveness of team teaching and single-instructor teaching. The results suggested that better performance was associated with the team teaching method. A researcher interested in investigating the phenomena involved would probably start his problem formulation with specific characteristics of team teaching already in mind. For example, he will probably speculate about just what it is that results in better learner performance: the subject matter sophistication of the teachers, the number of instructors constituting a team, the number of pupils taught by the team, the proportion of pupil time spent in large-group or small-group instruction, or in individual study, or simply the variation of teachers (i.e., the novelty of having different teachers). In doing so, he now has identified five possible variables, but he realizes that there are other variables relating to the set of activities called "team teaching" which he has not yet identified or considered. He would probably develop a comprehensive list of variables by:

1. Reviewing related research

2. Examining teachers' logs and discussing with them what it is about the set of team teaching procedures that seems to work

3. Observing and describing precisely what takes place in both the team teaching and the traditional instructional situations

Using the last technique, by analyzing the observed differences between two instructional situations it is sometimes possible to identify potentially relevant variables.

One might ask, Why bother to find out what it is in the team teaching activity that produces the improved student performance when all we want to know is whether it is better than the traditional method? Perhaps the most cogent argument on behalf of in-depth studies is that we have now developed the resources and abilities for undertaking investigations of those conditions thought to optimize the attainment of educational objectives under clearly specified, delimited conditions. Evaluative studies, although extremely helpful in making immediate decisions, have short-term utility. In some ways they resemble the actions of the old-timer in the film *No Time for Sergeants* who had found through experimentation that he could eliminate the static in his radio by spitting on the tubes and giving it a good whack. Unfortunately, he never found out what produced the static. Thus, every few minutes he had to repeat the spitting and whacking procedures to get rid of the static because the variables related to its cause remained unknown.

EXERCISE 5

STRATEGIES FOR SELECTING
INDEPENDENT VARIABLES

Summarize the three strategies or approaches that can be used to identify and select independent variables.

1. _____

_____

2. _____

_____

3. _____

_____

Three strategies that can be used in identifying and selecting independent variables are: 1) a search and analysis of related research, 2) analysis of extant data, and 3) analysis of an instructional situation.

STEPS IN SELECTING INDEPENDENT VARIABLES

Place a check beside the number of each step a researcher should take in selecting the independent variables to conduct an experimental study for improving the spelling performance of third-graders.

1. _____ Develop a comprehensive list of potentially relevant variables through the use of the three strategies defined above.

2. _____ Analyze the learner behaviors and select the specific learner behaviors he is most interested in changing.

3. _____ Select the independent variables after considering the first three or four that come to mind.

4. _____ Analyze the variables on the list for potential relevance.

5. _____ Select the most relevant non-manipulable variables as the independent variables for the experiment.

6. _____ Select the most relevant manipulable variables as the independent variables for the experiment.

The steps to be used in selecting independent variables for an experimental study are 1, 4, and 6. Step 2 is not applicable here although it is an important step in selecting the dependent variable. Step 3, although often practiced in educational research, usually results in important variables being overlooked in the formulation of the problem. Step 5 is not appropriate in selecting independent variables for an experimental study inasmuch as the independent variable in an experimental study must be a manipulable variable.

Pitfalls in Selecting Variables

Two major pitfalls that may trap the researcher in his formulation of the problem are (a) starting with a solution when seeking a problem and (b) failing to consider variables carefully.

STARTING WITH A SOLUTION
WHEN SEEKING A PROBLEM

In the preparation of a research proposal, a description of the general background of the problem precedes the description of the proposed solution of the problem. Thus, the format of the proposal suggests that the problem always occurs first conceptually, followed by an examination of potential solutions, the most promising of which is selected for the proposed research project. Although this is clearly a desirable strategy for the formulation and conduct of research, many researchers start not with a problem but with an "in-hand" solution. They then attempt to seek out an appropriate problem for their ready-made solution! Examples of this kind of approach are research questions such as:

1. What aspects of behavior can I study with my computer apparatus?

2. To what other courses can this technique (e.g., inquiry training, or computer-based instruction) be applied?

This type of behavior is often referred to as *The Law of the Instrument*. It may be formulated as follows: If you give a small boy a hammer, he will find that everything he encounters needs pounding. It is not surprising, therefore, that an educational researcher may formulate problems in a manner which requires "pounding" by his own favorite "hammer," whether it be flexible scheduling, self-contained classrooms, departmentalizing, team teaching, computerized classrooms, or homogeneous grouping. Too frequently, each touted technique comes to be regarded as a panacea for all educational ills.

It is for this reason that a researcher who continually applies one technique or procedure to a vast array of problems might be accused of being gimmick-oriented rather than problem-oriented. The gimmick-orientation in educational research is evidenced by the large number of ineffectual studies in the literature that are related to long-standing and poorly stated controversies such as "Does television teach?" and "Are overhead projectors better than printed material?"

Such studies often neglect more important questions and overlook important variables in a given learning situation. For example, the question which asks whether the use of overhead projectors results in improved learning, when compared to conventional printed material, may overlook critical variables related to the content that is being put *on* the overhead projector and into the printed material. For example, how it is sequenced and what kinds of responses are required of the student? In this way many gimmick-oriented studies in education have considered only the vehicle or transport system of instruction while neglecting the instructional content itself. Much research in programmed instruction has made this mistake, with studies concerning questions such as the effects of linear vs. intrinsic programming, feedback vs. no feedback, constructed vs. selected response, and the effects of overt and covert responding, to name some of the most prevalent. All are undoubtedly important questions to ask, but asking them is not appropriate until the instructional materials that are subjected to these techniques have been verified for quality.

FAILURE TO CONSIDER VARIABLES CAREFULLY

We have already mentioned the problems likely to result when a research project is initiated without the potentially relevant variables having been identified. This pitfall is elucidated by Gilbert (1964):

> Many Army officers were of the opinion that the superiority of one outfit over another in the matter of marksmanship was directly traceable to differences in the leadership provided by non-commissioned officers. The leadership hypothesis is a natural and prevalent one in the military. A strong devotee would have approached the problem of discovering means for improving marksmanship training by studying means of increasing the efficiency of leadership. Leadership no doubt has its effect on company marksmanship scores. The Army is, however, an organization in which the demands for "payoff" are over-prevalent. One military research group (HumRRO) directed itself toward the problem of marksmanship by setting aside the prevailing theories and allowing the task to direct its analysis. Its first job was to discover what the problem was. It was conceivable that there was no problem at all. Perhaps rifle firing training was near its maximal efficiency. An openminded research effort will not only reject the tendency to become a devotee of one particular construction of the problem, it will even question whether a problem exists. HumRRO eventually discovered how to increase the accuracy of marksmanship to such an extent that the HumRRO-trained companies, even with inferior non-commissioned officers, can outshoot other companies with the best non-coms. This does not [mean] that leadership is irrelevant. It does demonstrate that a plausible hypothesis indicated the study of variables (leadership) which were of minor importance to the task. When devotion to an hypothesis becomes greater than devo-

tion to a problem such may be the expected results. Hypotheses are trial guesses at answers, and devotion to them tends to change them into dogmatic truths.

IDENTIFICATION OF PROBLEM
FORMULATION PITFALLS

Place a check beside the number of each example of a pitfall, if you can discover it, in the three following items.

1. _____ A researcher interested in improving the reading performance of first-grade pupils reads an article describing the use of film-story books to improve reading performance. He then writes a research proposal for a study comparing the use of this technique with the use of the phonics approach currently being used.

2. _____ The following papers were authored by one researcher: (a) "A comparison of small group vs. large group classes in teaching history, 1969," (b) "The advantages of the small group in elementary school reading instruction, 1971," and (c) "The effects of small group instruction on third-grade arithmetic performance, 1970."

3. _____ The following papers were authored by another researcher: (a) "The use of advance organizers in the learning and retention of meaningful verbal material, 1970," (b) "A transfer of training approach to improving the functional retention of medical knowledge, 1970," (c) "Proactive inhibition in the forgetting of meaningful school material, 1968," (d) "The role of discriminability in meaningful verbal learning and retention, 1971;" and (e) "Meaningful learning and retention: intra-personal cognitive variables, 1971."

In item 1 the researcher starts with the learner behavior he wishes to alter but does not carefully consider all of the variables that may relate to the dependent variable. Item 2 gives clear evidence of a researcher who has fallen into the pitfall of starting with a solution when seeking a problem. In item 3, the researcher does not give any evidence of succumbing to either pitfall. He has focused his attention on the problem of retention of information and is directing his research efforts appropriately.

AVOIDING THE PITFALLS

The two pitfalls we have been discussing, although fairly easy to recognize, are so much in evidence in educational research that it is well for all researchers to bear in mind three simple rules stemming from problem-solving research that will help avoid the pitfalls:

1. Suspend judgment

2. Produce a second solution after the first

3. Evaluate your own ideas critically and evaluate those of others constructively

The rules sound almost like platitudes, but, if used regularly in research practice, they can make the difference between an insignificant study and one that is fruitful and worthy of respect.

RULE 1: Suspend Judgment.

Difficulties begin the moment the researcher identifies and selects the variables too quickly without carefully considering all the variables involved. Results of problem-solving studies indicate that a start in the wrong direction or a premature guess at a solution may actually prevent arrival at the correct solution. The results of one study showed that, once subjects have offered a solution to a problem, they have great difficulty in revising or discarding it, even in the face of contradictory evidence. Similar behavior can sometimes be observed in sophisticated researchers who become committed to a specific technique or theory. Any premature commitment to a so-called Great Theory or Great Method is tantamount to distorting the research problem so that it fits the theory or method. Often established theories and methods are nurtured by succeeding generations of educational researchers and protected from any damage which might be inflicted by the attacks of other researchers, who are in turn keeping their own menageries of pet theories and techniques. In general, a premature commitment to a theory or method usually results in a tendency on the part of the researcher to prove rather than to modify the theory or method.

RULE 2: Produce a Second Solution After the First.

Problem-solving studies indicate that individuals, in seeking their first solution to a problem, are dominated by strong pressures to achieve a solution, but that after they have derived an initial solution and are asked to provide another solution, the second is usually a more creative one. Transferring this to an experimental context, we might suppose that after analyzing a small amount of data related to reading performance and class size, a researcher had promptly designed and conducted a research program. According to problem-solving research, it is unlikely that he would have much to show for his efforts, even after expending considerable time and money, as he would if he had pushed on into further inquiries before starting the study. This all too common failing can often be prevented by thoughtful consideration of all relevant variables, hypotheses, and solutions which may apply to a given problem area. The hazards of not carefully considering the variables were also demonstrated in an earlier example in which "leadership" was so generally regarded as the most important variable in the learning situation that other variables were excluded from consideration. Only when a fresh approach was taken and all of the relevant variables carefully considered was it possible to find an effective instructional solution.

> RULE 3: Evalute Your Own Ideas Critically and Those of Others Constructively.

Compliance with this rule will enable the researcher to use previous attempts at solving identical or similar problems as sources of new ideas. It also helps prevent one from complaisantly accepting only his own idea for defining and solving the problem. In a problem-solving experiment using engineers as subjects, it was found that engineers who evaluated solutions "constructively" tended to produce better solutions than those who evaluated them "critically." Half of the engineers were asked to list reasons why a given group of solutions could not work, and the other half were asked to list as many strong points as they could regarding the same solutions. Following this task, the engineers wrote down their own solutions to a warehousing problem. The responses were scrambled and then presented to a committee of experts for evaluation. Results indicated that the group which had been asked to find strong points did significantly better than the group instructed to look critically at the solutions of others. Findings from this study suggest that one method of fostering a constructive attitude is by looking for weak points in your own initial formulations and for strong points in those of others.

In summary then, the two major pitfalls in the formulation of a research problem are starting with a solution when seeking a problem, and failing to consider all relevant variables carefully. Three rules for avoding the pitfalls are to suspend judgment, to produce a second solution after the first, and to evaluate your own ideas critically and evaluate those of others constructively.

AVOIDING THE PITFALLS

Identify each *failure* to observe the rules for avoiding pitfalls in the following examples. Answer each item by writing:

> S: if the researcher fails to *suspend judgment*
> P: if he fails to *produce a second solution*
> E: if he fails to *evaluate his own ideas critically*

1. _____ A researcher develops a theory about how organisms learn. He conducts several studies which produce results supporting his theory. Many other researchers, however, perform subsequent experiments with results that are not compatible with his theoretical system. The researcher critically analyzes these studies and indicates in a journal article where the other researchers have "gone wrong."

2. _____ A researcher is concerned about the problem of learning foreign languages. He identifies pronunciation of French words as the behavior of interest to him. He then analyzes this behavior into the following elements:

   a. *discrimination:* i.e., hearing the differences between phonemes which are common to French but not to English

   b. *articulation:* i.e., learning to make the motor movements adequate to proper production of the French phonemes.

   The researcher then develops a comprehensive listing of variables which may relate to the discrimination and articulation of French phonemes. He selects the most relevant of these for inclusion in his study.

3. _____ A researcher, excited about a new overhead projector his school has acquired, decides to conduct a study in which one class using the projector will be compared to another which will not have access to the projector.

In item 1 the researcher fails to both suspend judgment and evaluate his own ideas critically. In item 2, a brief account is given of a sound approach to formulating a research problem in which the researcher avoids the three pitfalls we have been discussing. The last item is an example of a researcher's selecting variables too quickly and starting with a solution (an overhead projector) rather than a problem. This researcher fails both to suspend judgment and to produce a second solution.

The Statement of the Research Problem

After final selection of the dependent and independent variables, the researcher has all the ingredients for a statement of his research problem. This statement usually takes the form of a question which specifies the independent and dependent variables (or the variate and criterion variable if the research is an associational or status study) and the type of relationship being studied between the variables. An example of a research problem statement might be:

> What are the effects of amount of practice on multiplication performance?

A causal relationship can be inferred between any two variables when a change in one produces a change in the other. Only in an experimental study, however, is the researcher able to manipulate the independent variable and observe its effect on the dependent variable. Thus, the problem statement of an experimental study is customarily phrased:

> What are the effects of type of reinforcement on the accuracy of French pronunciation?

The independent variable in this case is type of reinforcement, and the dependent variable is accuracy of French pronunciation. The words "effects of" and "on" indicate that one variable (pronunciation) will be observed, while the other (type of reinforcement) is varied.

In associational or status studies, in contrast, one is not able to infer a causal relationship between the variables. The problem statement should therefore be of the form:

> What is the relationship of college grade point average (GPA) to average earnings after graduation?

In this instance college GPA is the variate and average earnings after graduation is the criterion variable. The words "relationship of" indicate that the results of the study will enable us to say only that there is or is not a relationship between the two variables. It will not be possible, however, to make inferences regarding a causal relationship between the variables.

IDENTIFYING PAIRS OF VARIABLES

Mark *"ID"* for each pair of variables below that consists of an *independent variable and dependent variable*, and *"VC"* for each pair which consists of a *non-manipulable variate and a criterion variable*.

1. ____ Intelligence level of high school students; high school drop-out rate

2. ____ Amount of oral reading practice; reading performance

3. ____ Type of student grouping; mathematics achievement

4. ____ Age of parents; pupil attitudes toward school

The pairs of variables in items 2 and 3 consist of an independent and dependent variable (ID). Items 1 and 4 are comprised of pairs of non-manipulable variates and criterion variables (VC).

CONSTRUCTION OF PROBLEM STATEMENTS

Construct a research problem statement for each of the pairs of variables presented in the preceding exercise.

1. _____

   _____

2. _____

   _____

3. _____

   _____

4. _____

   _____

The problem statements for each pair of variables should have been similar to the following:

1. What is the relationship of the intelligence level of high school students to the high school drop-out rate?

2. What is the effect of amount of oral reading practice on reading performance?

3. What is the effect of type of student grouping on mathematics achievement?

4. What is the relationship of the age of parents to pupil attitudes toward school?

Summary

This sequence has stressed the importance of doing a thorough job of identifying all variables which might have significant effects on the results of a research study. It has also delineated techniques for avoiding the most frequent pitfalls when making the final selection of variables. Finally, the Appendix which follows provides sources, along with guidelines for their use, for reviewing the relevant literature.

REFERENCES

Dunnette, M. D. "Fads, Fashions, and Folderol in Psychology," *American Psychologist*, 21(1966), 343-352.

Educational Resources Information Center. *How to Use ERIC.* Washington, D. C.: U. S. Office of Education, National Center for Educational Communication, 1970.

Fry, E. "A Classification of Variables in a Programmed Learning Situation," in J. P. De Cecco (ed.), *Educational Technology.* New York: Holt, Rinehart and Winston, Inc., 1964.

Gilbert, T. F. "A Structure for a Coordinated Research and Development Laboratory," in J. P. De Cecco (ed.), *Educational Technology.* New York: Holt, Rinehart and Winston, Inc., 1964.

Gwynn, J. M., and Chase, J. B. *Curriculum Principles and Social Trends.* New York: The Macmillan Company, 1969.

Hyman, R., and Anderson, B. "Solving Problems," *International Science and Technology*, September, 1965, 36-41.

Kaplan, A. *The Conduct of Inquiry.* San Francisco: Chandler Publishing Company, 1964.

Lindvall, C. M. *Defining Educational Objectives.* Pittsburgh: University of Pittsburgh Press, 1964.

Siegel, L., and Siegel, L. C. "A Multivariate Paradigm for Educational Research," *Psychological Bulletin*, 65(1967), 306-326.

APPENDIX

SYSTEMATIC SEARCH AND ANALYSIS
OF RELATED RESEARCH

REVIEW OF THE LITERATURE

Usually the search for publications of related research should start with general reference sources such as *The Education Index, Psychological Abstracts,* or *Dissertation Abstracts.* These references have categorized documents by topic or subject, so that the researcher need search for research report titles and abstracts only in those categories that relate to his problem area. Many of the research reports listed under the topic headings in the above-mentioned sources can be eliminated from consideration by examining the titles. This is only possible, however, for those research reports which have clear, concise titles. A good research report title should specify clearly the independent and dependent variables as well as the particular population to which the results apply.

In reviewing the literature, the most efficient search strategies are (a) to work back from the new to the old, and (b) to work down from the general to the specific. Thus, a researcher would start with the most current reference sources and then work back through the preceding editions. Using the second method, he would start with general topics, systematically locating and searching the more specific areas of interest. Many of the reports of related research will be in the journals. There are a large number of journals, each of which has a different domain of interest. The researcher should always check through recent issues of those journals which publish research in his general area of interest. A listing of some of the more prominent published sources of educational and psychological research follows.

Acta Psychologia

AEDS Monitor

American Behavioral Scientist

American Educational Research Journal

American Journal of Mental Deficiency

American Journal of Psychology

American Psychologist

American Statistician

Annual Review of Psychology

Audiovisual Instruction

AV Communication Review

Behavior Research Therapy

Behavioral Research Methods and Instruction

Behavioral Science

Biometrics

Biometrika

British Journal of Educational Psychology

British Journal of Educational Research

British Journal of Psychology

California Journal of Educational Research

Canadian Journal of Behavioral Sciences

Canadian Journal of Psychology

Child Development

Child Psychology

Cognitive Psychology

Comparative Education

Contemporary Psychology

Current Index to Journals in Education

Data Processing for Educators

Dissertation Abstracts

Education Index

Educational Administration Abstracts

Educational Administration Quarterly

Educational and Psychological Measurement

Educational Leadership

Educational Media

Educational Product Report

Educational Record

Educational Research

Educational Technology

Educational Television

Educational Theory

Elementary School Journal

Exceptional Children

Harvard Educational Review

Human Factors

Journal of Abnormal and Social Psychology

Journal of Aesthetic Education

Journal of Applied Behavior Analysis

Journal of Applied Behavioral Science

Journal of Applied Psychology

Journal of Communication

Journal of Consulting Psychology

Journal of Counseling Psychology

Journal of Creative Behavior

Journal of Educational Data Processing

Journal of Educational Measurement

Journal of Educational Psychology

Journal of Educational Research

Journal of Experimental Child Psychology

Journal of Experimental Education

Journal of Experimental Psychology

Journal of General Psychology

Journal of Genetic Psychology

Journal of Learning Disabilities

Journal of Linguistics

Journal of Mathematical Psychology

Journal of Negro Education

Journal of Nervous and Mental Disease

Journal of Personality and Social Psychology

Journal of Psychology

Journal of Reading

Journal of Research and Development in Education

Journal of Research in Music Education

Journal of Social Psychology

Journal of Special Education

Journal of Speech and Hearing Disorders

Journal of Speech and Hearing Research

Journal of Systems Management

Journal of Teacher Education

Journal of the American Statistical Association

Journal of the Experimental Analysis of Behavior

Journal of Verbal Learning and Verbal Behavior

Language

Language and Language Behavior Abstracts

Language Learning

Language-Teaching Abstracts

Linguistics

Mind

Mirrors for Behavior

Modern Language Journal

Multivariate Behavior Research

Music Educators Journal

National Education Association Journal

National Society for the Study of Education

National Society of Programmed Instruction Journal

Occupational Psychology

Operations Research

Operations Research Quarterly

Organization Behavior and Human Performance

Perceptual Cognitive Development

Personnel and Guidance Journal

Personnel Psychology

Phi Delta Kappan

Planning and Changing—a Journal for School Administrators

Psychological Abstracts

Psychological Bulletin

Psychological Monographs

Psychological Record

Psychological Reports

Psychological Review

Psychology in the Schools

Psychology Today

Psychometrika

Quarterly Journal of Experimental Psychology

Reader's Guide to Periodical Literature

Reading Research Quarterly

Reading Teacher

Research in Education

Review of Educational Research	Sociology of Education
Science	Soviet Education
School Management	Soviet Psychology
School Research Information Service (SRIS Quarterly)	Studies in Art Education
	Teachers College Record
School Review	Technometrics

Useful sources of information concerning current research not in published form can be found in *Dissertation Abstracts* and *Masters' Abstracts*, which contain short summaries of doctoral dissertations and masters' theses completed by graduate students. If the description of the study indicates that it contains important information, the work may then be obtained through an interlibrary loan service or from the publishers of *Dissertation Abstracts*. For a title listing of dissertations in the field of education, both underway and completed, see Phi Delta Kappa's annual publication, *Research Studies In Education*.

EDUCATIONAL RESOURCES
INFORMATION CENTER (ERIC)

Perhaps the most promising source of information concerning educational research is the recently developed Educational Resources Information Centers (ERIC) of the U.S. Office of Education. ERIC is perhaps best described in its own helpful reference publication, *How To Use ERIC*, as:

> ... a national information system designed and supported by the U.S. Office of Education for providing ready access to results of exemplary programs, research and development efforts, and related information that can be used in developing more effective educational programs. Through a network of specialized centers or clearinghouses, each of which is responsible for a particular educational area, current significant information relevant to education is monitored, acquired, evaluated, abstracted, indexed, and listed in ERIC reference products. Through these reference publications any educator, anywhere in the country, has easy access to reports of innovative programs, conference proceedings, bibliographies, outstanding professional papers, curriculum-related materials, and reports of the most significant efforts in educational research and development, regardless of where they were first reported.

The particular educational areas in which the network of clearinghouses currently specialize are:

Adult Education	Library and Information Sciences
Counseling and Personnel Services	Linguistics
The Disadvantaged	Reading
Early Childhood Education	Rural Education and Small Schools
Educational Administration	Science Education
Educational Facilities	Teacher Education
Educational Media and Technology	Teaching of English
Exceptional Children	Teaching of Foreign Languages
Higher Education	Tests, Measurement, and Evaluation
Junior Colleges	Vocational and Technical Education

The researcher interested in using the ERIC system can begin his search by consulting the monthly issues of *Research in Education* (RIE) for current documents in his area of interest. If, for example, he were interested in improving reading performance, he could check RIE's subject index under the search term *Reading* and the applicable terms that follow (e.g., *Reading Comprehension*). Each document has its own identification number which can be used for obtaining it from the nearest ERIC microfiche collection (maintained by many educational and education-related institutions) or the ERIC Document Reproduction Service (EDRS). Using the same search term *(Reading)*, the researcher can also check the *Semi-Annual Index* and *Annual Index* to RIE for relevant documents. He can further extend his review of the literature by consulting the monthly indexes of *Current Index to Journals in Education* (CIJE) and issues of the CIJE *Semi-Annual* and *Annual Indexes.*

Searching the ERIC files for relevant research can be greatly facilitated through the use of a computer-based informational retrieval system. The QUERY system, for example, is available in many areas, and will enable the user (for a fee) to have the computer search for all documents that are coded to specific ERIC search terms or descriptors. This computerized search can save the researcher considerable time in locating studies relevant to his area of interest.

DATA RECORDING AND FILING   In making his comprehensive survey of related research, the investigator must develop a method for recording and filing notes which maximizes accuracy and minimizes time spent on clerical tasks. Note cards or identical-size sheets of paper provide convenient materials for recording data. The 4 × 6″ or 5 × 8″ note card or the 8½ × 11″ paper is preferred.

The entries should be arranged to facilitate ease of access when the materials are being used in writing his research report. The cards or sheets are usually filed in file boxes, indexed by subject and/or author. As shown below, the information cards or sheets should be arranged with the author's surname listed in the upper left-hand corner, using the standard bibliographic reference form. The data can then be filed alphabetically by author.

If more than a single topic is covered in the survey, and if large numbers of cards or sheets are collected, a system of coding by topic is desirable. One method involves placing colored marks or metal tabs in various positions on top of each card or sheet, the colors and positions of which can provide a key to indicate a number of separate topics.

1. Complete bibliographic listing (including the library call number) should be placed at the top of the card.

2. The page number from which each specific item of information has been taken should be included.

3. The exact wording of passages which may be used later as direct quotations should be recorded.

The following information will allow the researcher to make accurate references in writing the research proposal or report:

STANDARD BIBLIOGRAPHIC REFERENCE
INFORMATION CARD OR SHEET

Periodicals	*Books*
Author(s)	Author(s)
Article Title	Book title (include edition)
Source	Publication data: city, publisher, year
Volume (Volume number and issue number, or Month, Day, Year)	
Pages	Pages

Notes:

NOTES

NOTES

NOTES

COMPONENTS OF THE EDUCATIONAL RESEARCH PROPOSAL

Paul E. Resta

Robert L. Baker

CONTENTS

**Objectives
of
this
sequence**

To obtain financial support for a research project, one must first be able to explain the nature of the anticipated effort and its significance for education. This information is usually presented in the form of a research proposal.

Although the proposal formats of different funding sources vary, a few basic components can be identified as common to all well-constructed proposals. Funding agencies frequently attach unique labels to these components or specify a different order of structuring them into the overall research proposal, but such uniqueness poses no problem to the development of the component.

The general objective of this sequence is to put the reader in position to prepare a defensible research proposal by outlining the requirements and conditions of each of the basic components. Specifically, the learner who successfully completes this sequence should be able:

1. To rewrite project titles not possessing the specified characteristics of a well-formed title

2. To identify and construct problem statements meeting specified criteria

3. To propose a justification of the operations and procedures for a previously formed problem statement

4. To translate given research problem statements into substantive hypotheses and outline data collection and analysis procedures

5. To construct a proposal outline for a study formulated from a given problem area

Although the sequence is oriented toward an experimental research point of view, the components are equally applicable for correlational study proposals.

Proposal Title

The first part of any research proposal to be read is the title. An unclear, wordy, or poorly stated title will establish a negative predisposition in the reader toward what is to follow. The title identifies the proposed research project and must concisely and clearly indicate:

1. The key variables included in the study

2. The type of relationship between the variables

3. The population to which the results may be applied

IDENTIFICATION OF THE VARIABLES

The title should first of all identify the variables to be studied in the research project. What is meant by "variables" in this context? Variables in educational research may be categorized as either criterion (dependent) variables or variates. The criterion variable typically represents some aspect or product of student behavior such as achievement or dropout rate. The variate, on the other hand, usually represents a specific educational condition, or learner characteristics such as size of classroom, age of student, and so on. It is the relationship between the variate and the criterion variables that constitutes the heart of the study.

In an experimental study the researcher manipulates one variable (e.g., type of reading instruction) and observes its effects on another variable (reading performance). The manipulated variable is called the *independent variable* and the variable on which the effect is observed is called the *dependent variable*.

Remembering that the title for a proposed experimental study must include a statement of both the independent and dependent variables, look over the following title:

> The Effects of Mode of Presenting Instructions on the Mathematics and Biology Test Scores of Eighth-Grade Students

Here the independent variable is "mode of presentation." It might be manipulated by presenting instruction in either of two ways: (a) oral form, or (b) written form. The dependent variables are "mathematics" and "biology test performance."

EXERCISE 1

IDENTIFYING INDEPENDENT AND DEPENDENT VARIABLES

Write "I" beside the number of each *independent variable* and "D" beside the number of each *dependent variable* in the following research proposal titles.

The Effects of
1. ____ Subject Organization (Chronological and Problem-Centered) on
2. ____ the American History Achievement of Fifth-Grade Students

3. ____ The number of moving traffic violations of high school students receiving
4. ____ different types of driving instruction

Item 1 is the independent variable (I) and item 2 is the dependent variable (D). The second proposal title does not follow the usual sequence. In this instance the dependent variable (item 3) precedes the statement of the independent variable (item 4).

In non-experimental studies — that is, studies in which the variate is not manipulated by the researcher, the variables may be referred to simply as *variates* and *criterion variables.* A correlational (or associational) study is a non-experimental study in which the relationship (or association) between the variate and the criterion variable is investigated. The variates, however, are not manipulated.

An example of a correlation study proposal title might be:

> The Relationship Between Parental Income and Number of High School Dropouts

In this example the variate is parental income, and the criterion is number of dropouts.

EXERCISE 2

IDENTIFYING VARIATES AND CRITERION VARIABLES

Write "V" beside the number of each *variate* and "C" beside the number of each *criterion variable* in the following research proposal titles.

The Relationship between
1. ___V___ Amount of Teaching Experience
2. ___C___ and Teacher Acceptance of Objective-Based Instructional Programs

The Relationship between
3. ___V___ Socio-economic Status,
4. ___V___ Number of Children in Family,
5. ___C___ and Parental Participation in a Kindergarten Summer Reading Program

---

The variates (V) are items 1, 3, and 4. The criterion variables (C) are items 2 and 5.

SPECIFICATION OF THE TYPE OF RELATIONSHIP BETWEEN VARIABLES

A causal relationship can be inferred between two variables when change in one produces a change in the other, indicating that the one variable has an effect on, or is causally related to, the other variable. In an experimental study, the researcher manipulates the independent variable in order to observe its effect on the dependent variable. Thus, the title of an experimental study is customarily phrased: "The Effects of [the independent variable] on [the dependent variable]." This form of title conventionally indicates that the variable following "The Effects of . . ." is an independent variable and that its effects on the dependent variable will be observed. Another example of a proposal title for an experimental study is:

> The Effects of Tutoring by Fifth-Grade Pupils and Parents on the Reading Scores of First-Grade Pupils

This title indicates that the independent variable, "tutoring," will be manipulated by the researcher and that its effects on the dependent variable, "reading scores of first-grade pupils," will be observed.

The title of a correlational study should not be phrased "The Effects of . . . on . . . ," because in correlational studies one cannot make inferences about a causal relationship between the variables. One can state only that there is a relationship. Thus, these titles should be phrased, "The Relationship between [variate] and [criterion variable]." An example of a correlational study title is:

> The Relationship Between General Attitudes Toward School and Academic Achievement of Twelfth-Grade Students

Here the title indicates that the relationship between the variate, "general attitudes toward school," and the criterion variable, "academic achievement," will be observed.

EXERCISE 3

IDENTIFYING TYPE OF STUDY FROM THE TITLE

Write "E" beside the number of each *experimental* title and "NE" beside the number of each *non-experimental* title.

1. ____ The Relationship between Intelligence and Rate of Reading Comprehension of Second-Grade Students

2. ____ The Relationship of Sibling Position With Attitudes Toward School

3. ____ The Effect of Overt versus Covert Responding to Programmed Instruction on Long-Term Retention

---

Intelligence and Sibling Position are non-manipulable variates under the usual techniques employed in educational research. Title Number 1 and 2, therefore, are not experimental studies. Not only do the words "The Effect of . . ." label Title 3 as an experiment, but the manipulable variable (Response Mode) is obvious from the title.

Another important requirement for a good research title is that it identify the boundaries within which the research findings may be legitimately applied. These boundaries are frequently expressed in terms of a "target population." The target population must be precisely defined as a group or class of individuals that can be clearly differentiated from other groups or classes of individuals. The following research titles clearly indicate a "target population":

1. The Relationship Between The Family Social Position, School Expectations, and Peer Group Status of Fifth-Grade Rural Elementary School Children

2. The Effect of Computer-Assisted Instruction and Lecture Discussion Methods of Teaching General Science on the Science Achievement Test Scores of High School Students

The target population in the first title is "fifth-grade rural elementary school children." The target population in the second title is "high school students." The target population should always be defined as precisely and concisely as possible.

EXERCISE 4

TARGET POPULATION IDENTIFICATION

Identify the target population from the following research proposal titles in the spaces provided.

1. The Relationship Between Cognitive Style and Academic Achievement of High School Students Having Wechsler Adult Intelligence Scale (WAIS) I.Q. Scores of 140 or Higher

TARGET POPULATION: _____

_____

2. The Effects of Inquiry Training on the Scientific Interests of "High" Intelligence Junior High School Students Having College-Educated Parents

The first title indicates that the target population would be comprised of high school students having WAIS I.Q. scores of 140 or higher. In the second title, the target population consists of only those junior high school students who achieved a "high" score on an intelligence test and whose parents were college educated.

LENGTH OF TITLE

Titles longer than fifteen to twenty substantive words are usually too cumbersome to be useful. It is not possible to answer every question about the variables and the target population in a title. Even the long title

> The Effects of Inquiry Training on the Scientific Interests of 'High' Intelligence Junior High School Students Having College-Educated Parents

does not answer a number of questions, such as:

1. The sets of procedures and materials comprising "Inquiry Training"

2. Whether the junior high school students are drawn solely from a public school or whether students from a private school are included

3. Whether one or both parents have to be "college-educated"

4. The amount of college required to qualify as "college-educated"

5. The specific intelligence test and the I.Q. score for defining the "high" intelligence group

Some of these questions can be answered and operationally defined only later in the body of the proposal.

Titles are sometimes padded with unnecessary terms which make it difficult to find the essential information. Title lead-ins such as "A Study of . . . ," "An Investigation of . . . ," "An Analysis of . . . ," etc., are redundant and should not be used. Often procedural details are specified in a title instead of the variables, resulting in long, cumbersome titles, such as:

An Investigation of the Effect of the Traditional Approach to Teaching Introductory Psychology as Compared to an Interpersonal Approach to Teaching Introductory Psychology upon the Attitude Test Scores and the Personal Adjustment Ratings of College Students in a Course in Introductory Psychology

This long title could have been condensed with little, if any, loss of information to "The Effects of Different Methods of Teaching Psychology on the Attitudes and Adjustment of College Students."

CRITERIA OF A PROPOSAL TITLE

Write in the appropriate letters beside each item to indicate which of the following criteria apply to each proposal title.

> A: The variables are clearly specified.
> B: The target population is identified.
> C: The type of relationship being studied between the variables is correctly specified.
> D: The title includes no non-essential information.

In the spaces provided after each title, identify the variables if they have been clearly specified in the title (independent variables, dependent variables, and the like). Then specify any wording that should be deleted or changed if the title contains non-essential information.

1. ____ The Effects of Computer-Assisted vs. Teacher-Administered Diagnostic Testing on the Reading Performance of Third-Grade Pupils

VARIABLES: _____

_____

IMPROVED WORDING: _____

_____

_____

2. _____ An Analysis of the Relationship of Selected Factors to the Nature of the Voluntary Reading of Adolescents

VARIABLES: _____

_____

IMPROVED WORDING: _____

_____

_____

3. _____ A Study of Concept Learning and Generalization in Children

VARIABLES: _____

_____

IMPROVED WORDING: _____

_____

_____

Answers to the above are:

   1. a. The variables are specified, although the independent variable (mode of diagnostic testing) would be better phrased as "type of instructional procedures."
      b. The target population (third-grade pupils) is specified.
      c. The title correctly specifies the type of relationship being studied between the variables. "The effects of . . ." is correct, since "mode of diagnostic testing" will be manipulated in the experiment and its effects on the dependent variables will be observed.

d. No unnecessary information is included in the title.

2. a. The variables are not specified in the title. The terms "selected factors" and "nature of the voluntary reading" do not provide sufficient information about what, if anything, is to be studied or how it will be studied.

    b. The target population is defined as "adolescents," a rather broad term that could profitably be replaced by a more precise description such as "thirteen to seventeen-year-old students."

    c. The type of relationship implies a correlational study, but there is insufficient information to judge whether it meets the criteria for an associational study.

    d. The lead-in, "an analysis of . . ." is unnecessary. "The nature of . . ." is ambiguous.

3. a. The title does not specify the variables.

    b. Target population is identified, but "children" is too broad to be a good descriptor. We know only that the group to be used in this study includes none over the age of twenty-one. More precise descriptors should be used whenever possible: for example, "elementary school children" or "children aged two to eight."

    c. The type of relationship being studied between variables is not specified.

    d. "A study of . . ." is unnecessary.

EXERCISE 6

WRITING A PROPOSAL TITLE

Write a new title for the following, including all characteristics of a good title.

A Comparison of Varied Amounts of Time Devoted to Reading Instruction and Their Differential Effects on the Attitudes toward Reading Manifested by Fifth- and Sixth-Grade Children in a Public School Setting

IMPROVED WORDING: _____

_____

The title could be reworded as: "The Effects of Amount of Reading Instruction on the Reading Attitudes of Fifth- and Sixth-Grade Children."

In summary, a proposal title should identify, concisely:

1. The variables in the study

2. The type of relationship being studied between the variables

3. The population to which the results can be applied (or the sample, if no well-defined population can be identified)

Research Problem

The research problem statement is typically the first part of the body of the proposal. Because of its strategic location, it assumes special importance. A good problem statement will interest the reader and provide a frame of reference for evaluating the remainder of the proposal. If the problem is poorly stated or seems insignificant, there is little hope for proposal approval, no matter how well the rest of the proposal is executed. The Problem component of a proposal defines and delimits the specific area of the proposed research. It begins with the general background of the problem and ends with a concise statement of the problem. Thus, the structure of this component is much like a pyramid. It starts with a broad base of general problems and explanations, followed by a survey of previous relevant research. Development of this component should lead logically to the problem statement which forms the apex of the pyramid.

BACKGROUND OF THE PROBLEM

Every research problem is posed against some background of antecedent knowledge. This background of knowledge should be briefly defined in the proposal, for the researcher needs to indicate how his projected effort will refine, revise, or extend existing knowledge. Educational significance and specific applications of the refinements, revisions, or extensions proposed in the study should be carefully spelled out.

In building up to the problem statement, a researcher must show why he has selected the variables included in the problem statement. The selection of variables should be based either on empirical data or on information extracted from the research literature. The background section, therefore, should:

1. Identify the relevant variables

2. Discuss the variables selected for the study, as well as other important variables which were not included in the study

3. Specify the criteria used for the selection of the variables

This will provide continuity and a logical underpinning for the problem statement. It will also demonstrate to the reviewer that all relevant variables were methodically considered in selecting the specific variables to be included in the study.

Several ways to manipulate a specific variable are often available to the researcher. Should this be the case, he must include his rationale for selecting certain manipulations over others. He must demonstrate to the reviewer that something more than a personal bias led him to the selection of variables and the specific manipulations he plans for those variables.

The terms used in providing the background of the problem should be intelligible to a technically competent person who may be relatively uninformed in the area of the problem. One of the most common errors here is to assume that the reviewer is an expert in the proposed research area. Most reviewers will not be impressed by a lavish show of the researcher's mastery of the technical language of his research area. The use of esoteric and undefined terminology may actually reduce the chances of project approval. When a common or single syllable word will do, use it. If the reviewer does not understand the proposal content, he is unlikely to take the risk of approving it.

A proposal will usually be considered along with many others, and the person who reads it may even be tired, harassed, and irritable when he encounters it. It is imperative, therefore, that the entire problem section be written in clear language which holds the reader's attention from the outset and lets him know in precise, simple terms just what it is that you propose to do. If you fail to communicate with the reader in those first crucial paragraphs, his initial impression of inadequacy may well determine his final decision.

SIGNIFICANCE OF THE PROBLEM

The term "significance," as used here, is not the same as statistical significance. In education, a research problem is significant when its solution can make a practical difference in educational outcomes. The discovery of new knowledge or the elimination of erroneous beliefs or faulty practices can contribute to effecting such differences.

In many educational studies, the difference in the performance of treatment groups may be statistically but not *educationally* significant. An example would be a statewide study which investigates the effects of three different class sizes of fifteen, thirty, and forty-five pupils on mathematics achievement. Let us suppose that the mean scores of each class-size group were respectively 72.2, 71.4, and 70.2 on a 100-item test. Although the largest difference in means is only 2.0, this difference would most likely be considered statistically significant in a statewide study, but it would hardly be considered important *educationally*. Few educators would recommend that small classes be adopted on a statewide basis solely on the findings of this study. It does not require an economic analysis to conclude that the value of the effect is less than its cost.

Educational significance is also related to the type of study performed. For example, investigations designed to compare and assess the relative merits of specific instructional materials such as textbooks and teaching aids fail to yield educationally significant findings. The kind of statement that can be made upon the conclusion of such a study is only that textbook X is better than textbook Y and Z. It may be that all three textbooks are truly inadequate. The results of the study in this case would demonstrate only that text series X is the least inadequate of the three. This example is not intended as a condemnation of this type of research. However, those who engage in simple evaluative studies should be aware of the type of significance yielded by such studies.

The educational significance of the research problem may be justified with reference to such criteria as:

1. *Timeliness.* What is considered "timely" in research will change continually. Currently, ecology is a "hot" area of educational research. Projects related to this area tend to be considered "timely" now, but may not be a few years hence.

2. *Relation to a practical problem.* When a researcher can relate his research to a practical problem, he is more likely to obtain financial support. An example of a current practical problem would be that of maintaining the continuity of education for children in an increasingly mobile society.

3. *Relation to wide population.* A research project related to teaching kindergarten children to read would have wide applicability.

4. *Relation to an influential or popular population.* The Puerto Rican community in New York or the Black community in the Watts section of Los Angeles are examples. Research directed toward populations such as these may evoke more interest and support than might be the case with other populations.

5. *Sharpening of the definition of an important concept or relationship.* Once an important concept or relationship has been defined initially, a great deal of "mileage" can be obtained by refining it. "The Law of Effect" was first conceptualized by Thorndike at the turn of the century. Through the years, the initial concept has been sharpened and refined into the elaborate system of concepts related to reinforcement which hosts of researchers employ today.

6. *Creation or improvement of an instrument for observing and analyzing data.* New educational measurement instruments are continually being developed, many of which will serve as valuable tools for future research.

The same research problem may be considered significant or insignificant by different funding sources, according to their areas of concern. Each agency views some problems as central to its area of concern and others as peripheral. One agency may regard a study which explores the learning processes as having greater significance than a study of the political attitudes of high school students, while another agency may take an opposite point of view. Topic areas considered significant by a given funding agency can be determined by examining the types of research projects the agency has funded in the past.

STATEMENT OF THE PROBLEM

One of the last stones in constructing the Problem component should be the statement of the problem. Typically, this statement is often presented in the form of a question which specifies:

1. The variate and criterion variables (in an experimental study, the independent and dependent variables)

2. The type of relationship between the variables

3. The target population

The purpose of the proposed research effort will be to answer this question, so only a statement which indicates a relationship between variables or concepts qualifies as a research problem statement. Examples of adequate experimental study problem statements are:

> What is the effect of type of mathematics program on elementary school pupil achievement?

> Does provision of an advance organizer improve retention of a reading selection by high school students?

An example of a correlational study problem statement is:

> What is the relationship of car ownership to the grade-point average of college freshmen?

Problems such as "What is the history of modern math?" or "What are effective methods of reading instruction?" fail to satisfy the relationship criterion. In their stated form, these problems suggest the study of an educational phenomenon without relating it to another phenomenon.

EXERCISE 7

DISCRIMINATION OF PROBLEM STATEMENTS BY RELATIONSHIPS

Place a check beside the number of each problem statement which satisfies the relationship criterion.

1. _____ What is the effect of type of listening training on the listening comprehension performance of sixth-grade pupils?

2. _____ What is the relationship of high manifest anxiety and frequency of visits to the student infirmary?

3. _____ What is the administrative structure of the American university?

4. _____ What are the attitudes of Arizona field workers toward school?

Items 1 and 2 include statements of relationship between variables, while items 3 and 4 do not.

Another important criterion of a good problem statement is that it must be amenable to testing. A problem in which the relationship between variables cannot be empirically tested is *not* a scientific problem. Naturally, one may pose philosophical questions, but he should realize that unless the variables are amenable to evaluation, he is not asking a scientific question. Questions such as "What effect is the changing character of American education having on American children?" or "Are group processes good for children?" are not amenable to empirical testing in their stated form. Some of the above questions have specified neither the variables nor the relationship between the variables. Many of the concepts presented in the questions would be very difficult if not impossible to define in a measurable way.

EXERCISE 8

DISCRIMINATION OF PROBLEM STATEMENTS AMENABLE TO TESTING

Place a check beside the number of each problem statement which is amenable to testing in their present form.

1. _____ What are the implications of the aspirations of today's teachers for the school of tomorrow?

2. _____ What are the effects of pacing on the response accuracy of mentally retarded boys to two-digit multiplication?

3. _____ Do we need to return to fundamentals in education to reach our national potential?

Items 1 and 3 in the above exercise are not amenable to testing in their present form. Item 1 does not specify the variates or the criterion variable. Item 2 defines the variables and target population as well as specifying the type of relationship between the variables. The variates, criterion variables, and target population are not defined in Item 3.

OBJECTIVE VERSUS
VALUE STATEMENTS   A researcher ought to aim for maximum objectivity in his statement of the problem. He should not pose

his problem in a form loaded with value judgments. The question "Are aversive classroom controls bad?" asks a value question that science cannot answer. "Bad" and "Better than" are not objective, operational terms.

EXERCISE 9

DISCRIMINATION BETWEEN OBJECTIVES AND VALUE STATEMENTS

Mark with a "V" those statements which are *value laden or judgmental.* Mark with an "O" those which are *objective.*

1. _____ Is team-teaching better than single-teacher instruction?

2. _____ The problem is to make a comparison of the effects which team-teaching and single-teacher instruction have on achievement in high school physics.

3. _____ Does team-teaching result in higher achievement performance in high school physics than single-teacher instruction does?

4. _____ Is single-teacher instruction harmful to the student's personal development?

5. _____ What are the effects of teaching mode on the physics achievement test scores of high school freshmen?

Items 1 and 4 are value statements. Item 1 uses the term "better" while 4 uses the term "harmful;" nor does the structure of these problems meet the criteria for an adequate problem statement. Items 2, 3, and 5 are objective problem statements. Item 2, however, has an unnecessary "lead-in." The structure of items 2 and 3 does not satisfy the criteria of an adequate problem statement. Item 5 is an example of an adequate problem statement.

Problem statements commencing with "The problem is . . . ," or "The purpose of this study is . . . ," should be avoided; such beginnings tend to make the problem statement unnecessarily confusing. An example is a correlational study problem statement reading: "The problem is to determine the relationship of manifest anxiety and intelligence to the number of extracurricular activities participated in by academically talented high school students."

The "problem is to determine" portion of the statement conveys no information, yet it enlarges an already lengthy statement. The same is true of the following example:

The purpose of this study is to investigate the relationship of car ownership to the grade point average of high school students.

EVALUATION OF PROBLEM STATEMENTS

Write the appropriate letters beside each item, for those of the following criteria which apply to each example.

A: variables not specified
B: relationship not specified
C: not amenable to testing
D: includes value terms
E: contains unnecessary information
F: satisfies all criteria for a good problem statement

1. ____ The problem is to investigate the effects of delayed feedback on the performance of high school students.

2. ____ What is the relationship of parental national origin to the attitudes toward school of elementary school children?

3. ____ What is the best way to teach first-grade children?

4. ____ What are the effects of tutors in classrooms on reading achievement of first-graders?

5. ____ What are the effects of type of programmed instruction?

Items 2 and 4 satisfy all the criteria of a good problem statement. Item 1 has an unnecessary "lead-in" (E). Since the type of performance is not specified (A), it is not amenable to testing (C). Item 3 specifies no variables (A) and no relationship (B). Since no relationship exists, the problem statement is not amenable to testing (C). Item 5 does not specify the dependent variable (A) or a relationship (B), and it is not amenable to testing (C).

HYPOTHESIS STATEMENTS

An hypothesis statement is at a more sophisticated level of problem definition than a problem statement. Components of the research (or substantive) hypothesis are similar to those of a good problem statement, but they are presented in the form of an affirmative proposition rather than in the form of a question. Substantive hypotheses also go a step beyond the problem statement in that they state what is expected to occur if various conditions are evoked or presumed. Too often educational research proposals contain only the problem statement and no hypotheses, for it is far easier merely to pose a question about a relationship in advance. If the researcher reviews the literature carefully, however, there is almost always some empirical or theoretical basis for stating an hypothesis.

As an example, a poor proposal may contain only a problem statement, such as:

> What are the effects of team-teaching and single-teacher instruction on high school physics achievement?

In this instance the researcher has some pilot data that suggests that team-teaching will result in learner performance different from that attained under single-teacher instruction. Thus, the problem statement could be readily refined and translated into a specific hypothesis such as:

> Team-teaching will result in significantly higher physics achievement by high school students than will single-teacher instruction.

PROBLEM-HYPOTHESIS TRANSLATION

Translate the following problem statements into hypothesis form in the space provided.

1. What are the effects of a specially planned mathematics program, as opposed to conventional program, on pupil achievement in eighth-grade mathematics?

   HYPOTHESIS: _____

   _____

2. What effects will providing knowledge of results have on the spelling performance of fourth-grade pupils?

   HYPOTHESIS: _____

   _____

The first problem statement could be translated into the following hypothesis: "The specially planned mathematics program will result in higher pupil achievement than the conventional program."

The second problem statement could be translated: "Providing knowledge of results will result in greater accuracy in spelling new words than will providing no knowledge of results."

OPERATIONAL DEFINITION OF
TERMS IN THE HYPOTHESIS
A not uncommon difficulty in educational research is that a problem statement will be so broad and vague that it cannot be translated into a clear, testable hypothesis. One encounters in the literature statements of hypotheses such as: "Group educational processes enhance the self-insight of the individual." Yet terms like "Group educational processes" and "self-insight" lack adequate empirical referents and must be operationally defined before they can be used in the hypothesis. All terms in an hypothesis should be carefully defined either before or immediately following presentation of the hypothesis.

EXERCISE 12

DISCRIMINATION OF HYPOTHESES
REQUIRING OPERATIONAL DEFINITION

Place a check beside the number of those items which are adequately stated, as opposed to those which are vague and require operational definition.

1. _____ Democratic education results in a greater sense of personal identity than non-democratic education.

2. _____ Authoritarian classroom methods inhibit the creative impulses of students.

3. _____ The use of reading groups determined by scores on the Cosmopolitan Reading Test will result in higher first-grade reading achievement than will the use of reading groups determined by chronological age.

Items 1 and 2 are ambiguous in their present form. To be testable, concepts such as "democratic," "sense of personal identity," "authoritarian," and "creative impulses," must be translated into operational terms which can be observed and measured. The third hypothesis is acceptable because it uses unambiguous and well-defined terms.

THE NULL HYPOTHESIS
The substantive hypothesis, once formulated, must, of course, be translated into operational and

statistical terms in order to be tested. This requires that the statistical relations deduced from the substantive hypothesis be expressed by another conjectural statement — one using statistical terms. For example: A discovery method (Treatment A) will result in higher achievement than a lecture method (Treatment B).

This hypothesis, however, is untestable. It does not state how much higher A is expected to be than B. In actual fact, it is probably extremely difficult to predict in advance an expected difference of 1, 5, or 10 points. To circumvent this kind of problem, statisticians prefer working with the "null hypothesis" which, unlike the substantive hypothesis, states that only a chance difference is expected to occur between the groups. Thus, the null hypothesis is simply a statistical proposition which states that there is *no relationship* between the variables. If, for example, an independent variable such as "teaching method" were not related to the dependent variable of "pupil achievement," there would be no basis for expecting the mean of the discovery method groups (i.e., $\overline{X}_A$) to be larger than that of the lecture method group (i.e., $\overline{X}_B$). In fact, there would be no reason to expect that there would be any difference between the groups other than that resulting from chance effects. The null hypothesis asserts in effect that the directional substantive hypothesis is wrong, that there is in fact, no relation between the variables. Expressed in statistical terms it says, $\overline{X}_A - \overline{X}_B = 0$. The null hypothesis may also be used with correlation coefficients and other statistical techniques for examining relationships between variables.

In an experimental study, the null hypothesis takes the form of a statement asserting that the independent variable has no effect on the dependent variable. Given the substantive hypothesis that "Immediate feedback on test performance will result in higher mathematics achievement than delayed feedback," the associated null hypothesis is, "Type of feedback will have no effect on mathematics achievement." Similarly, the substantive hypothesis, "Team-teaching will result in higher reading achievement than single-teacher instruction," would yield a null hypothesis asserting: "Type of teaching method will have no effect on reading achievement."

EXERCISE 13

SPECIFICATION OF THE NULL HYPOTHESIS

Develop a null hypothesis from each substantive hypothesis below.

1.   Students assigned two hours of homework each day will make higher average grades than those assigned one hour of homework each day.

NULL HYPOTHESIS: _____

_____

_____

2. Distributed practice in learning to drive an automobile will result in fewer driving errors than will massed practice.

NULL HYPOTHESIS: _____

_____

_____

The null hypothesis for Item 1 could be: "Amount of homework will have no effect on pupil grade point averages." The null hypothesis for Item 2 might be stated as: "Type of practice in learning to drive an automobile will have no effect on number of driving errors."

Review the concept using another example. Suppose that, while observing classrooms in his school district, a researcher observed that Teacher A's class appeared to have a much lower frequency of disruptive classroom behavior than Teacher B's class. Upon closer scrutiny he noted that Teacher A frequently commended her pupils while they were pursuing assigned tasks. Teacher B, whose manner was equally positive, did not appear to be as selective of the pupil behavior to which she warmly responded. The following problem statement was subsequently formulated by the researcher:

What are the effects of teacher approval on frequency of disruptive classroom behavior (i.e., talking, out-of-seats, hitting)?

He could then translate this into a substantive hypothesis:

Classes receiving response-contingent approval will have a lower frequency of disruptive classroom behavior than classes receiving approval on a non-contingent basis ($\overline{X}_C < \overline{X}_{NC}$).

The null hypothesis paired with the above substantive hypothesis would be:

Type of teacher approval (contingent or non-contingent) will have no differential effect on frequency of disruptive classroom behavior ($\overline{X}_C = \overline{X}_{NC}$ or $\overline{X}_C - \overline{X}_{NC} = 0$).

The researcher then devises an experiment to test this hypothesis.

He randomly assigns subjects to the specified treatment conditions and builds in all the necessary safeguards against possible threats to validity. After the experiment is completed, he obtains a mean "on-task" time of 79% for the contingent group and 40% for the non-contingent group. These findings appear to support his substantive hypothesis. However, it is always possible that this difference could have occurred by chance. He thus uses the null hypothesis to test the data he has obtained against what might be expected to occur on the basis of chance fluctuations alone.

It should be noted that the substantive and null hypothesis are mutually exclusive. If one is accepted, the other must be rejected. Thus, statisticians commonly refer to the substantive hypothesis as the "alternative hypothesis." It is acceptable to use the null or alternative hypothesis alone in a proposal. However, as a matter of convention, the null hypothesis is customarily given with the accompanying alternative hypothesis either in the Problem or the Data Analysis components of the proposal.

CRITERIA FOR EVALUATING
HYPOTHESIS STATEMENTS   To assure the formulation
of testable and significant hypotheses, use the following criteria:

1. *The hypothesis must be clearly stated in operational terms.* The null and substantive hypotheses should be clearly stated and should include the operational specification of the concepts and variables employed in the study.

2. *The hypothesis must be specific and testable.* All operations and predictions included in the hypothesis must be thoroughly and unambiguously defined in order to assess the testability of the hypothesis. By operationally specifying the hypotheses, the potential validity of the experimental results is increased. Hypotheses are frequently stated in such general terms that they are simply not testable. By using broad terms one is able to resort to selective evidence in the interpretation of results. Although astrologists and palm readers make their living by stating predictions in a form that permits almost any occurrence to be construed as prophecy fulfillment, such a strategy is not legitimate in educational research. The more specific the prediction, the smaller the probability that the prediction will actually be borne out by collective evidence. It is imperative, then, that

the research hypothesis be as explicit and specific as possible in order to avoid the trap of selective evidence.

3. *Research problems should be selected which are directly related to previous research or theoretical formulations.* This criterion is usually ignored in research that seeks only an answer to an immediate local operational problem. It is often possible in such instances, however, to design a study which not only obtains the desired information related to the local problem, but also helps to classify the relevant knowledge base.

In summary, the Research Problem component should *begin* with the general background of the problem and *end* with a specific statement of the problem and the hypothesis. In the Background of the Problem, antecedent knowledge should be summarized and an indication given of how the proposed research will refine, revise, or extend existing knowledge. The educational significance of the problem should also be described.

The problem statement should usually be presented in the form of a question which satisfies the following criteria: (a) it must specify a relationship between the variables, (b) it must be amenable to testing, and (c) it must be free of value terms.

Procedures

The Procedures component of a research proposal describes the operations that will be performed to test the hypotheses. It is variously labeled "method," "procedure," or "method of procedure" and includes:

1. Target population and method of sampling
2. Research design and rationale
3. Stimulus materials and instrumentation
4. Data collection methods
5. Data analysis procedures

Careful attention will be given to the Procedures component by any funding agency reviewing the proposal for it contains the operational specifications for the entire project.

TARGET POPULATION AND SAMPLING

The population from which the sample will be drawn, the method of sampling, and the rationale for the sampling method will be examined closely by the funding agency, since the sampling procedures will largely determine the generalizability of the results. The specified characteristics of the target population will, in fact, be an operational definition of the group to which the results may be generalized.

DESCRIPTION OF THE TARGET POPULATION AND SAMPLE

Unless salient characteristics of the target population and sample are thoroughly described in the Procedures component, it will be difficult either to demonstrate that a representative sample was selected or to generalize appropriately from the results of the study. For example, to conduct a reading research project with all elementary school children, it is necessary to define the specific target population as including all grades from one to six, in both public and private schools, including special education classes of equivalent grades, and so forth. Too, if the reading instruction approach is not going to be used below the second grade, this limitation must be detailed.

If the sample is not thoroughly analyzed and precisely described, it is easy to make faulty generalizations from the research results. It was erroneously believed, at one time, that diptheria innoculations also afforded some protection against smallpox. The generalization was based on a sample of children who received diptheria innoculations and who also had a much lower incidence of smallpox. Subsequently, it was found that this was due not to the innoculation but to the fact that the children who were brought forward for the innoculations came from more highly educated families who practiced better hygiene and thus protected their children from smallpox exposure more effectively.

The questions that should be answered in this component include:

1. What is the target population to which the results will be generalized?

2. Are the proposed subjects representative of the target population?

3. To what extent have subgroups in the total population been taken into account?

An adequate description of a research study sample is, "The sample consisted of a random sample of fifteen public school, first-grade classes from a middle-class suburban area of Cleveland, Ohio." Although very brief, the description does indicate the population units used in the study (first-grade classes) and the target population to which the results may be generalized (all first-grade public school classes from Cleveland middle-class suburban areas).

EXERCISE 14

IDENTIFYING TARGET POPULATION FROM SAMPLE DESCRIPTION

Identify the target population to which results of the studies described here can legitimately be generalized.

1. Thirty students from two graduate educational psychology courses at State University were selected at random, and each was then randomly assigned to one of two treatment conditions.

    TARGET POPULATION: _____

2. An ad in newspapers in seven major cities (randomly selected) stated that volunteer female subjects were needed for a study of sex attitudes. Each subject would be paid $5.00 for the interview session. Three thousand women applied and two hundred were randomly selected for the study.

    TARGET POPULATION: _____

In item 1, the largest target population to which the experimental findings could legitimately be generalized would be graduate educational psychology students at State University. In item 2, the largest target population to which results could be generalized would be that of female subjects from large cities who volunteer for sex attitude surveys.

In some instances, the researcher may have to work with a small number of "intact" groups (naturally bonded groups, such as classrooms and professional associations) and may find it difficult to identify the target population from which the groups may be considered a sample. When this occurs, he should describe the sample to be used in detail so that a funding agency can make judgments about the potential generalizability of the results.

After writing the description of the sample in the proposal, the researcher should make sure that the target population named in his proposal title is consistent with the detailed description. Failure to do so may prove a source of embarrassment.

SAMPLING PLAN   The formal sampling plan, and the rationale for its use, should also be described in the proposal. This plan should describe: (1) how the units (one person or one class may be termed a "unit") in the target population will be selected, and (2) what controls (means by which conditions or variables affecting a study are controlled) will be used. The major criterion of a good sampling plan description is that it specifies:

> 1. How an accurate, current list of the target population units will be obtained or constructed
>
> 2. The method of drawing the sample (e.g., simple or stratified random, area, cluster)
>
> 3. The number of subjects or population units to be selected

Generalizations about a population are normally made from samples of that population. However, it is possible in some instances, to generalize about the larger population using an intact group as a sample. For example, in an eyelid conditioning experiment using students from a psychology class (intact group), there is no reason to believe that the subject's eyelid responses would differ systematically from those of other adult samples. However, if intact groups will be used because of convenience and accessibility, this must be justified in the proposal, and the effects on the generalizability of results should be discussed.

EXERCISE 15

SAMPLING PLAN EVALUATION

Write the appropriate letters beside each item, for those of the following criteria which apply to each example:

S: a formal sampling plan is used
R: the research unit is defined
T: the target population is identified

1. _____ The sample will be obtained by listing all the first-grade teachers in the Washington Unified School District and assigning a number to each. A simple random sample of twenty teachers will be selected using a table of random numbers. The sample will consist of all children in the twenty classrooms.

2. _____ The subjects will be one hundred American youths who will be selected from adjacent schools by the experimenter. No more than ten students will be used from the same school in the study.

3. _____ The subjects will be all 136 fifth- and sixth-grade students in the University School.

Item 1 uses a formal sampling plan. The research unit is a first-grade class, and the target population is all of the first-grade classes in the Washington School District. Item 2 does not indicate the use of a formal sampling plan. The research unit is the student. Neither the target population nor the sample is defined. The term "youth" does not denote a specific age range. The subjects, thus, could range from kindergarten to college age. In item 3, no formal sampling plan is used and the experimental unit is the student. In this instance, the entire population of fifth- and sixth-graders at the University School was used in the study. Strictly speaking, this is also the population to which the results may be generalized. To the extent, however, that this university school is similar to other university schools, the results may be applicable to the other schools.

SAMPLE SIZE   Increasing the sample size increases the *power* (i.e., the probability of correctly rejecting the null hypothesis) of a study. However, it is costly and inefficient to use more subjects than are actually needed. The researcher ought, therefore, to specify the rationale for the sample size selected and cite any pilot study data which indicates the sample size needed to obtain statistically significant results. Previous studies may also provide estimates as to the accuracy of the measuring instruments and methods used in the study. Once the variability of measures is estimated, statistical techniques can be employed on data obtained from pilot studies or previous studies by other researchers to estimate the sample size needed to detect a significant effect. If there is any doubt concerning the required sample size, the researcher should select a sample slightly larger than the minimum indicated. Most funding agencies see this as a means to increase the generalizability of the results. Research is expensive, hence an agency must have high confidence in the likelihood of a resulting payoff. The funding agency may not view the project as favorably if it is possible that results may have to be discounted because the sample was too small.

DESIGN

The design element of a proposal should indicate how the research setting will be arranged in order to yield the desired data with the least possible contamination by irrelevant variables. In an experimental study, the objective is to isolate the independent variable and then determine its effect on the dependent variable. To do this, the researcher must control all factors that may affect the results of the study. In animal behavior studies, it is possible to have complete control (twenty-four hours a day) over most environmental factors that may affect the subjects. Educational research is much more difficult, however, because there are so many variables operating in an educational situation and because there are many factors outside of the experimental situation that might affect the results. The proposal should carefully identify those variables that might affect the results, and it should specify how the variables will be controlled. Control is typically obtained through the careful:

1. selection of variables and treatments to be studied

2. selection of subjects to be used in the project

3. selection of the types of stimulus materials, tests, and instrumentation used

4. analysis of possible effects of other variables that affect the results

There is no single "correct" design that can be universally used. Individual researchers usually devise designs favoring their own methodological and theoretical predispositions. All research designs, in fact, represent a compromise dictated by the many practical considerations of educational research. A good design is one in which an optimal trade-off is made between what is easily controlled and what is desirable, but logistically impractical, to control. Thus, the researcher must specify the basis for the particular compromise proposed and the reasons for accepting it.

Many proposals neglect or ignore some of the research questions or hypotheses posed by the study they describe. The first step of the researcher in selecting an appropriate design, therefore, should be to ensure that every proposed question or hypothesis is covered by the design under consideration. In the design element he should justify the design selected as appropriate under the particular constraints imposed upon him.

These constraints might include inability to randomly assign subjects to treatment, limited size of the sample, and the like. Expediency, however, is not a justification for a weak design; if a "true" experimental design is not feasible, the researcher must demonstrate convincingly that the alternative design offered respresents an optimal compromise based on:

1. The extreme difficulty and/or cost of using a true experimental design for the proposed study

2. The control of the variables selected

3. The control of possible sources of error

A well explicated presentation and justification of a research design contains four key characteristics which:

1. *Specify its relationship to each research question or hypothesis.*

2. *Describe the way proposed controls anticipate specific confounding variables and threats to validity.* If specific sources of error are not completely controlled by the proposed design, the researcher should explain why they are not anticipated to constitute major threats to validity. For example, if interaction between testing and treatment remains a threat to validity, the proposal should indicate why such a threat is anticipated to have negligible effects. Supporting pilot study data should be cited if available. All possible sources of error should be pointed out in the proposal. If the researcher does not point them out, it is very likely that the reviewer will do so, to the detriment of the proposal.

3. *Describe the design in statistical or logical terms.* Describing the selected design in statistical or logical terms identifies and communicates the possible sources of error in the experiment.

4. *Identify the types of inferences that may be made.* The type of study, experimental or non-experimental, determines the types of statements of causal inference that may be made from the data. The researcher should verify that the desired kinds of statements can be made from the acquired data, using the selected design. Causal inferences can only be made in experimental studies. In correlational studies, all that can be inferred is that there is a relationship between the variables.

STIMULUS MATERIALS

All stimulus materials to be used in the study should be described in the proposal. Many kinds of stimuli may be used in educational research and can be presented in numerous ways. Stimuli are most commonly visual or auditory and can range in complexity from the presentation of a colored card to a complex verbal passage or a computer-generated visual display. The stimuli most commonly used in educational research are printed instructional materials. Descriptions of the instructional materials to be used should include at least the following elements:

1. Title

2. Author/editor

3. Producer (if appropriate)

4. Year of publication

5. Intended population including entering behavior specifications

6. Developmental and field test data summary

7. Time required for administration

8. Cost of materials

RESPONSE MEASURES

The researcher must specify clearly what raw data are required by the research design and how they will be collected. Each measurement instrument should be described in detail including the following items of information:

1. Title
2. Author/editor
3. Producer
4. Population
5. Forms
6. Test objectives
7. Descriptions of test, items, scoring procedures
8. Traits represented in score
9. Predictive/concurrent validity (including description of criterion, subjects and results obtained)
10. Reliability data
11. Normative data
12. Internal consistency or equivalence of tests
13. Time required for administration
14. Cost of materials
15. Date of publication

If the instruments used are well known, the above information can be condensed and appropriate reference information provided as to where full information may be obtained. In all instances, it must be shown how the device constitutes an acceptable operational definition of *all* the variables or terms contained in the research hypotheses. If more than one instrument is consistent with the variable definition, the proposal should indicate the rationale for the choice made. If a researcher must develop his own measuring instrument, he should specify the procedures for its development and validation.

Confounded with the above, but nonetheless a separate point for discussion in the proposal, is the way the device is to be used in decision making. For example, if a predetermined performance pattern is used to decide experimental group assignment or if a specified score is defined as "mastery," full justification for such uses is required.

DATA COLLECTION

The schedules and procedures for acquiring the data and accurately recording it must be included in the proposal. Explicit and formalized measurement procedures, if not already available, should be described in detail. Lengthy procedural forms and outlines, however, are best placed in an appendix and referenced in the body of the proposal. If recording is to be done by a human observer, tape recorder, or television camera, possible reactive effects should be discussed as well as the actions proposed to handle this problem (such as a long adaptation period for subjects or covert recording). A complete schedule for acquisition of all experimental data should be specified, including estimated man-hours for the data acquisition tasks.

DATA ANALYSIS

Data analysis involves the ordering and reduction of the data so that they can be related directly to the research problem. The major criterion used in assessing the data analysis section of the proposal is "Do the data analysis paradigms (statistical techniques used in the study) provide an adequate investigation of the problem?" An analytical paradigm is, in effect, another way to state a hypothesis.

All statistical procedures to be used in analyzing the data should be described in this section. One method of organizing the data analysis element is to state each null hypothesis and to follow it with a description of the statistical tests to be used in evaluating it. If the statistical test is well-known, a lengthy description is unnecessary; a brief statement, such as "a one-way analysis of variance will be used to analyze the data," will suffice.

If, on the other hand, a complex design or a relatively obscure statistical test is to be used, this section should describe the method of analysis and indicate clearly how it is consistent with the research design. If unequal frequencies occur among the cells of a complex design, the proposal should indicate how this problem will be handled.

In summary, the Procedures component should present the operational specifications for the entire research project. It should contain a complete description of all the proposed transactions from start to finish. Specific operations, techniques, instructions, and the mode in which individuals are to respond should be carefully described. Estimated time required for the various steps in the procedure should also be given. The major elements of this component include:

1. Target population and sampling.
   a. Salient characteristics of the target population
   b. Rationale for the formal sampling plan
   c. Characteristics of specific sample used

2. Design
   a. Name and description of the design selected
   b. Justification in terms of the research questions or hypotheses

3. Stimulus materials
   a. Description of materials selected and developed
   b. Requirements and procedures for their use

4. Response measures
   a. Description of each measurement device used
   b. Congruence of measures with research variables defined

5. Data collection
   a. Observation procedures used
   b. Recording procedures used
   c. Schedule for actual data acquisition

6. Data analysis
   a. Name and description of statistical procedures

EXERCISE 16

EVALUATION OF PROCEDURES COMPONENT

Evaluate the following excerpt from a research proposal abstract, indicating whether essential ingredients of any of the following elements are missing or are treated inadequately:

1. Target population and sampling
2. Design
3. Stimulus materials
4. Response measures
5. Data collection
6. Data analysis

THE EFFECTS OF AMOUNT OF TEST-TAKING PRACTICE ON PUPIL TEST PERFORMANCE *(excerpt)*

Hypotheses: 1. Pupils will improve their test-taking ability as a result of working through four discrete perceptual motor tests.

COMPONENTS OF THE EDUCATIONAL RESEARCH PROPOSAL **36**

2. Intelligence is related to acquisition of test-taking skills, thus the scores of intelligent children will show greater improvement across test administrations than will less intelligent pupils.

Method: The subjects to be used in this study will consist of approximately 600 fourth-grade pupils to be taken from 20 classes in eight Los Angeles County suburban schools. A Lindquist Type I Design (Lindquist, 1953, p. 267) will be employed in testing the hypotheses. Evidence for the first hypothesis will be obtained by: (1) a comparison of the mean scores obtained by experimental group classes on the first three tests; and (2) a comparison of final test scores of the experimental and control groups. Evidence for the second hypothesis will be obtained by dividing experimental and control group pupils into one of the three IQ categories (Hi = IQ $\geqq$ 105, Medium = IQ $\geqq$ 95, Low = IQ $\leqq$ 94). Mean scores on the first three tests will then be compared by category within the experimental group, a comparison will also be made between identical categories in the experimental and control groups on the final test.

All pupils will be given a group intelligence test before the start of the experiment. The experimental group will be administered the four perceptual motor tests in accordance with a balanced Latin Square arrangement. The second test will be administered after a one-week interval, the third test after a two-week interval, and the fourth test will be administered after a four-week interval. The control group will be given the initial and final test at identical times to those specified for the experimental group.

YOUR EVALUATION: _____

_____

_____

_____

_____

_____

The following points summarize the exercise:

1. The research proposal abstract specifies the target population but does not specify the sampling procedures used. Thus, it should be indicated that element number one has been treated inadequately.

2. The specific design to be used in the study is identified but there is no indication of why it was selected over other designs. Thus, number two needs additional attention.

3. No mention was made of the specific experimental set-up and stimulus materials requirement, other than referring to "working through . . . tests." Although the response measures themselves do constitute stimulus materials, there are other critical aspects of element number 3 that remain unspecified.

4. No information is furnished on the specific tests to be used in the study; element 4, response measures, requires completion.

5. The data collection description is concise and clear.

6. The types of data to be collected for each hypothesis are defined, but lacking any indication of the statistical tests to be employed, element 6 is incomplete.

Logistics

Logistics concerns itself with the business aspects of a research study, including:

1. Time schedule
2. Personnel
3. Facilities, equipment, and supplies
4. Travel
5. Publication costs and other direct costs
6. Budget forms

TIME SCHEDULE

Time schedules should be consistent with the tasks defined in the Procedures component. The estimated starting date on the project should be realistic and should take into account the availability of personnel and facilities at the time. If the funding agency to which the proposal has been submitted reviews proposals on a continuing basis, the start date should normally be set at least three to four months after the submission date. Some agencies will review proposals only at specific times of the year. If so, the start date should be at least three months after the review date.

A schedule of project tasks and activities can often be most clearly presented by diagrams and flow charts. If a large number of personnel and project tasks are required on the project, it may be desirable to use PERT (Program Evaluation and Review Technique) to display clearly the complex of tasks, target completion dates, and project milestones. Use of PERT on a large research project forces the researcher to define clearly the research project task sequence and it greatly simplifies the preparation of the time schedule and budget sections of the proposal.

PERSONNEL

All principal investigators and research associates should be identified in the proposal, together with a description of their specific research experience and research publications. A sample of five representative research publications per project staff member will suffice in the proposal. Other project personnel, such as graduate research assistants and secretaries need not be identified by name. If a project staff position requires special skills or experience, a job description for the position should be spelled out in the proposal. This section should also include: (1) percentage of time each person will spend on the proposed project; (2) present salary with rate of pay (i.e., 9 month or 12 month); and, (3) the total amount of salaries per year to be charged against the project for each staff member.

FACILITIES, EQUIPMENT, AND SUPPLIES

The proposal should specify all facilities, equipment, and supplies necessary for completing the project.

Office or laboratory space, for example, must be specifically identified. Special equipment such as tape recorders and television cameras, and general office equipment—calculators, typewriters, and dictating machines—must be described and often cost-justified as well. (That is, in addition to normal descriptive information, the equipment's relationship to the project requirements will have to be spelled out.) Even the quantity and cost of stationery items should be estimated and listed in the research proposal.

TRAVEL

Travel requirements of the research project should be carefully estimated, including both in-and out-of-town travel expenses such as air fare, car expenses and per diem. The applicability of the travel to the research must also be clearly defined.

PUBLICATION AND OTHER DIRECT COSTS

Estimate the cost of preparing the final report of the research project including clerical preparation, printing, and the cost of reprints.

Other anticipated direct costs such as consultants, use of computer services, and the like, should be described, including rate of compensation.

BUDGET FORMS

Most funding agencies supply special project budget forms for presentation of the proposal budget. The budget should present allocated time for all project personnel, plus associated costs for each time allocation.

If the proposed project is for more than a one-year period, normal salary increments should usually be estimated and included in the budget statement. Any budget items which are either quite expensive or unusual in any way should be accompanied by a justification for the item in the proposal.

Preparation and Submission of the Research Proposal

We have identified the major components of the research proposal. The organization and sequence of these components will vary according to the proposal formats of funding agencies, but before preparing a draft of his proposal, the researcher should already have clearly defined the proposal components so that he can relate them to any format he may be asked to use. The researcher should select the agency or agency program which he feels offers the greatest probability of funding the proposed research. Final selection of an agency as the recipient of the proposal is normally based on considerations such as the agency's special areas of interest and concern, the amount of funding available, and the ratio of number of projects funded to number of proposals received.

SELECTING THE AGENCY

In selecting an agency as a proposal recipient, the researcher must first ascertain what funding source is most appropriate for his project. One method of identifying appropriate funding agencies is by reviewing the following documents:

1. *Sources of Information on Funds for Education* (Publications Office, Oregon State University, Corvallis, Oregon). This booklet describes over 260 publications on funding sources. Using the index it is possible to quickly find a number of appropriate funding sources by subject area.

2. *Annual Register of Grant Support* (Academic Media, Inc., 10835 Santa Monica Boulevard, Los Angeles, California). This document presents detailed information on government, business and professional organization support programs.

3. *College and University Reporter* (Commercial Clearinghouse, Inc., 420 Lexington Avenue, New York). This is a comprehensive reference source which includes weekly bulletins on recent developments in Washington, D.C., in legislation relating to education and research.

Once the potentially appropriate funding sources have been identified, more detailed information can then be obtained by requesting the agency's published guidelines for proposal preparation. This document typically contains a statement of the agency's bounded area of concern and the type of research that it will support. From this information, the researcher can usually identify agencies whose interests are compatible with his proposed research project. Sometimes, however, an agency's area of concern is so broadly stated that the researcher is unable to assess the relevance of his proposed research project to the agency's interest. In this case, the researcher may be able to derive an operational definition of the agency's area of interest by examining a list of the projects recently funded by the agency.

AGENCY PROPOSAL GUIDELINES

After the researcher has selected a specific agency or agency program as the proposal recipient he should become thoroughly familiar with the agency's instructions for submitting a proposal. The agency's guidelines will indicate the format of the proposal and the items to be included. The researcher should also carefully attend to any deadlines. To avoid the charge of favoritism, most agencies adhere strictly to specified deadlines. In planning his proposal, the researcher, therefore, should allow enough time to write the proposal and to obtain official approval through his own administrative channels.

FORMAT

The researcher should adhere carefully to the proposal format specified by the agency. If the prescribed format is not followed, there is a greater risk of inadvertently omitting important information. Such an omission may result, at best, in a delay of evaluation until the information is provided. In the case of a substantive omission, it may greatly decrease the chances of obtaining approval for the proposed research project. Another hazard in deviating from specified format is that reviewers will have greater difficulty in finding particular items of information in the proposal. Reviewers examining a large number of proposals over a period of time become accustomed to locating certain items of information under certain headings. Thus, a reviewer may entirely overlook an important item of information because he expects to find it in one section of the proposal when the reseacher has placed it in another. Since even a matter of a few days will render specific proposal formats obsolete, it is important that the researcher attempt to maintain a current file of agency guidelines.

SOLICITED PROPOSALS

The sequence has presumed that the proposal originator generates each of the components. The trend within federal government agencies is to deemphasize such "unsolicited" proposals and to rely more heavily on "requests for proposals" (RFP) and "requests for quotations" (RFQ). The RFP and RFQ simply shift the responsibility for originating designated components or aspects of components from research personnel to internal agency personnel. An external researcher response to the RFP, therefore, must recognize the pre-planned specifications included in the RFP and integrate and elaborate his planning from the RFP perspective. The RFP and the response together would cover the same territory as that discussed earlier but frequently in a more detailed form. Since in order to write an RFP, the agency must be able to state what it expects to get out of the research, RFP research is necessarily highly directed and the proposal must be responsive to this direction.

REFERENCES

Davitz, J. R., and Davitz, L. J. *Guide for Evaluating Research Plans in Education and Psychology.* New York: Columbia University, Teachers College, 1967.

Feldt, L. S., and Mahmoud, M. W. "Power Function Charts for Specification of Sample Size in Analysis of Variance," *Psychometrika*, 23(1958), 201-205.

Finan, J. L. "The System Concept as a Principle of Methodological Design," in R. M. Gagne (ed.), *Psychological Principles in System Development.* New York: Holt, Rinehart and Winston, Inc., 1962.

Fox, D. J. *The Research Process in Education.* New York: Holt, Rinehart and Winston, Inc., 1969.

Goode, W. J., and Hatt, P. K. *Methods in Social Research.* New York: McGraw-Hill Book Company, 1952.

Guba, E. G. "Guides for the Writing of Proposals," in J. A. Culbertson and S. P. Hencley (eds.), *Educational Research: New Perspectives.* Danville, Ill.: The Interstate Printers & Publishers, Inc., 1963.

Guilford, J. P. *Fundamental Statistics in Psychology and Education.* 4th edition. New York: McGraw-Hill Book Company, 1965.

Hillway, T. *Handbook of Educational Research.* Boston: Houghton Mifflin Company, 1969.

Kerlinger, F. N. *Foundations of Behavioral Research.* New York: Holt, Rinehart and Winston, Inc., 1964.

Krathwohl, D. R. *How to Prepare a Research Proposal.* Syracuse, N. Y.: Syracuse University Bookstore, 1965.

Levine, S., and Elzey, F. F. *A Programmed Introduction to Research.* Belmont, Calif.: Wadsworth Publishing Company, Inc., 1968.

Rundquist, W. N., and Spence, K. W. "Performance in Eyelid Conditioning as a Function of UCA Duration," *Journal of Experimental Psychology*, LVII (1959), 249-252.

Sax, G. *Empirical Foundations of Educational Research.* Englewood Cliffs, N. J.: Prentice-Hall, Inc., 1968.

Smith, G. R. "A Critique of Proposals Submitted to the Co-operative Research Program," in J. A. Culbertson and S. P. Hencley (eds.), *Educational Research: New Perspectives*. Danville, Ill.: The Interstate Printers & Publishers, Inc., 1963.

————. "How to Write a Project Proposal," *Nation's Schools*, 76 (August 1965), 33-35, 57.

Symonds, P. M. "A Research Checklist in Educational Psychology," *Journal of Educational Psychology*, XLVI (1956), 101-109.

Willower, D. J. "Concept Development and Research," in J. A. Culbertson and S. P. Hencley (eds.), *Educational Research: New Perspectives*. Danville, Ill.: The Interstate Printers & Publishers, Inc., 1963.

NOTES

NOTES

NOTES

SIMPLIFIED DESIGNS FOR SCHOOL RESEARCH

W. James Popham

CONTENTS

Responsible professional innovation involves a concomitant account-ability to assess the merits of the new practices. The common tendency on the part of the public to assume that educational innovation auto-matically means improvement must be tempered by rigorous profes-sional evaluation of the effectiveness of every new educational practice. The need to evaluate prevailing procedures is, of course, a continuing responsibility of the educational research community. All such evalua-tion requires attention to research design.

This sequence, therefore, presents a series of research designs which are relatively simple to employ and are ideally suited for evaluative investigations in schools. At the conclusion of the material presented in this sequence, you should be able to distinguish between four powerful research designs, on the one hand, and three frequently used but weak designs from which few legitimate inferences can be drawn, on the other hand. You should also be able to decide which of the four recom-mended designs is most suitable for a given type of school investigation.

Specifically, the four primary objectives are:

1. To distinguish correctly between the four power-ful designs and three weak designs given examples of each

2. To name the designs on the basis of the given sym-bolic schema depicting particular design configura-tions

3. To construct the appropriate symbolic schema for given design names

4. To choose the most appropriate designs for given exemplar investigations and given descriptions of attendant constraints

Throughout this sequence, any specific practice such as an instruc-tional procedure, a teaching scheme, the use of special materials, and the like, is referred to as a *treatment*. Used in this sense, a treatment signifies the means by which an educator hopes to bring about a desirable end—namely, an intended change in learner behavior. Examples of such treatments include the introduction of supplemental self-study booklets in a mathematics class, or the deliberate increase in a teacher's use of praise with his pupils. Educators evaluate treatments such as these in order to decide whether they should be retained, modified, or discarded.

Weak Designs

UNASSESSED TREATMENT DESIGN

A schematic rendering of an inadequate but common procedure used in introducing a new instructional *treatment* (T) is depicted by the Unassessed Treatment design. The arrow means "then."

UNASSESSED TREATMENT DESIGN: $T \rightarrow$

In this approach, the instructional treatment developer simply implements a new instructional treatment or alters the existing instructional treatment without making any kind of systematic effort to measure whether the treatment is effective. Usually, of course, judgments have been made regarding whether the treatments are likely to prove worthwhile, but these evaluations are often made without any evidence whatsoever. A school administrator, for example, may introduce a new procedure requiring pupils to spend more time in the school library. At the end of the semester, he may "feel" it was a good idea and should be continued. Or a teacher may decide to alter the nature of his homework assignments so that students do half their assigned work during class sessions. Intuitively, he may decide that this new treatment worked out well, but he makes no attempt to measure the results produced by the innovation.

Inferences regarding the worth of a treatment without assessment are clearly to be avoided, as they are based on inadequate evidence and they tend, therefore, to impede the systematic collection of further data.

It is preferable for educators to remain open-minded, postponing all decisions about treatment until such time as appropriate measurements can be collected.

CASE STUDY DESIGN

Here is a second design used by school personnel for the *measurement* (M) of instructional treatments.

CASE STUDY DESIGN: $T \rightarrow M$

The Case Study design attempts to measure the results of a treatment or to gather information for more sophisticated investigations. A teacher may, for example, institute a new instructional technique and, at its conclusion, measure the performance of learners on some relevant criterion.

EXERCISE 1

THE CASE STUDY DESIGN

Write *Yes* or *No* in the space provided, depending on your own evaluation of the following Case Study model.

_____ The Case Study design for research is sufficiently free from major flaws to warrant its widespread use in public school research.

If you answered "Yes," you were not being very rigorous. Many uncontrolled factors might be influencing the measurement, so as to invalidate any judgment based on the Case Study. For example, the learner might have done just as well if the measurement had been made prior to, rather than after, the treatment. Perhaps the treatment didn't actually affect the measured performance at all. This design, then, makes it impossible to discover the impact of a treatment—and that, after all, is what we want to do.

ONE-GROUP PRETEST-POSTTEST DESIGN

Schools today are beginning to try to skirt the inadequacy of the Case Study by using the:

EXERCISE 2
ONE-GROUP PRETEST-POSTTEST DESIGN

Write *Yes* or *No* in the space provided, depending on your own evaluation of the following One-Group Pretest-Posttest model.

_____ The One-Group Pretest-Posttest design for research permits defensible judgments about the merit of a treatment.

Your answer should have been "No." Even though this design provides pretest and a posttest measurement of the learners, it contains a very serious weakness. Suppose a teacher using this design discovered that there was a sizable gain in pupil performance from pre- to posttest. Can he be confident that the gain is attributable solely to the treatment? No, for there are too many other equally plausible explanations. For example, it is possible that learners *without* the treatment would have made the same pre- to posttest gains as a consequence of maturation, or as a result of experiences totally removed from the school's control. Several other reasons tend to weaken inferences made on the basis of the One-Group Pretest-Posttest design, but its primary deficiency is that one cannot be confident that differences in the measurements before and after the treatment are a consequence of the treatment itself.

Thus far we have reviewed the three designs shown below (it seems excessively magnanimous to call them *research designs*) which, while perhaps useful during the early phases of an investigation, are inadequate for the rigorous final evaluation of an instructional program.

Unassessed Treatment	$T \to$
Case Study	$T \to M$
One-Group Pretest-Posttest	$M \to T \to M$

EXERCISE 3
THREE INADEQUATE DESIGNS

List the names of the three inadequate designs discussed above, and draw the symbol for each, in the spaces provided.

1. _____   _____

SIMPLIFIED DESIGNS FOR SCHOOL RESEARCH **6**

2. _____   _____

3. _____   _____

To check your recall, review the design names and symbols above before proceeding.

Powerful Designs

Let's turn now to four research designs which are recommended for school evaluation studies. It should be noted that, although we shall refer in this and subsequent examples to two contrasting groups only, a researcher might well make comparisons between more than two groups. For example, the experimental group might receive one treatment, one control group a second treatment, and a second control group no treatment. Such comparisons between more than two groups are often desirable, for educators are frequently interested in contrasting two or more new approaches. For ease of explication here, however, we restrict the discussions to contrasts between only one experimental group and one control group.

NONEQUIVALENT CONTROL GROUP DESIGN

We might start by examining the Nonequivalent Control Group design which is used with some frequency in school research. This design involves administering *one treatment* (T_1) to an experimental group and *another treatment* (T_2) to the comparison group known as the control group. Here is a schematic rendering:

NONEQUIVALENT CONTROL GROUP DESIGN
Experimental Group: $M \to T_1 \to M$
Control Group: $M \to T_2 \to M$

Nonequivalent Control Group designs involve a comparison between "intact" experimental and control groups. The term "nonequivalent" refers to the pre-treatment status of such groups. Often times in a natural school setting, it is impossible or impractical to select or arrange intact comparison groups that are equivalent with respect to all important pre-treatment conditions. The usefulness of these designs is dependent upon just how different at the experiment's outset the groups really are in regard to such variables as achievement or language ability.

NONEQUIVALENT CONTROL GROUP DESIGN

Write *Yes* or *No*, after studying the research design described.

_____ Usable data will be obtained by comparing the respective post-treatment measurements of two ninth-grade classes, following these procedures. One class is taught with the new method (T_1), while the other class continues with the old (T_2). Both classes are being taught by teachers who are enthusiastic supporters of their respective methods. A pretest covering basic social studies skills was administered and the results indicated that the performance means of the two classes differed significantly.

Although you may have been inclined to respond with a "Yes," you should not have done so. If the two groups used in this design differ in terms of their pre-treatment status (difference in social studies skills) with respect to the outcome of interest, it is impossible to make a sensible comparison of their post-treatment performance. We could not say with any confidence that the effects of the treatment produced the observable posttest differences, for the differences could have been present initially.

The thought may have occurred to you that one could use "gain" scores—that is, posttest minus pretest scores—to reflect the *relative* improvement of the two groups. But measurement specialists have identified serious limitations in the use of gain scores for this purpose. As one simple example of the problems introduced by gain scores, it is easier for a group with a very low average pretest score to make a large gain than it is for a group with a high average pretest score to make a comparable gain. Such a "test ceiling factor" works against the gain potential of the group scoring higher on the pretest.

Because it is true that the degree to which reasonable inferences can be drawn from the Nonequivalent Control Group design is dependent upon there being initial similarity between the two groups, it may have

SIMPLIFIED DESIGNS FOR SCHOOL RESEARCH **8**

occurred to you that we might match the groups. If so, you are thinking in the right direction. But if you have in mind "picking and choosing" matches, you need to think somewhat further. Such matching of groups for equilization has a time-honored tradition in educational research, but its only merits, according to current views, are historical. Although the matched groups may be equal on every variable selected, they may well be extremely different on many other relevant variables. Their many dissimilarities may, in fact, prove more influential than the few matching ones.

RANDOMIZATION AND SAMPLING UNITS   As an efficient alternative to matching, research specialists now recommend randomization procedures:

> Use randomization to ensure initial equivalence of groups.

Assigning experimental units (pupils, for example) to different groups at random through the use of devices such as a table of random numbers is an enormously efficient technique for equalizing groups prior to instituting an experimental treatment. Following is an example of equalizing procedures used by two researchers.

EXERCISE 5

SELECTING EQUALIZATION PROCEDURES

Place a check beside the number of the item which describes the research procedure offering the best likelihood of equivalent groups.

1. _____ Researcher A divides a class of thirty pupils into two groups according to the following procedure. He matches pupils on the basis of sex, IQ, and pretest scores so that Group One and Group Two contain (a) equal proportions of boys and girls, (b) equal average IQ scores, and (c) equivalent average pretest scores.

2. _____ Researcher B divides a class of thirty into two groups at random, so that Group One happens to contain (a) nine boys and six girls, (b) an average IQ of 112, and (c) an average pretest score of 92 correct, while Group Two contains (a) three boys and twelve girls, (b) an average IQ of 106, and (c) an average pretest score of 86 correct.

You should have selected Researcher B. Even though Researcher A's matching procedure produced two groups which appear to be equivalent on the three variables, there are undoubtedly many other relevant variables which were not involved in the matching scheme. There is actually a greater chance that the groups formed by Researcher B are equivalent, for, even though the second of his groups is superior on the basis of IQ and pretest scores, it is possible that certain other *unmeasured* variables, such as motivation, may favor Group One. These unmeasured variables, some perhaps even unmeasurable at present, are distributed without bias between Researcher B's two groups. His group, therefore, will tend to be more equivalent generally in all respects.

Random assignment of pupils to two or more groups is a relatively simple operation when a table of random numbers is used. As an example, a teacher wishing to divide a class of forty-five pupils into three groups, for purposes of evaluating three new tests, can consult such a table (found in most statistics textbooks), in which large sets of numbers are presented at random. Here is an excerpt from such a table.

A Portion of a Random Numbers Table

23157	54859	01837
05545	55043	10537
14871	60350	32404
38976	74951	94051
97312	61718	99755
11742	69381	44339
43361	28859	11016

The teacher might begin by numbering his pupils from one to forty-five. He then consults any point in the random number table as a starting place for selecting numbers between one and forty-five (to match the number of pupils). Once the first number is selected, he proceeds in an orderly fashion in selecting the remaining numbers. In the example below, the teacher has circled the numbers between one and forty-five. He arbitrarily selects number 23 as his first number and he chooses to read down the extreme left of each column (as indicated by the arrows) until all forty-five numbers appear. He then assigns the first fifteen numbers appearing in the table to Group One, the second fifteen to Group Two, and the third fifteen to Group Three. Thus the teacher has selected for Group One pupils numbered 23, 05, 14, 38, 11, and so on, until fifteen pupils for each group have been selected.

The teacher begins his selection process at ⟨23⟩157, reading down the columns

⟨23⟩157	54859	⟨01⟩837
⟨05⟩545	55043	⟨10⟩537
⟨14⟩871	60350	⟨32⟩404
⟨38⟩976	74951	94051
97312	61718	99755
⟨11⟩742	69381	⟨44⟩839
⟨43⟩361	⟨28⟩859	11016

. . . and continues systematically until forty-five numbers have been selected. You may be thinking that it is relatively simple for a classroom teacher to subdivide pupils by randomization, yet in point of fact the realities of the public school world make it difficult to employ randomization procedures with large numbers of pupils. The most conscientious administrator, no matter how strong his commitment to the use of rigorous research designs, will not always be able to move pupils randomly from classroom to classroom for research purposes. This may be all to the good, for usually research in the schools ought in most instances to use the most common unit, the classroom, rather than the pupil as the unit of sampling.

> Sampling by classroom units is a recommended procedure for conducting school research.

This is another way of saying that research investigations should employ the smallest *independent* sampling units available. In the public schools, because there are so many factors that make one class really different from another, such as the impact of the teacher and the interaction of a particular group of pupils, the smallest independent sampling unit tends to be the class. It is only logical that the social context in which group or class learning takes place makes it difficult for students to respond independently of one another. There is, in other words, considerable interdependence among pupils in a given classroom, so that, to secure independent sampling units when more than one class is involved in the study, we should routinely consider the class as our sampling unit. With extremely small numbers of classes this may, unfortunately, be impossible. In any two-group contrasts, for example, the researcher should have at least three classroom units in each of his two groups.

SELECTING EQUALIZATION PROCEDURES

Place a check beside the number of the item which describes the research procedure offering the best likelihood of equalization through randomization.

A. ____ A school researcher wishing to study the value of a new teaching procedure has available eight classes (of thirty pupils each) for evaluation. He randomly assigns four classrooms to the new treatment and four classrooms as controls, and he employs the eight class averages as his data.

B. ____ Another researcher, also having eight classes of thirty available to him, randomly assigns four classes to the new treatment and four as controls. He then contrasts the performance of the 120 experimental pupils with that of the 120 control pupils.

Although most school researchers employ procedure "B," the correct answer is "A." For reasons which it is beyond the scope of this program to demonstrate, the practice of sampling by classroom unit, where the average of the whole class provides the comparison scores, is to be preferred.

With this discussion of randomization and unit sampling in mind, we can turn now to a more powerful research design.

PRETEST-POSTTEST CONTROL GROUP DESIGN

The "R" in this model indicates that the two groups have been formed by randomization procedures. As before, the "M" refers to measurement while "T_1" and "T_2" refer to treatment:

PRETEST-POSTTEST CONTROL GROUP DESIGN		
Experimental Group:	R	$M \rightarrow T_1 \rightarrow M$
Control Group:	R	$M \rightarrow T_2 \rightarrow M$

Because the initial equivalence of the two groups has been maximized through the use of randomization, this design allows the educator to make clear inferences regarding the merits of the treatment. Its one drawback is that certain types of pre-treatment measures may have a confounding interaction with the treatment. It may be, for example, that the treatment, plus the cues received by the learner during his completion of the pretest, produces a posttest difference in favor of the treated group. Measurement procedures such as this—which may, by their use, produce a change in the subject's behavior—are known as *reactive measures*. If the pretest measure appears to be reactive, alternatives to the pretest-posttest control group design should be sought.

POSTTEST ONLY CONTROL GROUP DESIGN

A simple but powerful design all too rarely seen in school research is the Posttest Only Control Group Design:

POSTTEST ONLY CONTROL GROUP DESIGN

Experimental Group:	R	$T_1 \rightarrow M$	
Control Group:	R	$T_2 \rightarrow M$	

This design, as you can see, avoids the possible confusion introduced by reactive pretests. Comparison of the two groups' measurements permits one to make defensible judgments about the value of a given treatment. School researchers seem reluctant to employ this design because of their inability to determine, through a pretest, the initial similarity of the two groups, yet randomization procedure will resolve that problem satisfactorily.

INTERRUPTED TIME SERIES DESIGN

This final design is somewhat different from the previous models, as can be seen here:

INTERRUPTED TIME SERIES DESIGN
$$M_1 \rightarrow M_2 \rightarrow M_3 \not\!\!\!+ M_4 \rightarrow M_5 \rightarrow M_6$$

In this design a series of measurements (the more, the better) is taken both before and after the introduction of the treatment. Frequently these measurements are drawn from existing records such as regularly administered achievement tests, attendance reports, disciplinary referrals, and the like. Such so-called "archival" data are particularly well suited for the Interrupted Time Series design but are by no means the only kinds of data usable with the design.

EXERCISE 7

INTERRUPTED TIME SERIES DESIGN

Write in the space provided the letter or letters of the graph lines which support the conclusion that *improvement was due to the treatment.*

_____ In this hypothetical research situation, we have measured pupil performance on equivalent problem-solving tests every two months during the year, and we have introduced a three-week teaching unit (i.e., the treatment) on problem solving procedures during the middle of the year.

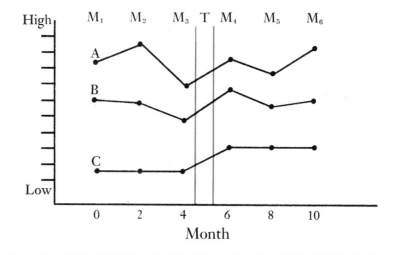

Even though there has apparently been an identical improvement in performance for all groups from the third to the fourth measurements — that is, on measurements immediately preceding and following the treatment — only to Group C should we attribute this increase to the treatment. Groups A and B reveal a fluctuating pre- and post-treatment performance record, thus indicating that the same stimuli

SIMPLIFIED DESIGNS FOR SCHOOL RESEARCH **14**

causing the pre-treatment fluctuations could also have caused the post-treatment fluctuations. Group C, on the other hand, appears to be unaffected by any stimuli other than the treatment because the pre- and post-treatment measurement periods are stable. This inference is made on the basis of an "eyeball" or graphic comparison only. Although certain types of results from the Interrupted Time Series design are difficult to interpret, many are quite straightforward and are easily interpreted when represented graphically.

Design Synopsis

We have now examined seven designs for evaluating the worth of instructional treatments in school research. The first three, as we have demonstrated, are particularly weak and should be avoided by school researchers. One, the Nonequivalent Control Group design, depends on the confidence the researcher can have that initial differences between the groups are unimportant but, in any case, it is preferable to the first three designs. Three additional designs which are strong and can yield readily interpretable evaluative data have been discussed. Summarily, all the designs can be represented schematically as here:

	Design		Symbol
weak	Unassessed Treatment		$T \rightarrow$
	Case Study		$T \rightarrow M$
	One-Group Pretest-Posttest		$M \rightarrow T \rightarrow M$
moderately effective	Nonequivalent Control Group		$M \rightarrow T_1 \rightarrow M$ $M \rightarrow T_2 \rightarrow M$
strong	Pretest-Posttest Control Group	R R	$M \rightarrow T_1 \rightarrow M$ $M \rightarrow T_2 \rightarrow M$
	Posttest Only Control Group	R R	$T_1 \rightarrow M$ $T_2 \rightarrow M$
	Interrupted Time Series		$M_1 \rightarrow M_2 \rightarrow M_3 \not\rightarrow M_4 \rightarrow M_5 \rightarrow M_6$

Spend a few moments reviewing the designs until you can recall their names by looking only at the symbols.

EXERCISE 8

SEVEN DESIGNS FOR RESEARCH: NAMES

Write the names of the seven designs opposite their symbols, in the spaces provided.

1. _____	$T \rightarrow$
2. _____	$T \rightarrow M$
3. _____	$M \rightarrow T \rightarrow M$
4. _____	$M \rightarrow T_1 \rightarrow M$ $M \rightarrow T_2 \rightarrow M$
5. _____	$R \quad M \rightarrow T_1 \rightarrow M$ $R \quad M \rightarrow T_2 \rightarrow M$
6. _____	$R \quad T_1 \rightarrow M$ $R \quad T_2 \rightarrow M$
7. _____	$M_1 \rightarrow M_2 \rightarrow M_3 \maltese M_4 \rightarrow M_5 \rightarrow M_6$

To check your recall, review the names and symbols listed on page 151.

EXERCISE 9

SEVEN DESIGNS FOR RESEARCH: SYMBOLS

Write the symbols of the seven designs opposite their names.

1. UNASSESSED TREATMENT _____

2. CASE STUDY _____

3. ONE-GROUP PRETEST-POSTTEST _____

4. NONEQUIVALENT CONTROL GROUP _____

5. PRETEST-POSTTEST CONTROL GROUP _____

To check your recall, review the names and symbols listed on page 151.

You should now be familiar with the names and symbols of the seven designs. Let's test that familiarity by presenting a few hypothetical descriptions of plans for school research in order to determine whether you can name the designs involved.

IDENTIFYING WEAK AND STRONG DESIGNS

EXERCISE 10

IDENTIFYING TYPE OF DESIGN

Write the *name* of the design employed in this example, in the space provided.

A school superintendent introduces a new music appreciation program throughout his school district which depends heavily upon tape recordings of classical masterworks. Although rather costly, the new program is considered a success by the superintendent and his staff at the close of the year.

DESIGN EMPLOYED: _____

You should have answered "Unassessed Treatment." If you catch one of your colleagues using this procedure to assess an instructional treatment, you have every right to hold him forever in contempt.

EXERCISE 11

IDENTIFYING TYPE OF DESIGN

Write the *name* of the design employed in this example.

A tenth-grade biology teacher institutes a new approach to the teaching of one-celled animal life based on a series of seven-minute single-concept films. Prior to starting the new unit, she develops a test covering the material and administers it to her class before and after the unit, noting with satisfaction a dramatic improvement by her pupils on the test.

DESIGN EMPLOYED: _____

This is an illustration of the One-Group Pretest-Posttest design. As indicated above, inferences from such a design must be made with considerable caution.

EXERCISE 12

IDENTIFYING TYPE OF DESIGN

Write the *name* of the design employed in this example.

A researcher uses a table of random numbers to subdivide 15 junior high school classes into three groups of five classes each (30 pupils per class) as follows: "Treatment A," "Treatment B," and "Control." The treatments are administered during the first four months of the school years, and at mid-semester a posttest is given to all of the 450 pupils involved.

DESIGN EMPLOYED: _____

In this example the researcher was employing the Posttest Only Control Group Design, using random assignment to obtain initial equality among the groups. He correctly sampled by classroom units and, hopefully, will analyze the posttest data by using the averages of the 15 classes. He should *not* lump together the scores of the pupils from each treatment into three groups of 150 each. Rather, he should consider the data to represent the samples of five, five, and five classroom averages.

EXERCISE 13

IDENTIFYING TYPE OF DESIGN

Write the *name* of the design employed in this example.

A school principal has received a federal grant to institute a new mathematics enrichment program. Using school records, he computes the average mathematics achievement score on a nationally standardized examination for his fifth-, ninth-, and twelfth-grade pupils during each of the preceding three years. He plans to have the same tests administered for the two years following the institution of the new program. He wishes to compare the relative positions of the three classes during the five-year period.

An example of the Interrupted Time Series design, this represents a class of problems faced by many practicing educators. They might like to set up an "untreated" control group but are, for one reason or another, prevented from doing so. One such reason might be that certain federal funds are given to school districts under strict provisions that *all* of the pupils must receive whatever educational benefits are provided by the funds, thus, ruling out the use of any group of untreated control pupils.

DESIGN ADAPTATIONS

One way of handling this situation would be to use a time series design such as that described in the previous example; all students would thus receive the treatment. But because intervals of data are not always available for a time series design, it might be wise to use another alternative—an adaptation of the Posttest Only Control Group design. To use this adaptation the research needs *two* new treatments: arithmetic and social science, for example. In this case, a design such as the following is set up, with *ss* signifying social science, and *a*, mathematics:

MODIFIED POSTTEST ONLY CONTROL GROUP DESIGN

Group 1:   R $T_{ss} \rightarrow M_{ss}$ $M_a \rightarrow T_a$
Group 2:   R $T_a \rightarrow M_a$ $M_{ss} \rightarrow T_{ss}$

Here two groups are constituted randomly, after which one group receives the social science treatment while the other receives the arithmetic treatment. At the conclusion of the treatments, Group 1 is administered the social science posttest and Group 2 the arithmetic posttest. Then, so that all pupils are given equal educational opportunities, the treatments between groups are reversed, but this time the tests are administered before the treatments. The test comparisons to determine the efficacy of the treatments are made below between Group 1's social science posttest and Group 2's social science pretest (dotted circles); and between Group 1's arithmetic pretest and Group 2's arithmetic posttest (solid circles).

19 DESIGN SYNOPSIS | 155

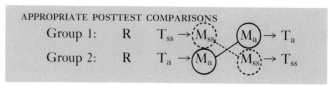

APPROPRIATE POSTTEST COMPARISONS

Group 1:   R $T_{ss} \rightarrow M_{ss}$ $M_a \rightarrow T_a$

Group 2:   R $T_a \rightarrow M_a$ $M_{ss} \rightarrow T_{ss}$

In order to employ this modified design, of course, the researcher must see to it that the two treatments are sufficiently different so that exposure to one will not contaminate posttest performance for the other.

IDENTIFYING STRONG DESIGNS

Now you will be given an opportunity to choose among the four recommended designs when presented with hypothetical research problems like those typically encountered by school personnel. Discarding for the moment (and, we hope, forever) the three weak designs described at the outset of this sequence, you should focus on the four strong models presented, including the modification of the Posttest Only Control Group design discussed above.

> *Recommended Designs:*
> NONEQUIVALENT CONTROL GROUP DESIGN
> PRETEST-POSTTEST CONTROL GROUP DESIGN
> POSTTEST ONLY CONTROL GROUP DESIGN
> INTERRUPTED TIME SERIES DESIGN

The Nonequivalent Control Group design is best used in situations where randomization is impossible, either within classes or by classroom units, and where one can make a strong case for the comparability of the groups involved.

The Pretest-Posttest Control Group design is best used when the educator is interested in a measure of student achievement change from pre-treatment to post-treatment measurement, and when he is willing to assert that the pretest is unlikely to interact with the treatment condition. The possibility for random assignment of experimental units must also be present.

The Posttest Only Control Group design is an excellent choice when randomization is possible, particularly when there is a danger that the pretest is a reactive measure. As noted earlier, this design can readily be modified to handle two instructional treatments when it is important that all learners be given essentially equivalent educational opportunities.

Use of the Interrupted Time Series design depends upon the availability of measurement data spread out over an extended period. In situations where randomization is impossible or where two parallel treatments are not readily available, it is an extremely useful model.

SELECTING THE APPROPRIATE DESIGN

Select the design best suited to the following research problem, and write its name in the space provided.

A school researcher hopes to test the merits of a new series of third-grade reading booklets. The booklets, commercially produced, are sold with a test which covers the skills ostensibly developed by learners during the four-week period when the booklets are to be used. The researcher suspects that the pretest may structure the thinking of pupils if it is administered to them prior to their exposure to the booklets. Twenty third-grade teachers have indicated a willingness to have their classes involved in the research, as members of either the experimental or control groups.

BEST DESIGN: _____

Because of the possibility for randomization, and because of the potentially reactive qualities of the pretest, this situation appears to call for the Posttest Only Control group design.

SELECTING THE APPROPRIATE DESIGN

Select the design best suited to the following research problem, and write its name.

A high school government teacher wishes to conduct a study in his class of the difference that weekly issues of current events newspapers will make in his pupils' scores on a current events test. He realizes that pupils will learn about current events outside of school, so he is particularly interested in their pretest to posttest growth. He has a series of literature selections which he can give to students in the class who are not assigned to read the current events newspapers.

BEST DESIGN: _____

This situation appears to call for the Pretest-Posttest Control Group design.

SELECTING THE APPROPRIATE DESIGN

Select the design best suited to the following research problem, and write its name.

A school counselor wishes to test the influence of students' attitudes toward narcotics of a particular commercial film dealing obliquely with the use of narcotics. He devises a self-report questionnaire but is afraid that if pupils complete the questionnaire prior to viewing the film they will become sensitized to the narcotics issue. Random assignment of pupils is possible.

BEST DESIGN: _____

Because of the reactive nature of the questionnaire, this is another case in which the Posttest Only Control Group design can be used.

SELECTING THE APPROPRIATE DESIGN

Select the design best suited to the following research problem, and write its name.

Faced with the necessity for evaluating a new set of general science kits, members of a small high school science department decide that they cannot randomly assign pupils among their first semester general science classes because there would be conflicts. They have, however, administered science aptitude tests and have found that their four classes are remarkably similar. They hope to use the science kits with two complete classes, since two teachers have indicated unwillingness to use the kits with only a portion of their class.

BEST DESIGN: _____

This seems to be a case where the Nonequivalent Control Group design might be employed, with the previously administered science aptitude test serving as the pretest. The performance of two of the nearly comparable groups will be contrasted with that of the other two. While the researchers' inability to randomize in this instance may force them to this "better than nothing" design, they should usually try to find means of randomly assigning subjects.

SELECTING THE APPROPRIATE DESIGN

Select the design best suited to the following research problem, and write its name.

> Mr. James Li, a school principal, wishes to assess the interest-building contribution of a school club program instituted four years ago. He decides to use average daily attendance rates as an index of pupils' interest in school. He discovers that such data has been accumulated (in the school's archives) for every year since the club program was inaugurated, as well as for the ten years before it was initiated.

BEST DESIGN: _____

This is, of course, a fairly clear instance in which the Interrupted Time Series design would be suitable. Would that all research design decisions were as simple!

Summary

This sequence has examined research designs used by school personnel in the conduct of evaluative investigations. Three were rejected as inadequate, and four were recommended for particular types of research situations. The techniques of equalizing groups through randomization and sampling by classroom units were strongly recommended.

REFERENCES

Barch, A. M., Trumbo, D., and Nangle, J. "Social Setting and Conformity to a Legal Requirement," *Journal of Abnormal Social Psychology*, 55(1957), 396-397.

Box, G. E., and Draper, N. R. *Evolutionary Operation.* New York: John Wiley & Sons, Inc., 1969.

Campbell, D. T., and Stanley, J. C. "Experimental and Quasi-Experimental Designs for Research on Teaching," in N. L. Gage (ed.), *Handbook of Research on Teaching.* Chicago: Rand McNally & Company, 1963, chap. 5.

Chapin, F. S. *Experimental Designs in Sociological Research.* New York: Harper & Row, Publishers, Incorporated, 1947; revised edition, 1955.

Cochran, W. G. "The Design of Experiments," in *International Encyclopedia of the Social Sciences.* New York: The Macmillan Company, 1968, vol. 5, 245-254.

Cox, D. R. *The Planning of Experiments.* New York: John Wiley & Sons, Inc., 1958.

Edwards, A. L. *Experimental Design in Psychological Research.* 3rd edition. New York: Holt, Rinehart and Winston, 1968.

Greenwood, E. *Experimental Sociology: A Study in Method.* New York: King's Crown Press, 1945.

Kerr, W. A. "Experiments on the Effect of Music upon Factory Production," *Applied Psychology Monograph*, No. 5, 1945.

Lindquist, E. F. *Design and Analysis of Experiments in Psychology and Education.* Boston: Houghton Mifflin Company, 1953.

Ray, W. S. *An Introduction to Experimental Design.* New York: The Macmillan Company, 1960.

Sanford, F. H., and Hemphill, J. K. "An Evaluation of a Brief Course in Psychology at the U. S. Naval Academy," *Educational and Psychological Measurement*, 12(1952), 194-216.

Schutz, R. E., Page, E. B., and Stanley, J. C. "Experimental Design in Educational Media Research," in *Curriculum Guide for a Course in Educational Media Research.* Washington, D. C.: U. S. Office of Education, NDEA Title VII Project B-236, 1962.

Selltiz, C., Johoda, M., Deutsch, M., and Cook, S. W. *Research Methods in Social Relations.* New York: Henry Holt and Company, Inc., 1951.

Sidman, M. *Tactics of Scientific Research.* New York: Basic Books, Inc., 1960.

Stanley, J. C. *The Improvement of Educational Experimentation.* Madison, Wisc.: University of Wisconsin, Laboratory of Experimental Design, 1965.

——— (ed.) "Improving Experimental Design and Statistical Analysis," *Proceedings of the Seventh Annual Phi Delta Kappa Symposium of Educational Research.* Chicago: Rand McNally & Company, 1967.

U. S. War Department Information and Education Division. "Opinions about Negro Infantry Platoons in White Companies of Seven Divisions," in T. M. Newcomb and E. L. Hartley (eds.), *Readings in Social Psychology.* New York: Henry Holt and Company, Inc., 1947.

CHOOSING AN APPROPRIATE STATISTICAL PROCEDURE

Richard M. Wolf

CONTENTS

At the outset of any research study, the researcher must decide how he will analyze the data to be obtained. It is only logical that this decision must be made before beginning the study if the appropriate data are to be collected. This sequence provides a strategy for choosing an appropriate statistical procedure for analyzing research data. Applying this strategy, the researcher identifies appropriate statistical procedures for analyzing data and for answering research questions.

Three main considerations are important in selecting an appropriate statistical procedure for analyzing data from a given study:

1. the types of variables

2. the number of variables

3. the scales of measurement of the variables

When you complete this instructional sequence, you should be able:

1. To identify variates and criterion variables, given sentences containing an example of each

2. To identify variates, criterion variables, and the number of each, given a description of a study

3. To identify the scale on which a variable is measured, given a list of variables

4. To write in cumulative order the three steps in selecting an appropriate statistical procedure

5. To identify the essential variates and criterion variables, their number, and scale of measurement, given a research study *or* a summary chart. Then, utilize this information to identify the appropriate statistical procedure, with the aid of a table provided in this instructional sequence

Types of Variables

A variable is any characteristic having two or more mutually exclusive properties or values. For example, sex is a variable because it has two mutually exclusive properties, maleness and femaleness. Reading achievement, as indicated by a test score, is also a variable because the potential test scores constitute mutually exclusive values. In planning a study, the researcher should identify and compile a list of all variables to be included. Then he should classify each variable into one of two categories:

1. Variate
2. Criterion variable (or criterion)

A *variate*, as used here, is a variable whose relationship to the criterion is being studied. The variate is a characteristic or experience shared in common by a group of individuals. It serves as the basis for classifying individuals into groups for study. As an illustration, consider the relationship between Head Start Training and student achievement; the Head Start Training Program is an experience shared in common by a group of students and presumably has a relationship to student achievement. Hence, it is the variate under study. In experimental studies, the variate is called the independent variable. It is directly manipulated by an experimenter as the experimenter assigns different levels of the variate to different groups of subjects. The term variate is the more general one; an independent variable is the variate in an experimental study.

A *criterion variable* represents an outcome or objective. In the above study of the relationship between Head Start Training and student achievement, the desired outcome is increased student achievement. Therefore, student achievement is the criterion variable. In experimental studies, the criterion variable is referred to as the dependent variable since it is presumed to be dependent on a variable described as the independent variable. The term "dependent variable" is applied

CHOOSING AN APPROPRIATE STATISTICAL PROCEDURE **4**

to experimental studies only; the term "criterion variable" can be applied to any type of study.

Variables cannot be designated as either criterion or variate once and for all time. In one study a particular variable may be the criterion variable and in another study the same variable may be the variate. The classification of variables must be carried out separately for each study. For example, in one study an investigator may be interested in studying the influence of teacher behavior on the anxiety level of students. In another study, an investigator may be interested in studying the influence of the anxiety level of students on achievement in reading. In the first study the anxiety level of students is the criterion variable while in the second study it is the variate, or more precisely, the independent variable.

While it is often necessary to distinguish between manipulable and non-manipulable variates in the correct *execution* of a statistical procedure, this distinction is unnecessary in the *initial selection* of the statistical procedure.

CLASSIFYING VARIATES AND CRITERION VARIABLES

Write "V" beside the number of each *variate* and "C" beside the number of each *criterion variable*.

Do
1. _____ variously controlled amounts of student-teacher contact affect
2. _____ student attitude toward school?

How is
3. _____ the dropout rate affected by
4. _____ a vocational training program?

How is
5. _____ reading achievement related to
6. _____ sex of student?

Items 1, 4, and 6 are variates. These are the characteristics or experiences serving as the basis for grouping. Items 2, 3, and 5 are C, criterion variables. These are the desired outcomes or objectives. The first con-

5 TYPES OF VARIABLES | 165

sideration a researcher must attend to in selecting an appropriate statistical procedure is to classify by *type* each variable as a variate or as a criterion variable.

Number of Variables

The second consideration in the selection of an appropriate statistical technique is the *number* of different variates and criterion variables involved. This requires merely counting the number of variables of each type—criterion and variate—but its importance cannot be overestimated.

Research studies may involve different numbers of variables—for a study may deal with one or more than one variate, in connection with one or more than one criterion variable. In studying the relationship between the type of teaching method used and student achievement on a spelling test, for example, one variate, teaching method, and one criterion variable, scores on a spelling test, are involved. In another example—a study of the effects of amount of teacher training and teacher age on subsequent student achievement in reading and math— one can identify two variates: amount of teacher training and teacher age. One can also identify two criterion variables: achievement in reading and achievement in math.

EXERCISE 2

IDENTIFYING NUMBER OF VARIATES AND CRITERION VARIABLES

Write in the spaces provided the *number of variates* and *number of criterion variables* inherent in this research situation.

> A study will be conducted to determine the effectiveness of a series of special community educational programs on PTA attendance, parental attitudes, and parent-teacher contact.

1. ＿＿ Number of variates

2. ＿＿ Number of criterion variables

In this situation there is one variate — series of educational programs and three criterion variables: attendance, attitudes, and parent-teacher contact.

IDENTIFYING NUMBER OF VARIATES AND CRITERION VARIABLES

Write the number of variates and number of criterion variables inherent in this research situation.

> To assess how recall of test scores, attitudes toward test scores, and achievement test scores are affected by two methods of interpreting test scores and by sex of student, the researcher plans to select four schools in which to conduct his experiment.

1. ____ Number of variates

2. ____ Number of criterion variables

The variates in this exercise are two: methods of interpreting test scores and sex of students. The criterion variables are three: recall of test scores, attitudes toward test scores, and achievement test scores.

IDENTIFYING NUMBER OF VARIATES AND CRITERION VARIABLES

Write the number of variates and number of criterion variables inherent in this research situation.

> A researcher plans to study the influence of private tutoring sessions and in-class surprise quizzes on math achievement. He will use four classes: one receiving tutoring, one receiving the quizzes, one receiving both tutoring and quizzes, and one receiving neither.

1. ____ Number of variates

2. ____ Number of criterion variables

There is only one variate, which can be called instructional procedure. The number of criterion variables is also one — math achievement.

IDENTIFYING NUMBER OF VARIATES AND CRITERION VARIABLES

Write the number of variates and number of criterion variables inherent in this research situation.

> A study is being planned to determine the effect of varying the amount of in-class practice on grammar structure on teacher made and standardized achievement tests. The researcher will use three classrooms: one receiving twenty minutes of practice per day, one receiving ten minutes per day, and one receiving no in-class practice.

1. _____ Number of variates

2. _____ Number of criterion variables

The one variate in this exercise is amount of in-class practice. The two criterion variables are the teacher-made achievement test and the standardized test. Remember that, even though both criteria are achievement, each is considered a separate criterion variable.

Levels of Each Variate

In addition to counting the number of variates being considered, the researcher also needs to determine the number of levels of each specific variate. In a study of the effectiveness of different methods of teaching *and* different kinds of instructional materials, for example, there would be two variates — methods and materials — but there could also be several different methods and several types of materials. The researcher, then, is obliged first to count the number of variates under consideration and second to distinguish among the individual types, or *levels*, of each variate in the study.

The following three exercises provide an opportunity not only to classify variables as variates or criterion variables but also to indicate number of levels for each variate.

EXERCISE 6

IDENTIFYING VARIATES, LEVELS OF VARIATES, AND CRITERION VARIABLES

Write, in the spaces provided, the *variates*, the *number of levels of variates*, and the *criterion variables* inherent in this research situation.

A study to determine which of three different methods of teaching spelling would lead to the highest level of student achievement in spelling and to the most positive attitude toward spelling.

VARIATES: _____

_____

NUMBER OF LEVELS OF VARIATES: _____

CRITERION VARIABLES: _____

_____

The study involves only one variate—methods of teaching spelling. There are, however, three levels (three methods) of that single variate being studied. Levels of a variable apply only to the variate; criterion measures are always considered unitary measures because they are handled separately in the statistical analysis. The criterion variables in this study are (1) achievement in spelling, and (2) attitude toward spelling.

EXERCISE 7

IDENTIFYING VARIATES, LEVELS OF VARIATES, AND CRITERION VARIABLES

Write the variates, the specific levels of variates, and the criterion variables inherent in this research situation.

In a study to determine whether length of lecture affects interest and achievement in subject matter, four lecture lengths will be used: thirty minutes, fifty minutes, seventy-five minutes, and ninety minutes.

VARIATES: _____

_____

NUMBER OF LEVELS OF VARIATES: _____

CRITERION VARIABLES: _____

_____

The variate is the length of lecture. The levels of variate are the four time periods being used. Subject matter interest and subject matter achievement are the two criterion variables.

EXERCISE 8
IDENTIFYING VARIATES, LEVELS OF VARIATES, AND CRITERION VARIABLES

Write the variates, the specific levels of variates, and the criterion variables inherent in this research situation.

A researcher will study the influence of class size and class organization on student achievement in reading. He plans to use five class sizes of 20, 25, 30, 35, and 40 pupils per class. He will use two types of class organization: graded and ungraded.

VARIATES: _____

_____

NUMBER OF LEVELS OF VARIATES: _____

_____

Class size and class organization are the two variates in this study. The class size variate has five levels, each of the different classes, while the class organization variate has two levels, graded and ungraded organization. Reading achievement is the criterion variable.

You have been presented with two considerations in selecting statistical techniques. Can you recall them?

EXERCISE 9
TWO STEPS IN SELECTING STATISTICAL PROCEDURES

Write the first two primary considerations for selecting an appropriate statistical procedure to analyze data. (Exclude the number of levels of a single variable as a possible response.)

1. _____

_____

2. _____

_____

The first two steps are: (1) identifying the types of variables — variate and criterion variable, and (2) determining the number of variables.

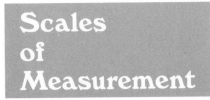

Scales
of
Measurement

A third major consideration in the selection of an appropriate statistical technique is the type of measurement scale most appropriate for each variate and criterion variable. In general, three types of measurement scales are recognized in the behavioral sciences:

1. nominal

2. ordinal

3. interval

The *nominal* scale is the lowest level of measurement. This scale or measure assigns numerals, letters, or some other identifying label to each subject or object. Identifying two methods of teaching spelling as *A* and *B*, *1* and *2*, or *alpha* and *beta* is an example of using a nominal scale. It should be stressed that no ordering of the various categories of a variable is intended with the use of a nominal scale. Each category is discrete and does not necessarily represent a scale position. When in doubt as to whether the measurement ought to be nominal, merely pose this question:

> Is there some order inherent in the categorization?

If there is no order, the scale involved is nominal.

EXERCISE 10

CLASSIFYING NOMINAL SCALES

Place a check beside the number by each variable which involves a nominal scale.

1. _____ Methods of teaching beginning reading

2. _____ Intelligence test scores

3. _____ Type of class organization—graded vs. ungraded

4. _____ Instructional materials—programmed texts vs. conventional texts

5. _____ Scores on the Stanford Reading Test

Items 1, 3, and 4 involve nominal scales, as there is no order inherent in the various categories of each of these variables. In the case of intelligence and reading achievement test scores, on the other hand, an order is inherent in the various score levels. That is, students with higher scores are said to possess greater amounts of the characteristic being tested. These, then, are not nominal scales, since there is an ordering inherent in the various categories or score levels.

An *ordinal* scale or measure assigns numerals to subjects or objects which are rank-ordered with respect to some characteristic. For example, the highest achieving student in a class may be given a rank of 1, the second highest achieving student a rank of 2, and so on. Because the numerals indicate a student's position in the class, this is an ordinal scale. It does not indicate, however, the amount of difference between the individuals. For example, the difference between the first- and third-ranked students is not necessarily the same as the difference between the seventh- and ninth-ranked students. The ordinal scale shows only that the first-ranked student is higher than the third-, or the seventh-, or the ninth-ranked student. When determining whether a measure is ordinal, ask this question:

> Is some order inherent in the categorization, but do we nevertheless lack knowledge of the magnitude of the differences?

If order is present without specified magnitude, the scale involved will be ordinal.

CLASSIFYING NOMINAL AND ORDINAL SCALES

Mark each item as: "N" *(nominal scale)* or "O" *(ordinal scale)*.

1. _____ Rank in class

2. _____ Type of teaching method employed

3. _____ Percentile scores on a standardized test

4. _____ The order of finalists in a Science Fair

5. _____ A list of textbook publishers

Items 2 and 5 are nominal scales, as they involve categories having no inherent order.

Items 1, 3, and 4 are ordinal scales, as each of the various categories is rank-ordered. But we do not know the magnitude of differences between categories. For example, on a percentile scale the difference in performance between the 50th and 70th percentile is not the same as the difference between the 70th and 90th percentile.

An *interval* scale or measure defines a unit of measurement such that the difference between units is equal. It may be a difference between 4 and 5, or 16 and 17, or 28 and 30, and the like. Scores on well-constructed intelligence or achievement tests can be regarded as measures on an interval scale. Thus, an interval scale permits statements not only as to whether one individual ranks higher than another, but also as to the difference between the two in comparison with the difference between another pair of subjects.

CLASSIFYING NOMINAL, ORDINAL AND INTERNAL SCALES

Mark each item as: "N" *(nominal scale),* "O" *(ordinal scale),* or "I" *(interval scale).*

1. ___ Aptitude scores on standardized arithmetic test

2. ___ Responses to the question, "How much do you like your teacher?" (little? some? much?)

3. ___ Type of school (academic, vocational, comprehensive)

4. ___ Type of classroom organization

5. ___ Scores on the Metropolitan Spelling Test

6. ___ Admittance or rejection by the college of one's choice

7. ___ Scores on the Lorge-Thorndike Intelligence Test

8. ___ Sequence in which students turn in papers after a test

9. ___ Type of textbook used

10. ___ Socioeconomic status of students

The appropriate answers are: 1, I; 2, O; 3, N; 4, N; 5, I; 6, N; 7, I; 8, O; 9, N; and 10, O. It should be mentioned that some of the above items could be considered to involve *either* an ordinal scale *or* an interval scale. For example, one might consider raw scores on the Metropolitan Spelling Test to imply an ordinal scale, but this might well be considered an interval scale if there is general agreement as to what is going to be meant by the equal unit of measurement, as is the case when one decides on a standard scale of some sort. By the same reasoning, item 10, socioeconomic status, could be considered an interval scale if it were a composite of income and profession which had been numerically developed and standardized.

A number of variables which are treated as if they were measured on an interval scale are, in fact, measured on an ordinal scale. This is particularly true of many variables included in questionnaires, and rating scales. Consider the following attitudinal item.

Marriage is the most significant institution in the United States today.

1	2	3	4	5
STRONGLY AGREE	AGREE	UNDECIDED	DISAGREE	STRONGLY DISAGREE
_____	_____	_____	_____	_____

The numerical values 1 through 5 are assigned to the five response categories. However, this does not imply that the difference between *strongly agree* and *agree* is the same as the difference between *undecided* and *disagree*. Thus, since no unit of measurement exists which permits legitimate statements of the differences here, an ordinal scale is involved.

There exists a fourth scale, the *ratio* scale, which is the highest level of measure. This measure is an interval scale having an absolute zero point, so that it is meaningful to speak of one scale value being twice as large as another. Examples of this scale include weights, heights, and lengths of objects. If one object has a measurement value of five feet and another a value of ten feet, one can say that the second object has twice as much length as the first. Because ratio scales are rarely used in educational and psychological measurement, they will not be referred to in classifying the various statistical techniques in this material. The classification scheme used here, so far as type of scale is concerned, will refer only to variables measured on nominal, ordinal, and interval scales.

The scale of measurement involved in measuring *each* of the variables under study is an important determiner of the statistical procedures that should be employed when analyzing data.

Let us review the primary aspects of the best strategy for selecting an appropriate statistical procedure.

THREE STEPS IN SELECTING
STATISTICAL PROCEDURES

Write the three main steps in the selection of an appropriate statistical procedure for analyzing data.

1. _____

---

2. _____

_____

3. _____

_____

The three steps are: 1) determining whether the variables are variate or criterion variables, 2) determining the number of variables, and 3) determining the scale of measurement of the variables. A summary chart containing the three necessary steps in selecting the statistical techniques can be set up as follows:

Variates			*Criterion Variables*		
NAME	NUMBER	SCALE OF MEASUREMENT	NAME	NUMBER	SCALE OF MEASUREMENT

Answering the following six questions will make completing this type of summary chart an easy task.

1. What are the variates in the study?

2. What are the criterion variables?

3. How many variates are there in the study?

4. How many criterion variables are there?

5. What scale of measurement is appropriate for each variate?

6. What scale of measurement is appropriate for each criterion variable?

SUMMARY CHART

Fill out a summary chart for this research situation.

A researcher plans to study the relationships between method of teaching geometry, attitude toward geometry, and geometry grades. One method will utilize the regular text only. Method Two will employ the test and two-dimensional visual aids. Method Three will use the regular text and three-dimensional figures.

Variates			*Criterion Variables*		
NAME	NUMBER	SCALE OF MEASUREMENT	NAME	NUMBER	SCALE OF MEASUREMENT

Your chart should look more or less like this.

Variates			*Criterion Variables*		
NAME	NUMBER	SCALE OF MEASUREMENT	NAME	NUMBER	SCALE OF MEASUREMENT
methods of teaching geometry	1	nominal	geometry attitudes and geometry class grades	2	ordinal ordinal

There is only one variate—methods of teaching—although the study includes three levels of that variate. Both of the criterion measures—geometry attitudes and geometry grades—are ordinal variables.

SUMMARY CHART

Fill out the summary chart for this research situation.

A researcher plans to study the effects of two different instructional approaches, programmed and conventional, on the teaching of driver training material, through aptitude scores on a standardized achievement test.

Variates			*Criterion Variables*		
NAME	NUMBER	SCALE OF MEASUREMENT	NAME	NUMBER	SCALE OF MEASUREMENT

Your chart should look something like this.

Variates			*Criterion Variables*		
NAME	NUMBER	SCALE OF MEASUREMENT	NAME	NUMBER	SCALE OF MEASUREMENT
type of instructional materials	1	nominal	achievement scores	1	interval

Using the charted information for the example above, you will be able very soon to locate the appropriate statistical procedure. Knowing the type of variables, the number of variables, and the scale of measurement of variables are the only requirements for pinpointing the correct statistical procedure.

Using a
Table
of
Statistical
Techniques

Everything discussed thus far in this sequence has been preliminary to using a table of statistical techniques. Remember: the purpose of this sequence is to help you select an appropriate statistical technique for any study you will undertake. Mastery of the technique, or procurement of a statistical consultant, is a relevant but independent consideration.

Using the summary chart in Exercise 15 with the information in Table 1 on the next page, you can now determine the appropriate statistical technique for conducting the study. The variates are listed vertically according to *number* of variates, either "one" or "two or more." These divisions are further broken down into scales of measurement: nominal, ordinal, and interval. Horizontally across the top are the criterion variables, which also are divided first according to number of criterion variables and then subdivided into scales of measurement.

From your summary chart in Exercise 15, you can determine that only one variate is being studied. Therefore, in Table 1, locate the first set of three rows, which is set off by horizontal double lines and headed by "one."

According to your summary chart, the scale of measurement of the variate is nominal. Therefore, in Table 1, locate the first row labeled "nominal" in the set of three scales which have been identified. This row is shaded in the table so that there is no question as to the row you should select in this example.

Having located the correct row of the table for one variate and for the nominal scale of measurement, you need to consult your summary chart entry for the criterion variable being studied. In the case of Exercise 15, it is a single criterion variable (achievement score); therefore, in Table 1, locate the first set of the three columns set off vertically by double lines. These are the columns under the heading "one." Looking at your summary chart once more, you see that the scale of measurement for the criterion variable is interval. This means that the column under the "interval" heading is appropriate. This column has also been shaded for your convenience.

The box where the two shaded areas intersect indicates the correct statistical procedure to be used with this study. This procedure is Analysis of Variance.

One more example-exercise will be presented to provide practice using the table.

TABLE 1

STATISTICAL TECHNIQUES CLASSIFIED ACCORDING TO TYPE, NUMBER, AND MEASUREMENT SCALE OF VARIABLES

VARIATES		CRITERION VARIABLES — One			CRITERION VARIABLES — Two or More		
		NOMINAL	ORDINAL	INTERVAL	NOMINAL	ORDINAL	INTERVAL
One	NOMINAL	Chi-Square Test for Independence Contingency Coefficient Cochran Q Test Fisher Extract Probability Test for 2 x 2 Tables	Sign Test Median Test Mann-Whitney U Test Kruskal-Wallis One-Way Analysis of Variance	Analysis of Variance			Multiple Discriminant Analysis
	ORDINAL		Spearman's Rank Correlation Kendall's Rank Correlation	Analysis of Variance with Trend Analysis			
	INTERVAL	Analysis of Variance		Regression Analysis (Multiple Coefficient) Correlation	Analysis of Variance		Multiple Regression Analysis
Two or More	NOMINAL		Friedman Two-Way Analysis of Variance	Analysis of Variance (Factorial Design)			
	ORDINAL						
	INTERVAL	Multiple Discriminant Analysis		Multiple Regression Analysis	Multiple Discriminant Analysis		Canonical Correlation

SUMMARY CHART

Fill out the summary chart for this research situation.

A researcher plans to conduct a study to determine the relationship between scores of the Scholastic Aptitude Test (SAT) and the American College Test (ACT), acceptance by college of one's first choice, and the number of subjects who finished college. He will divide the scores on the two tests into low, average, and high and then calculate the percentage for each category who were accepted by their first-choice college and those who finished college.

Variates			*Criterion Variables*		
NAME	NUMBER	SCALE OF MEASUREMENT	NAME	NUMBER	SCALE OF MEASUREMENT

Your chart should closely resemble this one.

Variates			*Criterion Variables*		
NAME	NUMBER	SCALE OF MEASUREMENT	NAME	NUMBER	SCALE OF MEASUREMENT
SAT scores	2	interval	students accepted by their first-choice college	2	nominal
ACT scores		interval	number of students who finished college		

This summary chart information enables you to turn to the table and find the most appropriate statistical technique quickly.

SELECTING A STATISTICAL PROCEDURE

Write the appropriate statistical procedure for the research situation described in Exercise 16, using Table 1.

STATISTICAL TECHNIQUE: _____

The answer is Multiple Discriminate Analysis. Be sure of how you obtain this answer. The first consideration is the variates—of which there are "two," so the horizontal rows will be involved. The variates are measured on an "interval" scale, which leads you to the last horizontal row.

Turning to the criterion variables, note that there are "two"—which means that the last three columns across the top of the table will be involved. To find out which of the three columns to use, you need only identify the scale of measurement, which in this case is "nominal." The vertical "nominal" column intersects with the last horizontal column, labeled "interval," to pinpoint the correct statistical technique: Multiple Discriminate Analysis.

Some additional considerations will be involved in the most effective use of Table 1. First, notice that the table contains, for the most part, the *general* title for various statistical procedures. Thus, the term "Analysis of Variance" is used in several places, although there are a variety of analysis of variance procedures. A researcher, then, would have to determine which particular analysis of variance procedure to employ by consulting one of the references at the end of this sequence (page 30). In some cases, however, the statistical procedure listed in the table is quite specific. For example, the Kruskal-Wallis One-Way Analysis of Variance is a specific statistical procedure, not a general class of procedures. In such a case, one would simply refer to the appropriate reference to obtain precise details of the procedure.

Concerning the hierarchical nature of the scales of measurement, a second point can best be made using Table 2. An interval-scale variable can be analyzed using the statistical procedures appropriate for an ordinal scale or a nominal scale, while an ordinal-scale variable can be analyzed using procedures listed for a nominal scale. Thus, a statistical

TABLE 2
MODIFIED TABLE 1 TO SHOW THE
DIRECTION OF INCREASING POWER OF
STATISTICAL ANALYSIS

		CRITERION VARIABLES		
		One		
		NOMINAL	ORDINAL	INTERVAL
VARIATES One	NOMINAL	Chi-Square Test for Independence Contingency Coefficient Cochran Q Test Fisher Exact Probability Test for 2 x 2 Tables	Sign Test Median Test Mann-Whitney U Test Kruskal-Wallis One-Way Analysis of Variance	Analysis of Variance
	ORDINAL		Spearman's Rank Correlation Kendall's Rank Correlation	Analysis of Variance with Trend Analysis
	INTERVAL	Analysis of Variance		Regression Analysis (Multiple Coefficient) Correlation

procedure which can be used with a nominal scale can also be used with ordinal- or interval-scale data; a procedure that can be used with an ordinal scale may also be used with interval-scale data. For example, analysis of variance may be used if there is one variate measured on a nominal scale and a criterion measured on an interval scale. However, the criterion variable may also be analyzed with techniques appropriate for an ordinal- or nominal-criterion variable such as the Sign Test, Median Test, etc.

Although interval-scale data may be analyzed using procedures appropriate for the other scales, the reverse is not true. That is, nominal- or ordinal-scale variables may *not* be analyzed using the procedures listed for interval-scale data. The arrows in Table 2 indicate that statistical procedures for lower-order scales may be used with data from higher-order scales. However, this feature applies only to any one subsection of Table 1 (which is subdivided by the heavy intersecting lines).

While it is possible to use a statistical technique intended for data of a lower-order scale, it is usually not advantageous to do so because statistical procedures for lower-order scales are generally *less powerful* than those for higher-order scales. This means that the statistics are more likely to overlook an important difference. Thus a researcher is generally better off using the highest-order procedure available. This will not be possible if the data fails to meet the assumptions required for the use of a particular technique. In these cases an investigator may be forced to resort to the use of a less precise technique.

There is another case in which the researcher may be required to use a less precise statistical procedure. That is when the research situation involves two or more variates or criterion variables which are measured on different scales. If, for example, the researcher wishes to determine the relationship between scores on a college entrance exam and success in college, as ascertained by whether a subject completed college and by scores on a standardized achievement test given the senior year, he is dealing with one variate (scores on a college entrance exam, which is measured on an interval scale) and two criterion variables for success in college (measured by two different scales). One criterion (completion of college) is measured on a nominal scale, and the other (scores on an achievement test) is measured on an interval scale. The question for the researcher is which scale—nominal or interval—to use in order to determine the appropriate statistical procedure. Because he already knows that lower-order statistical procedures can be used with higher-order scales, he might arrive at the solution of treating both variables in terms of the lower-order scale. In this example the lower-order scale is nominal. Using the table, it can be determined Analysis of Variance would be the correct statistical procedure.

Although more time and facilities are required, greater precision will be obtained when each level of measurement for the two variates or criterion variables is treated separately statistically. Using the example given, the researcher would employ the Analysis of Variance procedure with the nominal measure (completion of college) and the Regression Analysis Correlation procedure with the interval measure (the standardized achievement test). This is the recommended procedure.

Finally, you should realize that each statistical technique requires that certain assumptions be made about the data to be analyzed. Some assumptions may be quite simple, others more complex. Analysis of Variance, for example, assumes that the scores for individuals in each treatment group are normally distributed and have equal variances. You can determine the assumptions underlying a particular statistical procedure by checking the reference or references for that technique listed at the end of this sequence. It should be mentioned that under certain circumstances these assumptions can be violated. Sometimes a statistical technique is considered "robust," which means that the assumptions can be violated and still give accurate results. "Robustness" will not be covered in this material.

The following exercises give you an opportunity to fill out summary charts by writing the variates, the criterion variables, and the scale of measurement of each variable, and then to select the appropriate statistical procedure from Table 1.

EXERCISE 18

SUMMARY CHART AND SELECTION OF
A STATISTICAL PROCEDURE

Fill out the summary chart and select the appropriate statistical procedure for this research situation, using Table 1.

A researcher plans to study social and psychological factors related to achievement in reading. He plans to collect information about five background factors measured on an interval scale for one hundred randomly selected fifth-graders. He also plans to obtain standardized test scores for these individuals.

Variates			Criterion Variables		
NAME	NUMBER	SCALE OF MEASUREMENT	NAME	NUMBER	SCALE OF MEASUREMENT

STATISTICAL TECHNIQUE: _____

The appropriate technique is Multiple Regression Analysis. The five background factors are the variates, which are measured on an interval scale. Reading achievement is the criterion variable. It is measured on an interval scale.

SUMMARY CHART AND SELECTION OF A STATISTICAL PROCEDURE

Fill out the summary chart and select the appropriate statistical procedure for this research situation, using Table 1.

A researcher plans to study the relationship between type of instructional material used and performance in arithmetic. Three kinds of instructional materials will be used: a conventional text, a linear programmed text, and a branching programmed text. Three randomly selected groups of students will be used, each group using one type of instructional material. At the end of a semester, students will be administered a test of arithmetic computation and a test of arithmetic reasoning.

Variates			Criterion Variables		
NAME	NUMBER	SCALE OF MEASUREMENT	NAME	NUMBER	SCALE OF MEASUREMENT

STATISTICAL TECHNIQUE: _____

The appropriate statistical technique is Multiple Discriminant Analysis. Type of instructional material is the sole variate. Scores on the two arithmetic tests are the two criterion variables. Thus, the single variate is measured on a nominal scale, and the two criterion variables are measured on interval scales.

SUMMARY CHART AND SELECTION OF A STATISTICAL PROCEDURE

Fill out the summary chart and select the appropriate statistical procedure for this research situation, using Table 1.

A researcher wishes to compare a group of ninth-grade students' scores on a standardized arithmetic test with their scores on the Otis Quick Scoring Intelligence Test.

Variates			*Criterion Variables*		
NAME	NUMBER	SCALE OF MEASUREMENT	NAME	NUMBER	SCALE OF MEASUREMENT

STATISTICAL TECHNIQUE: _____

The appropriate technique is Regression Analysis (Multiple Correlation Coefficient). In any comparison of this nature, one test is considered the variate and the other the criterion variable. Both are interval scales, and the number for each is one.

SUMMARY CHART AND SELECTION OF A STATISTICAL PROCEDURE

Fill out the summary chart and select the appropriate statistical procedure for this research situation, using Table 1.

An experiment is planned with third-grade students to determine the effect of two types of science instructional materials, programmed text and conventional text, on a standardized science achievement test.

Variates			Criterion Variables		
NAME	NUMBER	SCALE OF MEASUREMENT	NAME	NUMBER	SCALE OF MEASUREMENT

STATISTICAL TECHNIQUE: _____

The appropriate technique is Analysis of Variance. Type of instructional materials is the sole variate, measured on the nominal scale. The scores on the criterion variable (achievement test) would involve an interval scale.

Absence of A Criterion Variable

It is possible that a researcher may be involved in a study where there is no criterion variable, as such. The most common case is that in which the researcher is interested in determining how certain variables "hang together," rather than trying to discern how given variates affect a measured outcome, or criterion. Explanations of such research studies may be found in the Tatsuoka and Tiedeman chapter referenced at the end of this sequence.

Summary

The research worker using Table 1 will be able to select the statistical procedure that is most appropriate for analyzing data. Such selection should be made before collection of the data, and, once the statistical procedure is identified, that technique (found in the index of most statistics books, including those listed on page 30) should be fully studied so that any special considerations or problems involved in meeting the requirements for use of the technique will be identified at the outset of the investigation. In this way, adequate provision can be made for data to be collected in ways that will satisfy requirements for the use of the procedure. Adherence to the above procedures should result in improved data-analysis procedures in educational research studies.

REFERENCES

Anderson, T. W. *An Introduction to Multivariate Statistics.* New York: John Wiley & Sons, Inc., 1958.

Dubois, P. H. *Multivariate Correlation Analysis.* New York: Harper & Row, Publishers, Incorporated, 1957.

Eisenhart, C., et al. *Selected Techniques of Statistical Analysis.* New York: Dover Publications, Inc., 1970.

Guilford, J. P. *Fundamental Statistics in Psychology and Education.* New York: McGraw-Hill Book Company, 1965.

Harmon, H. *Modern Factor Analysis.* Chicago: University of Chicago Press, 1960.

Hill, J. E., and Kerber, A. *Models, Methods, and Analytical Procedures in Educational Research.* Detroit: Wayne State University Press, 1967.

Lohnes, P. R., and Cooley, W. W. *Introductory Statistical Procedures: With Computer Exercises.* New York: John Wiley & Sons, Inc., 1968.

Popham, J. W. *Educational Statistics: Use and Interpretation.* New York: Harper & Row, Publishers, Incorporated, 1967.

Siegel, S. *Nonparametric Statistics for the Behavioral Sciences.* New York: McGraw-Hill Book Company, 1956.

Tatsuoka, M. M., and Tiedeman, D. V. "Statistics as an Aspect of Scientific Method in Research on Teaching," in N. L. Gage (ed.), *Handbook of Research on Teaching.* Chicago: Rand McNally & Company, 1963.

Winer, B. J. *Statistical Principles in Experimental Design.* New York: McGraw-Hill Book Company, 1962.

NOTES

NOTES

THE
USE
OF
LIBRARY
COMPUTER
PROGRAMS
FOR
STATISTICAL
ANALYSES

Richard M. Wolf

CONTENTS

The necessity of performing intricate mathematical computations and statistical analyses of data has played its part in impeding the flow of worthwhile educational research. The use of computers can now reduce these functions to the level of routine mechanical operations, for it is neither laborious nor difficult for a researcher to prepare data for analysis by a computer program. But exactly where and how does the researcher avail himself to computer services and facilities? To answer these questions is the objective of this sequence. More specifically, at the completion of this sequence the researcher will be able:

1. To identify and describe the major procedures in using library computer programs

2. To prepare punch card decks meeting the specified computer program and punch card format requirements

3. To read and interpret standard computer printouts of specified statistical routines

Fortunately, just as there exist libraries for books, films, and records, there now exist libraries of computer programs that perform various kinds of analyses. (These libraries are simply repositories for computer programs that have been written and designed to perform specific statistical analyses on raw data. Most computer centers maintain such a library and store their computer programs on cards, disks, or magnetic tapes in specially designed canisters, thus giving rise to the term "canned" computer programs.)

The researcher, or *user*, need only select the program that will perform the desired statistical analysis. Using computer library programs improves the accuracy and reliability of data analysis and makes conducting research easier and more efficient.

Computer Programs

A computer program is merely a set of instructions to a computer that enables it to perform a specified set of operations. For example, a computer program may consist of a set of instructions that enables the computer to read a set of test scores for a group of individuals, compute the arithmetic mean of these scores, and print out the results. There are computer programs to perform almost any kind of statistical analysis, ranging from simple computations of means, standard deviations, and standard errors, to complex multivariate analyses.

The set of instructions comprising the computer program, arranged in the proper order, are often referred to as a *job*. The job is submitted for processing. In most computer installations this usually involves leaving the job in a specified place and having personnel at the installation process it on the computer. The job and the printed results, called the *output*, are returned to the user (the researcher) after processing. The user, in most cases, does not come into direct contact with the computer as trained computer operators do the actual processing.

In most cases the set of instructions which comprise a computer program is punched onto punch cards, with each instruction appearing on a separate card. The researcher simply obtains the computer program in the form of a deck of such cards, together with a printed description of the program. It is not necessary for the user to know anything about computer programming. He should know, however, how to put his data into a form that will be acceptable to the particular program he has chosen even if he doesn't understand a program's specific instructions to the computer. To aid him in this regard is the general purpose of the program description.

The printed program description usually consists of several sections. The first part describes what analyses the program will perform, what information must be submitted along with the program deck, and what kinds of results the program will produce. Reviewing the program description and the computer program should be sufficient to enable the user to select the appropriate program.

A second section of the description usually sets forth the methods of calculation used by the program; these methods are usually stated in conventional statistical notation.

A third section furnishes precise instructions about the input to the computer and the ordering of all punch cards. The *input* consists of all information, including the program deck, which must be submitted to the computer. All such information must be submitted in the form and order specified in the program description. The common means for the data input is the punch card.

Punch Card Format

A *punch card* is a rectangular piece of cardboard consisting of eighty vertical columns and twelve horizontal rows (Figure 1). Only ten rows (0 through 9) are actually designated on the card. The remaining two rows, referred to as the "x" and "y" rows, are in the blank area above the "0" row, and will be discussed momentarily.

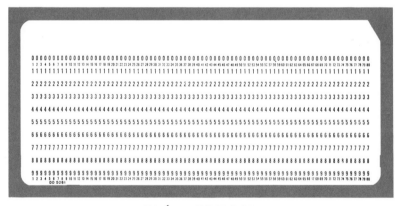

FIG. 1.   A PUNCH CARD

When information is recorded on a punch card, a single digit, letter, or punctuation mark is punched into each column by means of a special device, not unlike a typewriter, called a *keypunch machine*. All that is necessary to record a single character, therefore, is to depress that character on the keyboard of the keypunch machine; the machine will automatically punch the correct holes. A device called a *card reader* will sense these holes and transmit the information to the computer.

Usually, cards are punched by being inserted into the keypunch machine and, beginning at column 1 (the columns are numbered 1 through 80 under the "0" and "9" rows), punching sequentially whatever information is to be recorded (Figure 2). Notice also in Figure 2 that the information recorded on this particular card is in the form of punched holes with the corresponding "translation" at the top of the card (145 19 96 THIS IS A SAMPLE). Of course, the computer senses only the holes. The characters at the top simply provide the researcher or keypunch operator with a quick check of the data on the card. The printing of characters at the top of the card is optional. Figure 2 also shows what holes form a particular character. For example, for each printed digit at the top of the card, one corresponding digit has been punched out below. However, each letter is represented by two punched holes. Let's quickly analyze the letters "T", "H", and "M" of "THIS IS A SAMPLE." The computer senses or reads a "T" when a "0" and "3" are punched out in the card. It reads an "H" when the upper blank row ("x" row) and the "8" are punched out. And it reads an "M" when the lower blank row ("y" row) and the "4" are punched out. As can now be seen, the blank "x" and "y" rows referred to earlier are used for forming certain letters of the alphabet, and also for special characters, such as a plus or minus sign.

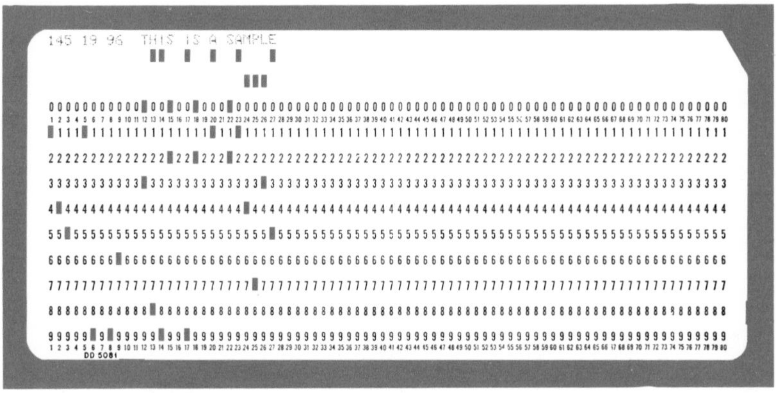

FIG. 2.   INFORMATION RECORDED ON A PUNCH CARD

Features for skipping columns and for backspacing in case of over-skipping are provided on most keypunch machines. Most also provide for the duplication of any card, by depressing a single key.

It is customary that each punched card will contain information — or several items of information — about an individual subject. Consider, for example, an individual whose identification number (assigned arbitrarily by the researcher) is 3167428, who has an IQ of 112, whose reading comprehension score is 29.3, and whose arithmetic problem-solving score is 37.4. This information would be prepared for key-punching as follows:

Columns	Data	Type of Information
1-7	3167428	identification number
8-10	112	IQ
11-13	293	reading comprehension
14-16	374	arithmetic problem-solving

Figure 3 illustrates how this information would appear after being recorded on a punch card. The individual's identification number is customarily punched on the far left of the card, and other information about the individual in subsequent columns.

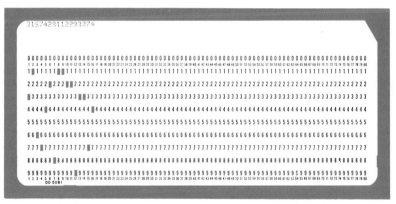

FIG. 3.   A PUNCH CARD ILLUSTRATING HOW SPECIFIC DATA WOULD APPEAR

Note that no decimal points have been recorded. When data from the card are read by the computer, decimal points are added appropriately through use of a variable format card, a device which will be described later.

EXERCISE 1

PREPARING THE PUNCH CARD

Record the following data in the appropriate columns, treating the boxes below as columns on a punch card.

Columns	Information	Data
1-2	Identification Number	13
3-4	Height (in inches)	64
5-7	Weight (in pounds)	106
8-9	Age (in years)	26

1	2	3	4	5	6	7	8	9	10	11	12

Your answer should appear as:

1	2	3	4	5	6	7	8	9	10	11	12
1	3	6	4	1	0	6	2	6			

Additional data can be coded (translating the character on a key-punch machine, by depressing the appropriate key, into the proper numeric code on the punch card) by punching subsequent columns. If it is desired to keep a record of a large number of variables (say 100) for each individual, it becomes necessary to use more than one punch card per individual. The common practice is to reserve the last column on a card, column 80, to indicate the number of the card. Thus, if it is desired to have two cards for an individual whose identification number is 3167428, they might be laid out as shown in Figure 4. Note that the individual's identification number appears in the first seven columns of both cards, and that the card number for each card appears in column 80. If more than one card is used for a single individual, therefore, it is necessary to punch his identification number on each card and the card number on each card. Most programs do not place any limit on the number of cards that can be used for a single individual.

Once a card layout (arrangement of data items on the punch card) has been formulated, it is necessary to follow this layout for all cards in a program. Thus, if four-digit identification numbers are used, and if two-digit scores are to be the data, then one possible layout for all the cards would be:

Columns	Information
1-4	identification number
5-6	score on ABC Test

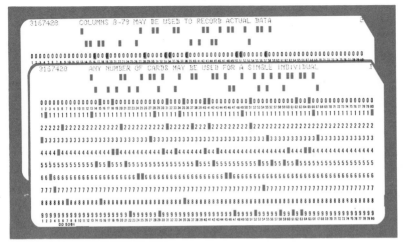

FIG. 4. LAYOUT OF PUNCH CARDS WHEN MORE THAN ONE
CARD IS NEEDED FOR A SINGLE INDIVIDUAL

All cards for a particular group of individuals *must* be punched according to the specified layout because they will be read according to that layout as specified by the user.

The number of columns allotted to a particular variable is called a *field*. If three columns are allotted for IQ data, for example, these three columns constitute a field. When data is punched onto cards, it must be adjusted to the *right* within the field. For example, if columns 7-9 are allocated for IQ data, each individual's IQ should be punched in the three columns of this field. Column 9 would contain the units digit of the IQ, column 8 would contain the tens digit, and column 7 the hundreds digit. To avoid punching data in the wrong columns, zeros should be punched in all columns of a field to the left of the actual data. An IQ score of 90, for example, should be punched as 090 (not 900) in a three-column field. The computer simply ignores the "leading zero." Further examples are shown below.

Individual	IQ Score	Column Number		
		7	8	9
1	104	1	0	4
2	97	0	9	7
3	92	0	9	2
4	109	1	0	9

For individuals 2 and 3 in the preceding example, column 7 is punched with a zero.

Note that each piece of data is punched as far to the right as possible in the appropriate field. Data recorded on punch cards in this manner are said to be "right-justified" or "right-adjusted."

EXERCISE 2
RECORDING RIGHT-JUSTIFIED DATA

Record each individual's age (in months) in the appropriate column, making sure that the data are right-justified.

Individual	Age in Months	Column Number		
		5	6	7
1	120			
2	96			
3	60			
4	9			

Your answers should appear as follows:

Individual	Age in Months	Column Number		
		5	6	7
1	120	1	2	0
2	96	0	9	6
3	60	0	6	0
4	9	0	0	9

Program Requirements

The computer systems available to users of the library program vary, so that punch cards must always be prepared and arranged according to the format specified for the particular library program being used. Examples for the local computer system are usually available and are best illustrated by their personnel. However, most programs do have common requirements for preparing data as input for the computer. Nine common requirements of many programs, in the order in which they are fed to a computer, are:

1. System cards
2. Program deck
3. Execute card
4. Control cards
5. Title card
6. Variable format card
7. Data cards
8. Finish card
9. End-of-file card

SYSTEM CARDS

In submitting a program to a computer, it is almost always necessary to precede the actual program deck, the data cards, and the various other control cards (cards telling the computer what to expect and how to arrange itself internally in order to handle that particular set of cards or deck) with a set of cards referred to as *system cards*. These cards enable one's job, in effect, to "get into" the computer. There is little standardization with respect to system cards. Each computer manufacturer has developed his own conventions for system cards, so that the user must find out what system cards are necessary for use on a particular computer. Most computer installations have a guide for the preparation of system cards.

PROGRAM DECK

The program deck, as we have mentioned, contains the instructions that enable the computer to perform the desired statistical procedures on the researcher's data. Selection of a program deck is determined by the type of data available and the type of analysis to be performed. Here again, we might emphasize that it is not necessary for the user to understand the program deck instructions. All library computer programs have been designed to yield specific statistical analyses; it is necessary only that the user make certain that his data are in a form acceptable for the particular program he has chosen.

EXECUTE CARD

Immediately following the program deck, a special card must be inserted. The purpose of this card is to inform the computer that the end of the program deck has been reached and that what is to follow is the information (the data) for a particular job. Without this card, the computer has no way of distinguishing between the end of the program deck and the beginning of subsequent information.

What appears on this card is dependent on the particular program and computer that is used. Some programs require that "*DATA" be punched on this card, others require the word "EXECUTE," and still others require "DATA." The researcher should check the program description for exactly what must appear on the execute card.

CONTROL CARDS

Control cards specify basic information to the program in order for it to operate. If the program is to compute the mean for each one of a number of variables, for example, it is necessary to inform the program of exactly how many variables it will need to process. Similarly, if the program is to perform an analysis of variance, the cards must inform the program of the number of groups on which the analysis will be carried out. It is not usually necessary to indicate the number of cases on which the program will operate, for this can be determined by the computer as it goes through the program.

Other kinds of information often needed on control cards include the number of cards required for the variable format statement (see below) and the options in the program which are available to the user.

For example, a computer program might be designed to generate an intercorrelation matrix for a large number of variables but may be capable of providing an optional factor analysis on this intercorrelation matrix. If the researcher wishes to use this option, he indicates this fact on the control cards.

TITLE CARD

Many computer programs contain a provision for the insertion of a title card. Its purpose is to enable the computer to print an appropriate label along with the results of the statistical analysis. The user merely punches the title of his analysis as he wishes it to appear on the computer printout of his results and then submits the card along with the program deck and other input cards.

VARIABLE FORMAT CARDS

If the layout, more accurately referred to as the format, for the data cards was fixed in advance, all data would have to be punched in precisely the same way for every study. Since this is not convenient, most programs are written so that a user can vary the format according to the way he has punched his data onto cards. For this reason, the cards are referred to as *variable formats*. Variable format cards indicate to the program the format that is to be used in interpreting the information contained on the data cards. As mentioned previously, the number of cards required to specify the variable format must be indicated by the user on the control card.

The variable format card or cards also instruct the program how to "read in" a set of cards in those instances when more than one card is used to store data for a single individual.

Specifications in a variable format card also instruct the program as to which fields or columns of the cards to ignore, which fields to regard as one number, and which fields to regard as several numbers in a row. Thus, it is the variable format card which tells the program whether a card bearing the sequence of digits 326715849 is to be read as 326, 7.1, 58.49, or as 3267, 1.58, .49, and the like. It does this by giving the program a sequence of specifications which indicate the "size of a field"—that is, how many columns a variable occupies—and the method of handling each field: ignoring it, for example, or entering it as an integer, or entering it as a decimal number. In most programs the format describes the variables for all the data cards. That is, each data card is punched according to the same format.

In addition to providing an efficient method of preparing cards for the input of data, the variable format card allows the user to exercise considerable control over the data input, by permitting him:

1. to select only those fields which interest him from among all the fields on each card

2. to select, if there are several cards for each individual, only those cards containing fields of interest to him

Several formats are available for describing the manner in which data should be analyzed. However, the F-type format is the one most frequently used in computer programs designed to perform statistical analyses. The F-type format is necessary when decimal points have been keypunched on the card, or when decimal points are to be inserted by the program. In order to avoid keypunching errors, it is advisable to allow the program to insert the decimal point according to the researcher's specifications. When the F-type format is used, all data input values must be signed (+ *or* −) or unsigned *numbers*, with or without a decimal point.

The general form of an F-type format is as follows:

Fw.d

"F" indicates that the data are numeric, the usual form of input data for statistical programs. The "w" denotes the *width* (the number of columns) of the field, and the "d" indicates the number of *digits* to the right of the decimal point. The total width of the field must include a column for the sign (+ *or* −) if one is used. If there is no sign, the value is assumed to be positive. Consider a specification:

F3.2

The "F" indicates a variable that is numeric, the "3" indicates it is three columns wide, and the "2" indicates that it contains two digits to the *right* of the decimal point. Suppose a card were punched with the digits 794 in columns 1-3, and the format specification was F3.2. The number would be read by the computer as 7.94.

Note that the absence of a sign assumes the number to be positive. If the same three digits had been punched on a card, but had been preceded by a minus sign (−794), and the same format specification (F3.2) had been used, the number would have been interpreted by the computer as −.79. The last digit (4) would not have been read because the format specification F3.2 indicates to the computer that the field is only three columns wide; hence the computer reads only the first three columns, starting with the first column on the left. In order to interpret the sequence of digits −794 as the decimal number −7.94, the format specification would have to be F4.2.

Consider another illustration. The format specification F3.0 indicates a field three columns wide with all three digits to the *left* of the decimal point. If the digits 241 were punched in columns 1-3 of a card, and if it was desired that this sequence of digits be interpreted by the computer as the decimal number 241.0, then the format specification would be F3.0. The computer automatically inserts the decimal point followed by a zero in such cases.

Here is an illustration depicting the first six columns of seven punched cards, along with the way in which each is to be read by the computer, and the format specification of each.

Example	Digits in Columns 1-6	Read As	Format Specification
Card A	4 8 6 3 1 5	4863.15	F6.2
Card B	4 8 6 3 1 5	486315.0	F6.0
Card C	4 8 6 3 1 5	486.3	F4.1
Card D	4 8 6 3 1 5	48.631	F5.3
Card E	− 4 8 6 3 1	−4.863	F5.3
Card F	− 4 8 6 3 1	−4863.1	F6.1
Card G	− 4 8 6 3 1	−48631.0	F6.0

On Card A, the reasoning used to determine the format specification would be as follows: all six digits are to be read; therefore, the F6. component is appropriate, indicating that six columns are to be read. Because two digits are to appear to the right of the decimal point, the complete specification is F6.2.

The reasoning used to determine the format specification for Card C would be as follows: only four of the six digits are to be read; therefore, the F4. specification is correct. Because one digit is to appear to the right of the decimal point, the complete specification is F4.1.

Suppose the situation had been reversed. That is, suppose the problem had been to determine how the computer, given the format specification, would read the data. The reasoning for Card D would be as follows: the F5. component of the format specification indicates that only the first five columns are to be read; the 3 component indicates that three digits are to appear to the right of the decimal point, so that the decimal point would fall between the 8 and the 6. Thus, the data would be read by the computer as the decimal number 48.631.

For Card F the reasoning would be as follows: the F6. component of the format specification indicates that the first six columns of the card are to be read; therefore, the minus sign and the following five digits would be read by the computer. The 1 component of the format specification indicates that one digit is to appear to the right of the decimal point; therefore, the decimal point would fall between the 3 and the 1. Thus, the data would be read by the computer as the negative decimal number −4863.1.

EXERCISE 3

F-TYPE FORMAT SPECIFICATIONS

Write the F-type format specification for each of the following problems, where you are given digits for the first five columns of a punch card plus the way in which the digits will be read by the computer.

Problem	Digits in Columns 1-5	Read As	Format Specification
1	3 7 2 1 5	372.15	
2	4 8 5 1 3	48.513	
3	2 6 7 9 8	26798.0	
4	3 8 2 4 4	3.8244	
5	5 8 6 7 9	58.67	
6	− 9 4 5 1	−94.51	
7	− 7 3 2 6	−7.32	
8	− 9 3 1 4	−9314.0	

Answers are: (1) F5.2, (2) F5.3, (3) F5.0, (4) F5.4, (5) F4.2, (6) F5.2, (7) F4.2, and (8) F5.0.

F-TYPE FORMAT SPECIFICATIONS

Write the number as it would be read by the computer for each of the following problems, where you are given digits for the first five columns of a punch card plus their format specifications.

Problem	Digits in Columns 1-5	Format Specification	Read As
9	1 3 6 7 2	F5.3	
10	1 8 3 2 5	F4.2	
11	7 2 8 4 6	F5.0	
12	− 1 3 9 7	F3.1	
13	− 2 8 7 3	F3.2	
14	1 4 7 9 3	F3.0	
15	+ 7 2 8 4	F4.2	

Answers are: (9) 13.672, (10) 18.32, (11) 72846.0, (12) −1.3, (13) −.28, (14) 147.0, and (15) 7.28.

If more than one variable is to be read from a single card it is, of course, necessary to specify the format for each variable, in proper succession. Three cases are possible in this regard:

1. each variable is of a different width

2. all variables occupy fields of equal width

3. a combination of 1 and 2 above

VARIABLES OF DIFFERENT WIDTHS   When each variable on a card occupies a field of a different width, the specification format for each variable must be written separately — with a comma separating each specification from the others. The specifications are

17 PROGRAM REQUIREMENTS | 209

written in an unbroken line, with no space skipped after the comma. The general form is:

Fw.d,Fw.d,...,Fw.d

Consider an example in which columns 1 and 2 of a data card represent an individual's grade placement in vocabulary, to the nearest tenth (4.8 for example), while columns 3-5 represent his IQ, and columns 6 and 7 give his age in years. As shown in Figure 5, the variable format card required in this case to enable the computer to read the data in the desired manner would consist of three format specifications, each separated from the others by a comma:

F2.1,F3.0,F2.0

Using this variable format card, the computer would read only the first seven columns of any data card.

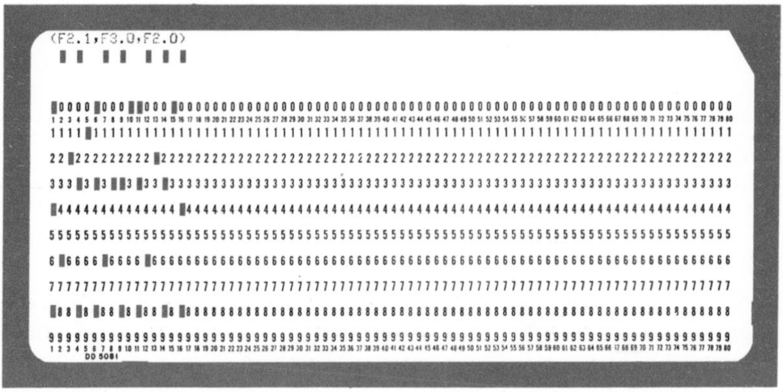

FIG. 5. A VARIABLE FORMAT CARD ILLUSTRATING FORMAT SPECIFICATIONS WHEN MORE THAN ONE VARIABLE IS TO BE READ FROM A SINGLE CARD AND WHEN EACH VARIABLE OCCUPIES A FIELD OF A DIFFERENT WIDTH

VARIABLES OF EQUAL WIDTHS   When all variables on a card occupy fields of equal width, the user can elect to write the variable format card in the manner described above. However, he can save time and reduce the possibility of error by using what is termed a *multiple field* format specification. Use of this technique requires not only that all variables occupy fields of equal width but that all variables contain the same number of digits to the right of the decimal point. In setting up multiple fields of equal width and specification, the researcher indicates the number of fields desired by placing a number before the F in the format specification. The general form is:

nFw.d

Here, n stands for the number of fields desired.

Suppose for example, that the researcher wishes to read from each single card a total of six different variables, each of which occupies a field five columns in width and contains two digits to the right of the decimal point. Following the procedure described above for variables of different widths, he could prepare the variable format card as follows:

F5.2,F5.2,F5.2,F5.2,F5.2,F5.2

Using the multiple field format specification, however, he could write the variable format card (much more simply) as:

6F5.2

Both format specifications would cause the computer to read the first thirty columns of a data card.

VARIABLES OF DIFFERING AND EQUAL WIDTHS   In most cases, data does not automatically group itself into fields of equal width. This requires that the researcher using the program determine in advance the manner in which the data is to be recorded on cards. Such planning allows him to organize the data cards so as to permit him to use a combination of the two cases described above when preparing the variable format card.

Consider the following illustration. A researcher has collected data including the following variables on a group of subjects: (a) IQ, (b) age in months, (c) vocabulary grade placement to the nearest tenth (10.7 for example), (d) arithmetic problem-solving grade placement to the nearest tenth, (e) reading grade placement to the nearest tenth, (f) standard score on a mathematical achievement test to the nearest hundredth, and (g) standard score on a reading comprehension test to the nearest hundredth. One way to prepare the variable format card for such data would be to use the procedure described for variables of different widths. The card would then appear as follows:

F3.0,F3.0,F3.1,F3.1,F3.1,F4.2,F4.2

Using a combination of the procedures described in variables of different widths and variables of equal widths, however, the card could be prepared, less complicatedly, in the following manner:

2F3.0,3F3.1,2F4.2

Note that three multiple field format specifications have been used, and that each has been separated from the others by a comma.

WRITING FORMAT SPECIFICATIONS WHEN A CARD WILL CONTAIN MULTIPLE VARIABLES

Write the format specification for each of the following problems, where you are given digits for the first eight columns of a punch card plus the way in which the digits will be read by the computer.

Problem	Digits in Columns 1-8	Read As	Format Specification
1	4 8 9 5 1 3 6 2	4.89, 51.362	
2	7 3 6 9 4 3 1 2	7.369, 4.3, .12	
3	2 1 8 3 5 3 4 6	2.1, 8.3, 5.3, 4.6	
4	5 9 3 4 4 8 7 3	5.934, 4.873	
5	6 3 2 8 7 9 1 4	6.3, 2.8, 7.9, .14	
6	1 9 3 7 2 5 1 8	.19, 3.7, 2.5, .1, .8	

Answers to the above problems are: (1) F3.2,F5.3, (2) F4.3,F2.1, F2.2, (3) 4F2.1 *or* F2.1,F2.1,F2.1,F2.1, (4) 2F4.3 *or* F4.3,F4.3, (5) 3F2.1,F2.2 *or* F2.1,F2.1,F2.1,F2.2 and (6) F2.2,2F2.1,2F1.1 *or* F2.2,F2.1,F2.1,F1.1,F1.1.

WRITING FORMAT SPECIFICATIONS WHEN A CARD WILL CONTAIN MULTIPLE VARIABLES

Write the number as it should be read by the computer for each of the following problems, where you are given digits for the first eight columns of a punch card plus their format specifications.

Problem	Digits in Columns 1-8	Format Specification	Read As
7	3 6 4 9 5 8 7 1	F3.2,F2.1,F2.2,F1.1	
8	4 7 3 6 5 4 1 5	F5.3,F3.2	
9	3 5 9 8 1 4 3 6	3F2.1,F2.2	
10	9 1 3 7 4 2 1 5	F1.1,2F2.1,F3.2	
11	8 4 6 3 5 2 1 3	F4.2,F4.3	
12	1 4 5 7 9 0 4 2	2F4.3	

Answers to the above problems are: (7) 3.64, 9.5, .87, .1, (8) 47.365, 4.15, (9) 3.5, 9.8, 1.4, .36, (10) .9, 1.3, 7.4, 2.15, (11) 84.63, 5.213, and (12) 1.457, 9.042.

Frequently the researcher may not wish to have the computer read all the data on a card. The format specification which will accomplish the skipping of columns on a data card is:

mX

Here, m indicates the number of columns to be skipped, and X is the format code which causes the computer to skip the specified number of columns. Thus, 7X indicates that seven columns are to be skipped. Analyze the following specifications:

F4.0,5X,F3.1

They denote that the first four columns are to be read as F4.0, the next five columns are to be skipped, and the next three columns are to be read as F3.1. If the format above were used to read data punched as shown in Figure 6, the computer would read the input as: 4671.0, 69.5. Note that the information in columns 5-9 was not read, because of the 5X specification. Note also that information from column 13 on was not read because of the absence of any format specifications to dictate reading of variables beyond column 12. In fact, only two variables were read, for that was all the computer was instructed to read: that is, F4.0 and F3.1, with a skip of five columns between the two variables.

If, because of the way data is keypunched, it is necessary to skip

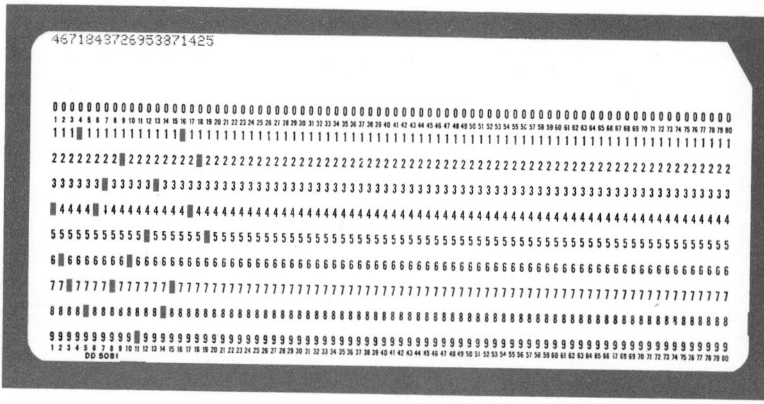

FIG. 6.   A DATA CARD

columns at the beginning of a card, then the skip instruction should come at the beginning of the variable format statement. Suppose, for example, that one wished to read only columns 71 and 72 on a data card, and that he wished to read them as a two-digit number with the decimal point after the last digit (F2.0). The correct format statement would be:

70X,F2.0

This causes the computer to skip the first 70 columns on the card, and to read the next two columns as a two-digit number with the decimal point after the last digit.

Consider the following examples, paying particular attention to the way the format specification has been set up to cause certain parts of the data to be skipped.

Example	Digits in Columns 1-7	Read As	Format Specification
A	3 7 1 5 6 2 8	2.8	5X,F2.1
B	4 3 9 4 7 6 2	4.3, 7.62	F2.1,2X,F3.2
C	7 2 1 9 4 6 5	2.19, 4.65	1X,2F3.2
D	5 3 8 4 2 7 6	6.0	6X,F1.0
E	2 6 0 5 1 4 3	2.60, 1.43	F3.2,1X,F3.2

WRITING VARIABLE FORMAT SPECIFICATIONS
USING THE SKIP OPTION

Write the format specifications for each of the following problems, where you are given digits for the first seven columns of a punch card plus the way in which the digits will be read by the computer. Note that certain parts of the data are to be skipped in each problem.

Problem	Digits in Columns 1-7	Read As	Format Specification
1	9 3 8 6 7 1 4	9.3, 1.4	
2	2 5 7 4 1 3 6	25.7, 0.36	
3	4 3 6 7 9 8 2	4.0, 79.82	
4	5 1 4 8 9 6 3	0.14, 0.63	
5	7 3 5 6 2 4 9	7.3, 0.62, 9.0	

Answers are: (1) F2.1,3X,F2.1, (2) F3.1,2X,F2.2, (3) F1.0,2X,F4.2, (4) 1X,F2.2,2X,F2.2, and (5) F2.1,1X,F2.2,1X,F1.0.

WRITING VARIABLE FORMAT SPECIFICATIONS
USING THE SKIP OPTION

Write the number as it would be read by the computer for each of the following problems, where you are given digits for the first seven columns of a punch card plus their format specifications.

Problem	Digits in Columns 1-7	Format Specification	Read As
6	4 7 3 6 5 1 7	2X,F5.4	
7	3 8 2 1 9 6 6	1X,2F3.2	
8	5 7 1 2 3 4 3	F2.1,3X,F2.1	
9	2 3 9 6 8 9 5	F3.2,3X,F1.1	
10	1 7 3 8 4 2 5	3X,2F2.1	

Answers are: (6) 3.6517, (7) 8.21, 9.66, (8) 5.7, 4.3, (9) 2.39, 0.5, and (10) 8.4, 2.5.

It is sometimes necessary either to skip part of the data on a card or to skip an entire card or cards when "reading in" data. In order to accomplish this latter operation, the researcher should insert a "slash" (/) at that point in the format statement when he wishes the computer to go to the next data card. Depending on its position in the format statement, the / mark can direct the program either to go immediately to the next card, ignoring any further information on the current card, or to skip one or more cards altogether.

There are several special applications of the slash. If, for example, a format statement begins with /, the program will automatically skip the first data card, read the second, skip the third, and so forth. If a format statement ends with /, the program will automatically read the first data card, skip the second, read the third, and so forth.

Two slashes (//) at the beginning of a format statement cause the program to skip the first two cards, read the third, skip the fourth and fifth, read the sixth, and the like. Two slashes at the end of a format statement cause the program to read the first card, skip the second and third, read the fourth, skip the fifth and sixth, and the like. Any number of slashes can be used, depending on how many cards the user wishes skipped.

Use of the / can be illustrated in the following example in which two cards are used for each individual. Figure 7 illustrates how the two data cards appear for a single individual. Note that the identification number appears in the first three columns of both cards, and that the card number for each card of the individual's set appears in its column 80.

The information punched in columns 11 and 12 of card 1 for each individual denotes a grade placement score on a spelling test. The information punched in columns 34-36 of card 2 denotes the individual's IQ. If it is desired to read these two items of information, the appropriate format statement would be:

10X,F2.1/33X,F3.0

The 10X indicates that the first 10 columns of the first card are to be skipped. The F2.1 indicates that columns 11 and 12 of card 1 are to be read and a decimal point inserted between the two digits (6.2 in this example). The / indicates a skip to the next card (card 2). The 33X indicates that the first 33 columns of the second card are to be skipped. Finally, the F3.0 indicates that columns 34, 35, and 36 are to be read and a decimal point inserted after the last digit in the three column field, yielding 115.0.

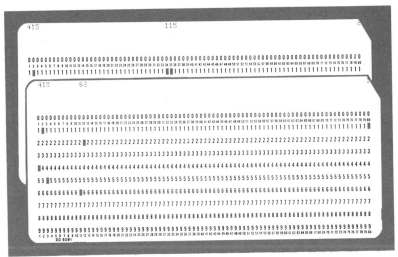

FIG. 7.   TWO DATA CARDS FOR A SINGLE INDIVIDUAL

Two additional points should be made with regard to variable format statements. First, each variable format statement for reading a set of data must be enclosed in parentheses. The above format statement, actually, should appear as:

(10X,F2.1/33X,F3.0)

Second, usually only columns 1-72 of a card are available for punching variable format statements. Columns 73-80 of variable format cards are generally not read by the computer. If a variable format statement requires more than 72 columns, including enclosing parentheses, then more than one variable format card must be used. The researcher is usually required to specify on the control card exactly how many variable format cards are necessary to inform the program how the data are to be read.

Below is an example which contains specifications for a variable format statement plus the statement itself as it would be written by a researcher. Study the example fully, for you will be asked to complete similar problems.

- There are two cards for each individual.
- Skip the first six columns of card 1.

- Read a five-digit number and insert a decimal point after the last digit.
- Skip to card 2.
- Skip the first five columns of card 2.
- Read a two-digit number and insert a decimal point between the digits.

The variable format statement here would be:

(6X,F5.0/5X,F2.1)

Consider a second example:

- There are two cards for each individual.
- Skip the first column of card 1.
- Read a three-digit number and insert a decimal point after the first digit.
- Skip ten columns.
- Read a three-digit number and insert a decimal point after the last digit.
- Skip to card 2.
- Skip the first three columns of card 2.
- Read a two-digit number and insert a decimal point after the last digit.

Here the variable format statement would be:

(1X,F3.2,10X,F3.0/3X,F2.0)

EXERCISE 9

WRITING COMPLETE VARIABLE FORMAT CARDS

Write the appropriate variable format statement, in the space provided, for each of the following problems containing the specifications listed.

- There are two cards for each individual.
- Skip the first three columns of card 1.
- Read a four-digit number and insert a decimal point after the last digit.
- Skip to card 2.
- Skip the first five columns of card 2.
- Read a one-digit number and insert a decimal point after the digit.

VARIABLE FORMAT STATEMENT: _____

The answer to this problem is (3X,F4.0/5X,F1.0). Did you remember to include the enclosing parentheses?

WRITING COMPLETE VARIABLE FORMAT CARDS

Write the appropriate format statement for each of the following problems containing the specifications listed.

- There are two cards for each individual.
- Skip the first five columns of card 1.
- Read a three-digit number and insert a decimal point before the last digit.
- Skip the next four columns.
- Read a two-digit number and insert a decimal point before the last digit.
- Skip to card 2.
- Skip the first ten columns of card 2.
- Read a two-digit number and insert a decimal point after the first digit.

VARIABLE FORMAT STATEMENT: _____

The answer to this problem is — in parentheses — (5X,F3.1,4X,F2.1/10X, F2.1).

WRITING COMPLETE VARIABLE FORMAT CARDS

Write the appropriate variable format statement for each of the following problems containing the specifications listed.

- There are three cards for each individual.
- Read a four-digit number from card 1 and insert a decimal point after the last digit.
- Skip the next six columns.
- Read a three-digit number and insert a decimal point after the last digit.
- Skip to card 3.
- Skip the first five columns of card 3.
- Read a two-digit number and insert a decimal point before the last digit.

VARIABLE FORMAT STATEMENT: _____

The answer to this problem is (F4.0,6X,F3.0//5X,F2.1).

DATA CARDS

The data cards contain the information to be processed, in the form of punched holes. There are usually one or more cards for each individual. Data for all individuals are punched according to a layout specified in the variable format card discussed above.

The data are usually prepared for punch card entry on standard commercial forms available from most computer centers. Such centers also usually provide instructions for the use of forms as a part of the library computer program. In many cases the data can be recorded on such forms and submitted to a trained keypunch operator at the center. Where this service is available, time and trouble can be saved at little cost to the user.

FINISH CARD

Most data that is processed involves the comparison of group scores. The function of the finish card is to indicate that the end of the data for a given group has been reached. Some computer programs require that a blank card follow the last data card for each group; other programs require a card with the letters F-I-N-I-S-H punched into columns 1-6. The printed description of a particular program will indicate how the end of each group is to be signaled to the program.

END-OF-FILE CARD

The last card of every deck is the end-of-file card. It signals that all input has been entered into the computer. Not until the end-of-file card has been encountered does the computer actually carry out the calculations for which it received instructions on the program deck and the control cards. As the calculations are completed, the printout is produced. The computer operator then returns the program cards and the results of the analysis to the researcher.

The order in which cards are to be arranged for any particular job is specified in the written program description. In general, however, the order is as depicted on page 29. This order is usually followed on most makes of computers and in most computer installations. Any deviations from this general set-up would have to be determined at an individual computer center.

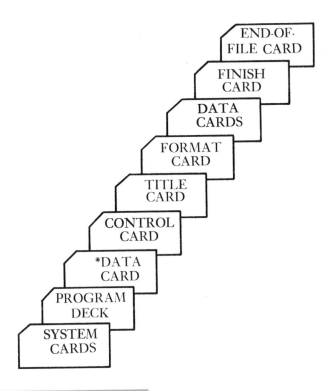

An Illustrative Program

Following is the complete program description of a program to compute summary statistics for any number of groups. All operations are handled internally by the programs so that the user need not be concerned with details of the statistical procedures.

Read the program description, paying particular attention to the order and form of punched input cards.

PURPOSE OF THE PROGRAM

This is a computer program for univariate statistics. Its purpose is to compute the mean, to compute the standard deviation, to perform an analysis of variance, and to obtain a count of the number of cases in a group. Up to fifty groups can be processed at one time.

INPUT

The data consists of two items for each individual: (a) an identification number, and (b) a score or measurement for each. Usually, the identification number and the score are contained on a single data card.

OUTPUT

For each group, the following information will be computed and printed out: (a) the number of cases in the group, (b) the mean for the group, (c) the standard deviation for the group, and (d) an analysis of variance showing the sum of squares, degrees of freedom, mean square, and the F-ratio. Figure 8 is an example of the output of a program whose purpose it is to compute means, standard deviations, and analysis of variance. Although the output is simple in terms of the statistics reported, the operations involved in using the computer program are the same as those that would be involved in using a highly complex program for multivariate analysis.

```
                    SOUTHWEST REGIONAL LABORATORY
                FOR EDUCATIONAL RESEARCH AND DEVELOPMENT

BMD01V          ANALYSIS OF VARIANCE FOR ONE-WAY DESIGN

PROBLEM CODE   VAR = 3
NUMBER OF TREATMENT GROUPS    3
NUMBER OF VARIABLE FORMAT CARDS    3


TREATMENT GROUP         1       2       3

SAMPLE SIZE             5       5       5

MEAN                    5.00    3.50    2.50

STANDARD DEVIATION      3.03    2.44    1.78


                    ANALYSIS OF VARIANCE

                    SUM OF SQUARES    DF    MEAN SQUARE    F RATIO

BETWEEN GROUPS          63.33         2       31.65         4.13

WITHIN GROUPS           92.00        12        7.67

   TOTAL               155.33        14
```

FIG. 8.   SAMPLE OUTPUT OF A COMPUTER PROGRAM

ORDER OF PUNCHED CARDS FOR INPUT

The order of input will be as that which we have followed throughout this sequence (see most recently, page 29). For each additional group to be processed, the sequence of title card — control card — variable format card — data cards — and — blank cards should be repeated.

INFORMATION FOR VARIOUS CARDS FOR EACH ADDITIONAL GROUP

The information to be contained on each type of card is:

TITLE CARD: Punch the title for each group in columns 1-60.

CONTROL CARD: Punch the number of the variable format cards to follow in column 1.

VARIABLE
FORMAT CARD: Begin in column 1 with a left parenthesis. A format specification for the identification number must be included first. Then designate the column in which the scores appear and close the format statement with a right parenthesis.

DATA CARDS: These must be punched according to the specifications set forth in the variable format card.

BLANK CARD: Insert a blank (non-punched) card after the last card in the group

All scores for individuals in each group need to be punched into cards in a standard manner, with identification numbers punched into the first few columns of each card and scores on a particular test following in certain specified columns for each group. This specification would then be used to develop a variable format card for each group. Assume that the data cards for each of, say, three groups are punched in the following manner:

Card Columns	Information
1-3	identification number
4-5	blank
6-8	test score

After the cards have been punched, you would have one deck of data cards for each group:

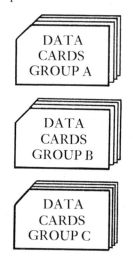

Using the Illustrative Program described above, construct answers to the problems in Exercise 12.

THE MAKEUP OF COMPUTER CARDS

Print the information requested at the top of each card for each of the six blank punch cards supplied below.

on card 1: Make up a title card for Group A.

on card 2: Write the control card for Group A.

on card 3: Write the variable format card for Group A.

on card 4: Make up a title card for Group B.

on card 5: Write the control card for Group B.

on card 6: Write the variable format card for Group B.

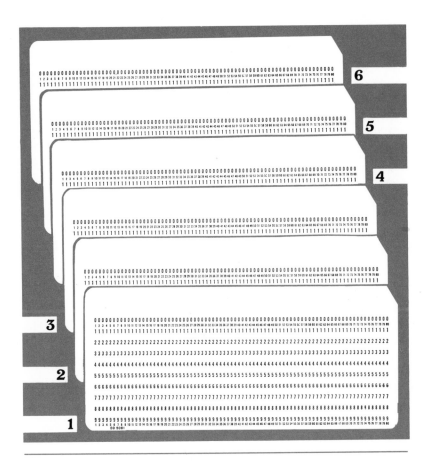

The answers are as follows:

1. *Title Card for Group A:* This can vary, but it must be no more than 60 characters in length including blank spaces. One example might be: TEST RESULTS FOR GROUP A.

2. *Control Card for Group A:* Punch a 1 in column 1 since only one variable format card is needed.

3. *Variable Format Card for Group A:* The format statement should appear as: (F3.0,2X,F3.0).

4. *Title Card for Group B:* This should be similar to item 1, above. One example might be: TEST RESULTS FOR GROUP B.

5. *Control Card for Group B:* Punch a 1 in column 1, as only one variable format card is needed.

6. *Variable Format Card for Group B:* The format statement should appear as: (F3.0,2X,F3.0).

The complete arrangement of the cards and decks for this program would be as follows:

1. system cards
2. program deck
3. execute card
4. title card for Group A
5. control card for Group A
6. variable format card for Group A
7. data cards for Group A
8. blank card
9. title card for Group B
10. control card for Group B
11. variable format card for Group B
12. data cards for Group B
13. blank card
14. title card for Group C
15. control card for Group C
16. variable format card for Group C
17. data cards for Group C
18. blank card
19. end-of-file card

Summary

Now that the generalized instruction of this sequence has removed the "chill" surrounding the purpose and use of computer programs, the researcher, equipped with a cogent computer terminology and an ability for pertinent question-asking, can confidently solicit the aid of his local computer center (found in most educational institutions) in using a library computer program for analyzing his data.

REFERENCES

Dial, O. E. *Computer Programming and Statistics for Basic Research*. New York: Van Nostrand Reinhold Co., 1968.

Sterling, T. D., and Pollack, S. V. *Introduction to Statistical Data Processing*. Englewood Cliffs, N. J.: Prentice-Hall, Inc., 1968.

Veldman, D. J. *FORTRAN Programming for the Behavioral Sciences*. New York: Holt, Rinehart and Winston, Inc., 1967.

Weiss, Eric (ed.) *Computer Usage Fundamentals*. New York: McGraw-Hill Book Company, 1969.

NOTES

NOTES

NOTES

NOTES

THE
RESEARCH
REPORT

Paul E. Resta

CONTENTS

Even the most carefully conducted research effort is of little value if it is not communicated to others. The research report serves as the vehicle for communicating what research was done and what results were obtained.

There are at least three types of research reports that can be identified as useful to the research and research-user communities. The first is a detailed or "base" report that provides complete documentation of what was done, results obtained, and implications warranted. This type report should be written in sufficient detail to enable another researcher to replicate the study; examples include technical reports to funding agencies and graduate study dissertations.

In addition to the completely detailed report, the researcher may also wish to prepare a condensed account of the study for publication in a specified research or technical journal. The major criterion to be satisfied by the condensed report is that it provide the reader sufficient information to evaluate the problem, design, results, and conclusions. The interested reader can request a copy of the detailed report.

Another type of report is responsive to special audiences. For example, a study related to the identification of an initial word list for beginning reading instruction will have both theoretical and practical interest. While the more detailed account is appropriate for the researcher who has theoretical and/or methodological interests, it is not appropriate for the person responsible for developing instruction. Development personnel will be more concerned with the actual list of words and the decision rules optimized in the generation of the list than with such things as analytic techniques and instrumentation. Here, too, the detailed report should be referenced for ready acquisition.

The nature of the research will determine the specific content of the report, and the requirements of the audience to which the report is submitted will determine its emphasis and format. However, a few basic components can be identified as common to all well-constructed research reports. This sequence describes the major components of the research report. Throughout this sequence, the term *component* refers to the major parts making up the research report, while *element* refers to the parts of the component.

The general objective of this sequence is to put the reader in position to prepare a defensible research report by outlining the requirements and conditions of each of the basic components. Specifically, the learner who successfully completes this sequence should be able:

1. To identify report titles which possess the specified characteristics of a well-formed title

2. To distinguish appropriate content to adequately communicate the problem, design, procedures, results, and conclusions of a given research effort

3. To describe the conventional function of the following components:
   a. Title
   b. Problem
   c. Method
   d. Results
   e. Discussion
   f. Conclusions
   g. Summary
   h. Abstract

Title

A good research proposal and report title should concisely identify: (a) the variables included in the study, (b) the type of relationship between the variables, and (c) the population to which the results may be applied. Obviously, the title is the first thing seen in any research paper. If it is wordy, unclear, or poorly sequenced, a negative initial impression toward the contents of the paper may result.

IDENTIFYING THE VARIABLES

The report title should first identify the variables that were studied in the research effort. This is appropriate since learning about the variables and the relationship between them is what any research study is all about. If an experimental study was conducted, the title should identify the variable that was manipulated (e.g., type of reading instruction, class size, etc.) as well as the criterion variable upon which its *effects* were observed (e.g., reading performance). An example of an experimental study title is, "The Effects of Hierarchically Structured Biological Principles on the Biology Test Scores of Eighth-Grade Pupils."

If a correlational study (i.e., one in which the *relationship* between two or more variables is studied, but none of the variables is manipulated) was performed, each variable should be identified briefly in the title and prefaced by something like "the relationship between. . . ." An example of a correlational study title is: "The Relationship Between Frequency and Type of Disruptive Classroom Behavior and the Wechsler Intelligence Scale for Children (WISC) Scores of Third-Grade Students."

In preparing the report title, one of the following paradigms will usually be appropriate:

EXPERIMENTAL STUDY

> The effects of . . . on . . .

CORRELATIONAL STUDY

> The relationship between . . . and . . .

> A comparison of . . . and . . .

The above are only examples of the types of paradigms that may be used. While there is no reason why other paradigms cannot be used, neither is there any obligation to originate a paradigm if one of these will do.

SPECIFYING THE TARGET POPULATION

Another important requirement for a good report title is that it identify the boundaries within which the research findings may legitimately be applied. These boundaries are ordinarily expressed in terms of a "target population." A *population* is simply a group or class of individuals who can be clearly differentiated from other groups or classes of individuals. The following research title clearly indicates a target population from which subjects in the study were drawn:

The Relationship Between the Family School Expectations and Level of Aspiration of Fifth-Grade Rural Elementary School Children

Remember to keep the title brief. Titles longer than fifteen to twenty substantive words are too cumbersome to be useful. Having completed a highly complex and precise experimental study, there is a strong urge to detail its unique characteristics in the title. This tendency, if unbridled, may result in the entire Methods component suddenly appearing on the cover of your research report. Try to make the title an aid to efficient reading rather than a deciphering task.

Wherever possible, avoid padding the title with unnecessary terms and vague lead-ins such as "A study of . . . ," "An investigation of . . . ," and the like. The following is an example of a padded title:

An Investigation of the Effect of the Traditional Approach to Teaching Introductory Psychology as Compared to an Interpersonal Approach to Teaching Introductory Psychology upon the Attitude Test Scores and the Personal Adjustment Ratings of College Students

This long title could be condensed with little, if any, loss of information to:

The Effects of Method of Teaching Psychology on the Attitudes and Adjustment of College Students

---

EVALUATING TITLES OF REPORTS

Mark the following examples of report titles with one or more letters, using the following marking system:

V: if both the *variables and relationships* are indicated
P: if the *population* to which the results are applicable is indicated
T: if the *title* is not excessively long

1. _____ The Effects of Computer-Generated vs. Teacher-Generated Diagnostic Tests on Word Attack Performance

2. _____ The Relationship Between Spelling-to-Sound Performance and Speech Comprehension Vocabularies of 6- to 9-Year-Old's

3. _____ Parent-Assisted Learning

4. _____ An Analysis of the Relationship of Selected Educational Factors to the Nature of the Voluntary Reading of Adolescents

---

Title 1 concisely indicates the variables and their relationship but does not identify the target population. You should have written "V" and "T." Title 2 suggests a correlational study and briefly presents all desired elements of information. Title 3, on the other hand, has at best only one variable defined; thus you should have written nothing. Title 4 contains extraneous words such as "An analysis of" and "nature of." It defines only the target population and, at best, one variable. Only "P" should have been written.

Research Problem

The Research Problem is, typically, the first component presented in the body of the report. It usually begins with a description of the background and educational significance of the problem and ends with a formal statement of the research problem and hypothesis.

BACKGROUND OF THE PROBLEM

In presenting the background of the problem, identify the general problem area or major issues and their educational significance. A research problem is significant when its solution contributes to existing educational practice, research, or theory. Usually, in funded research efforts, the impact of the study on education has to be carefully defined in the proposal. Similar information on the educational importance of the study should also be included in the research report.

Avoid becoming encyclopedic in describing related research. Rather, briefly describe only those studies whose results or methods have direct relevance to your study. Avoid also "put-downs" of previous studies such as implying that others have only groped toward the fundamental truths you have discovered in your study. Be simple, brief, and objective in reviewing the literature and describing the research of others.

Ideally, the background of the problem should:

1. Identify the relevant variables

2. Discuss those that were selected for the study, as well as other important variables not included

3. Specify the criteria used for selection of the variables

Although brevity is desirable, acceptable lengths for the background element depend upon the type of report. In journal articles, for example, the review of related research is usually very brief, consisting of only synoptic statements of the most critical antecedent studies. In contrast, the literature review in a dissertation or thesis may be comprehensive and detailed. Funding agencies usually fall somewhere between the two.

STATEMENT OF THE PROBLEM

Typically, the statement of the problem specifies:

1. The variables in the study
2. The type of relationship between the variables
3. The target population

An example of an adequate experimental study problem statement might be:

> What is the effect of teacher vs. tutor-administered remediation on first-grade reading achievement?

Problem statements such as, "To investigate the problems in individualized instruction" or "What are effective strategies for preventing disruptive behavior in the classroom?" are vague and fail to satisfy the three criteria. The major weakness of these statements is that they suggest the study of educational phenomena without relating it to other phenomena. The problem statement should also be free of value statements such as, "Is computer-assisted instruction better than computer-managed instruction?" A more appropriate problem statement is, "Does computer-assisted instruction result in higher pupil achievement than does computer-managed instruction?"

Finally, avoid redundancies such as "The problem defined for this study was . . ." or "The purpose of this investigation was . . ." The problem statement will usually be long enough without such a tedious beginning.

EVALUATION OF PROBLEM STATEMENTS

Mark the following examples of problem statements with one or more letters, using the following marking system.

V: Variables and Relationships are not specified.
U: Unnecessary information is present.
A: All the criteria for a good problem statement have been met.

1. ＿＿ What is the relationship of the aggressive behavior of kindergarten teachers to the school attitudes of children in their classes?

2. ＿＿ The problem is to investigate the effects of immediate and delayed reinforcement on cooperative play behavior by pre-school children.

3. ＿＿ What is the nature of creativity as reflected in children's problem solving patterns?

4. ＿＿ What are the effects of type and frequency of computational practice on the multiplication performance of third-grade pupils?

Items 1 and 4 satisfy all the criteria of a good problem statement. Item 2 has an unnecessary "lead-in" (U). Item 3, at best, only vaguely intimates a criterion variable (V) and certainly does not indicate what, if any, variate is intended by the term "creativity."

HYPOTHESIS

In an experimental study, the problem statement should be followed by the research hypothesis. The elements of the hypothesis are similar to those of a good problem statement except that the hypothesis is phrased in the form of an "if . . . then" proposition rather than as a question. For example, the problem statement, "What are the effects of computer- and teacher-administered tests on the mathematics performance of fourth-grade pupils?" might be translated to the hypothesis that "Computer-administered tests will yield higher mathematics performance scores than teacher-administered tests." As was true of the problem statement, the hypothesis should be stated in operational terms, be free of value terms, and, if possible, be related to a body of theory which is clearly described.

There are two types of research hypotheses in which a prediction is made before the study is conducted, concerning the relationship of the variables in the study. A *directional hypothesis* predicts the direction in which a difference is expected to occur. An example of a directional hypothesis would be, "Classes using a multi-group instructional system will have higher reading performance than those using single group instruction." A *non-directional hypothesis* predicts a difference but does not specify its direction (e.g., type of grouping will affect reading performance). In other words, the expected difference could be in favor of either the multi-group or single-group condition.

Suppose a researcher advances the directional hypothesis that pupils in multi-group reading instruction will demonstrate higher reading achievement than those in single-group reading. After completing the study he finds, however, that the results favor single-group instruction. It would violate all scientific principles for him to change the directional hypothesis to a non-directional one and then pretend that it was the hypothesis he held at the beginning of the study.

It is expected that new and better hypotheses will emerge during or after the conduct of a research study. These hypotheses are usually presented as recommendations for future studies in the Conclusions of the research report.

SYNOPSIS OF RESEARCH PLAN AND PROCEDURES

Sometimes the research problem may also include a brief description of the overall research plan and/or the experimental treatments incorporated into the study. In a final report to a funding agency, it is also customary to present a brief review of the entire research report and to indicate the organization of its contents.

SUMMARY OF RESEARCH PROBLEM ELEMENTS

The following is a summary of the sequence of elements that provide a logical development of the Research Problem component:

1. *Background of the problem*   The background of the problem should include: (1) a statement of the general problem area within which the research project falls, or a statement of major issues toward which the project is directed; (2) an indication as to the educational significance of the problem area; and (3) a synopsis of the most relevant studies which

have preceded the present study. The "benchmark" studies related to the general problem area should be mentioned first, followed by a brief discussion of the studies most closely related to the specific research problem. The review of the studies should identify the relevant variables and discuss those selected for study.

2. *Statement of the problem*   Element 1 above should lead logically to the statement of the research problem or objective. The criteria for stating the research problem are that the statement should specify the variables, the relationship between the variables, and the target population.

3. *Hypothesis*   The next logical element is the presentation of the research hypothesis. This hypothesis should be specific, testable, and free of value terms. Whenever possible, the hypothesis should be related to a theoretical position, and the theory and the nature of the relationship must be made clear.

4. *Specification of the research plan and procedures*   The hypothesis should be followed by a synoptic description of the research plan and/or the specific procedures which comprise the study.

The following paragraphs comprise the introductory section of a research report actually published in a journal (Van DeReit, 1964). All the elements of the research problem are contained in this example.

BACKGROUND OF THE PROBLEM (GENERAL PROBLEM AREA): An enigmatic phenomenon with which all teachers and many parents are familiar is the child who manifests an inability to learn in school in spite of test indications of normal or superior ability. One view of learning disabilities, and the one with which this study is concerned, is that the disability is a neurotic learning inhibition in which the learning problem is the major symptom. As Pearson (1952) points out, the learning process itself becomes involved in conflict.

BACKGROUND
OF THE
PROBLEM
(SYNOPSIS OF
RELATED
RESEARCH): Underlying many of the contributing factors
involved in the neurotic condition appears to
be the existence of a "need to fail" (Kunst,
1959) for any of a number of reasons. Among
these reasons are the confusion between aggres-
sion and achievement (Klein, 1931; Liss, 1940),
negative reinforcement in early mental exploratory experience (Oberndorf, 1939), and dis-
turbance in experiences of receiving from the
environment (Fenichel, 1937; Strachey, 1930).

HYPOTHESES: If a need to fail is present in children with
learning disabilities, then it would be experi-
enced as threatening and would act as a detriment to further learning. Indeed, the factor of
level of achievement may be one of the uncontrolled variables which contributes to the contradictory results of prior research on the effects
of praise and reproof on learning.

This study tested the following experimental
hypotheses concerning the variables of praise
and reproof in learning by these children:
1. Educationally retarded children require
more trials to reach criterion of learning
than do children who are not educationally retarded on initial paired-associate learning.
2. For educationally retarded children,
praise results in a significantly larger
number of trials to reach criterion on
the second task than does reproof because success constitutes a threat.
3. For normal children, praise results in a
significantly smaller number of trials to
reach criterion than does reproof.

STATEMENT
OF THE
PROBLEM: The present study sought to determine whether
praise of underachievers would result in a
decrement in subsequent learning performance.

PROCEDURES: Underachieving boys in Grades 4, 5, and 6
were matched with respect to ability. Two

> equated lists of paired associates were learned
> by Ss. Between lists one-third of the Ss were
> praised, one-third were reproved, and one-third
> were told nothing.

ELEMENTS OF THE RESEARCH PROBLEM

Identify each of the four elements of the research problem component in the following Introduction to a research journal article (Muehl, 1960). Circle and label in the margin each passage containing one of the following elements:

1. Background of the Problem
2. Hypotheses
3. Statement of the Problem
4. Procedures

INTRODUCTION

To master beginning reading, a child must be able to associate word names, or meanings, with their printed symbols. To make these associations, a beginning reader must be able to see and respond to the printed symbols themselves as distinctive and stable stimulus compounds.

How does this visual discrimination skill develop? Theories of perceptual development attempt to relate sensory input to the learning process. The perceptual theories developed by such writers as Hebb (1940), Gibson (1940), and Murphy (1951) stress the contribution of sensory experience to perceptual differentiation of a stimulus field. Thus, for beginning readers, the question can be asked: What types of sensory experiences facilitate visual discrimination of complex stimuli represented by printed words in a reading task? The answer has practical implication for visual discrimination training in the reading readiness program. McKee (1948, p. 147) has noted that commercial reading readiness books concentrate on visual discrimination exercises using geometric or animal forms rather than printed words. Educational research (Goins, 1958) has never confirmed the effectiveness of this type of discrimination training for beginning reading.

Although not directly concerned with the learning process defined in terms of reading performance, psychological studies in the area of discrimination pretraining provide hypotheses, research procedures, and findings which may contribute to understanding the relation between visual discrimination skills and reading performance. Studies in this area have investigated the effects of different types of stimulus discrimination pretraining on performance in a subsequent discrimination learning task. These studies provided tests of either Miller's (1948) acquired distinctiveness of cues hypothesis, or of Gibson's (1940) transfer of discrimination hypothesis. Both hypotheses state, in effect, that if differences are established among similar stimulus items or situations, then learning will be facilitated in a subsequent task using these same stimuli. An analysis of this research by Spiker (1956), and the later findings of Kurtz (1955), indicated that stimulus differentiation pretraining does result in positive transfer to a second task employing the same visual stimuli but different responses as used in the pretraining task.

The general objective of the present study was to extend the experimental procedures used in the stimulus pretraining research to investigate the question raised above: What types of sensory experiences facilitate visual discrimination among printed words occurring in a reading task? Specifically, the purpose was to investigate the effects of different types of discrimination pretraining on the performance of kindergarten children in learning to read a vocabulary list. Prior to learning the same vocabulary list, kindergarten children were given matching pretraining with three types of stimulus material: the same words as those appearing in the vocabulary list; different words; and geometric forms. Based on the results of the previous experimental work in stimulus pretraining, the prediction was made that the group given visual discrimination pretraining matching the same words would learn the vocabulary list faster than the groups given pretraining with different words or geometric forms.

All the necessary ingredients of a good introductory section are present in the above Introduction. The procedures and hypothesis elements are not in the same order as presented earlier, but this is of little importance. Study their place in this Introduction once again, as they are highlighted and labeled here in blue.

BACKGROUND OF THE PROBLEM (GENERAL PROBLEM AREA): To master beginning reading, a child must be able to associate word names, or meanings, with their printed symbols. To make these associations, a beginning reader must be able to see and respond to the printed symbols themselves as distinctive and stable stimulus compounds.

How does this visual discrimination skill develop? Theories of perceptual development attempt to relate sensory input to the learning process. The perceptual theories developed by such writers as Hebb (1940), Gibson (1940), and Murphy (1951) stress the contribution of sensory experience to perceptual differentiation of a stimulus field. Thus, for beginning readers, the question can be asked: What types of sensory experiences facilitate visual discrimination of complex stimuli represented by printed words in a reading task? The answer has practical implication for visual discrimination training in the reading readiness program.

BACKGROUND
OF THE
PROBLEM
(SYNOPSIS OF
RELATED
RESEARCH):   McKee (1948, p. 147) has noted that commercial reading readiness books concentrate on visual discrimination exercises using geometric or animal forms rather than printed words. Educational research (Goins, 1958) has never confirmed the effectiveness of this type of discrimination training for beginning reading.

Although not directly concerned with the learning process defined in terms of reading performance, psychological studies in the area of discrimination pretraining provide hypotheses, research procedures, and findings which may contribute to understanding the relation between visual discrimination skills and reading performance. Studies in this area have investigated the effects of different types of stimulus discrimination pretraining on performance in a subsequent discrimination learning task. These studies provided tests of either Miller's (1948) acquired distinctiveness of cues hypothesis, or of Gibson's (1940) transfer of discrimination hypothesis. Both hypotheses state, in effect, that if differences are established among similar stimulus items or situations, then learning will be facilitated in a subsequent task using these same stimuli. An analysis of this research by Spiker (1956), and the later findings of Kurtz (1955), indicated that stimulus differentiation pretraining does result in positive transfer to a second task employing the same visual stimuli but different responses as used in the pretraining task.

STATEMENT
OF THE
PROBLEM: The general objective of the present study was to extend the experimental procedures used in the stimulus pretraining research to investigate the question raised above: What types of sensory experiences facilitate visual discrimination among printed words occurring in a reading task? Specifically, the purpose was to investigate the effects of different types of visual discrimination pretraining on the performance of kindergarten children in learning to read a vocabulary list.

PROCEDURES: Prior to learning the same vocabulary list, kindergarten children were given matching pretraining with three types of stimulus material: the same words as those appearing in the vocabulary list; different words; and geometric forms.

HYPOTHESIS: Based on the results of the previous experimental work in stimulus pretraining, the prediction was made that the group given visual discrimination pretraining matching the same words would learn the vocabulary list faster than the groups given pretraining with different words or geometric forms.

Method

The function of this component is to present a complete description of what was done in the study. It is variously labeled "method," "procedure," or "methods and procedures," and includes these major elements:

> Target population and method of sampling
> Materials and instrumentation
> Research design and the rationale for its selection
> Type of data and the method of collection
> Data analysis methods
> Pilot study data

The usual rule of thumb for the researcher to follow in writing the Method component of a research report is to describe the procedures in sufficient detail to permit another researcher to: (1) replicate the study, and (2) assess the adequacy of the methods and procedures used in collecting and analyzing the data. This rule should always be applied in writing the final technical report to a funding agency or in preparing a dissertation. However, it is difficult to apply the rule to writing a report for submission to a journal because of space limitations. Consequently, most journal articles do not provide the detailed specifications necessary to permit someone else to replicate the study. This does not mean that the researcher should abandon the completeness criterion in writing the report for publication. Rather, it suggests that he should strive to meet this criterion as best he can, within the constraints imposed by a journal.

TARGET POPULATION AND METHOD OF SAMPLING

An accurate description of the target population is critical to the research report, for without it the reader cannot determine the generalizability and relevance of the results. A statement of the target population used in a study might be:

> Mexican-American preschool children who have participated in the Head Start Program.

Following the identification of the target population, this element should then describe the sampling plan and procedures that were used. Here the following questions should be answered.

How many subjects were selected? You should carefully identify all factors related to the final number of subjects included in the study. Were the subjects volunteers? If so, how many were invited and how many of that number actually chose to participate? What was the attrition rate (if any) during the study and what implications did it have for generalizing from the results of the study to the target population? It is desirable to include descriptive data about the sample in the report. If extensive data in the form of tables has been obtained, it is less disruptive to the reader to place these in the appendices and present a condensed summary in the body of the report. Be sure to point out the basis for the sample size used in the study. If, for example, a high attrition rate was anticipated on questionnaire returns, this should be indicated in this section. In a complex experimental design, show that there are enough subjects per cell to allow use of the selected statistical techniques.

What random sampling procedures were used?   Detailed explanations are usually not required if simple random sampling is used. However, if some other type of sampling method was used (e.g., matching, systematic, cluster, stratified random, etc.) be sure to describe the procedure fully.

MATERIALS AND INSTRUMENTATION

The materials and instrumentation element of the report should name and, when appropriate, describe: (1) the instructional or stimulus materials presented to the subject; and (2) the instruments used to collect the observations or maintain experimental control.

STIMULUS MATERIALS   If formal instructional materials were used in the study, at least the following descriptive information should be provided:

> Title
> Author/editor
> Producer (if appropriate)
> Population; entering behavior specifications
> Developmental and field test data summary
> Time required for administration
> Cost of materials
> Date of publication

If the above information is published elsewhere, the researcher may, after naming the materials, cite the reference where the information can be obtained. If special stimulus materials were developed, they should be carefully described in the report and tryout data obtained prior to using the materials in the experiment should be included in the appendices.

MEASUREMENT DEVICES USED   All measurement devices used in the study should be described in detail, within the body of the report including the following information:

> Title
> Author/editor
> Producer
> Population
> Forms
> Test objectives
> Descriptions of test, items, scoring
> Traits represented in score
> Predictive/concurrent validity (including description
>   of criterion, subjects, and results obtained)
> Reliability data
> Normative data
> Internal consistency or equivalence of tests
> Time required for administration
> Cost of materials
> Date of publication

If a well-known instrument was used, the above can be abbreviated and references listed to indicate where more detailed information may be obtained. Following this, a description should be provided of how the instruments were used in the study, including instructions, procedures for their use, time allocations, and the like.

DESIGN

The design element should clearly demonstrate how the study was planned to answer the research questions or hypotheses. The primary purposes of this element are:

1. To specify the relationship of the experimental treatments and hypotheses to the design selected

2. To describe the way the design served to control specific confounding variables. It should be shown that the design tactics used were the most effective for purposes of answering the research question or responding to the stated hypothesis

The reader will also want to know if there were any possible "side-effects" of the procedures that might bias the results. For example, has the researcher been careful to minimize the possible influence of his own wishes and expectations? Unfortunately, in conducting research in the schools, it is very easy unintentionally to cue the teachers of the experimental groups that higher performance is expected from their classes. In their desire to please the experimenter, they may make an extra effort to produce the desired results. The design element should indicate how such threats to the validity of the study were controlled.

In some instances, irrelevant factors or confounding variables may become apparent during the conduct of the study. This should be fully described in the report as well as any changes made in the planned design as a function of unforeseen problems.

DATA COLLECTION METHODS

This element should describe the data collection plans and procedures including schedules, descriptions of observer training (if appropriate), instructions used, etc. The procedural forms used in the study may be placed in the appendix.

The researcher should also provide a complete description of what was actually done during the conduct of the study. Brief instructions used by the experimenter should be presented verbatim, while longer instructions can be accurately paraphrased. The method of presenting the stimuli, the way in which the subject was asked to respond, and the time required for the various steps in the procedure should also be reported. In a product development study the type of teacher training, program monitoring, and data acquisition procedures should be carefully described.

DATA ANALYSIS

The Method component of the research report concludes with a description of the data analysis performed in the study. Normally, this element is limited to a description of the analysis that was performed, the statistical procedures used, and the rationale for the statistical procedures and level of significance; the actual data is reserved for the Results component.

SUMMARY OF METHOD ELEMENTS

The following is a summary of the sequence of elements for the Method Component:

1. *Target population and sampling*   This element should precisely define the target population, the sample size and procedures used and their rationale.

2. *Stimulus materials and instrumentation*   All stimulus materials and measurement devices used in the study should be described in detail. Abbreviated information and references may be provided for well-known materials and instruments.

3. *Research design and rationale*   This element should specify the relationship of the research hypothesis or question to the design and show how the selected design was the most effective for dealing with the question or hypothesis.

4. *Type of data and method of collection*   This type of data and collection methods should be described including a complete description of what was done during the data acquisition phase of the study.

5. *Data analysis methods*   All statistical procedures used for analyzing the data and the rationale for their use should be included in this element.

EXERCISE 4

ANALYSIS OF METHOD COMPONENT

Identify any missing elements in the following selection from a research report. Look for the following:

1: Target population and sampling procedure
2: Stimulus materials and instrumentation
3: Research design and rationale
4: Data collection methods
5: Methods used in analyzing the results

TITLE: The Effects of Phonetics-based and "Look-and-Say" Approaches to Teaching Reading on the Reading Performance of Elementary School Children

METHOD: Two approaches to teaching reading were used in the study: 1) a phonics-based reading approach and 2) a "look-and-say" reading approach.

The two approaches were tested on 260 pupils in nine second-grade classrooms of the Washington Elementary School District. Teachers were asked to take part in a program of in-service education that would prepare them to teach one selected approach for a period of time, ruling out the other approach. Following the teachers' participation in the in-service training sessions, the teachers were all given required instructional materials. They then conducted reading instruction using the specified approach for a period of three months. Following exposure to the two teaching approaches all groups were administered the *Gates Advanced Primary Reading Tests.*

MISSING ELEMENTS: _____

_____

_____

_____

The above example, clearly, contains insufficient information to allow someone else to replicate the study. The target population is specified in the example, but the sampling procedure is not. Numbers 3 and 4 are also inadequately specified. The only measurement device apparently used in the study is the reading test battery. Yet no information is presented on how the tests were used, on reliability, on validity, or on references as to where such information might be found. Nor is it indicated why this test was selected over other possible tests. Number 2 therefore, is missing. Number 5 is also missing, because no method of analyzing results is indicated.

Results

The major purpose of any research effort is to obtain data that may answer the specified research hypotheses or questions. The Results component is where the answers are presented. Let us review some simple guidelines for the preparation and presentation of the results, and consider several criteria for evaluating their completeness and objectivity.

ORGANIZING THE RESULTS

Many times, a research report will contain both a Results component and a Discussion component. Using this format, the Results should be limited to a straightforward exposition of the data. The interpretation of the findings should be reserved for the Discussion component.

The mark of a well organized Results component is that the data are sequenced and presented in such a way that it is easy to see whether the data support or fail to support the research hypothesis or question. One method of accomplishing this is to restate each research problem, hypothesis, or question, and then present the data that specifically relates to it.

Tables usually display data relevant to a single hypothesis. However, in some cases, it may be desirable to organize the data relevant to several hypotheses in a single table to facilitate comparison and discussion. In this case, the table should be placed next to the first textual reference and then referred back to in later discussions of other hypotheses.

SPECIFYING STATISTICAL METHODS USED

All statistical methods used to test each hypothesis should be named in the Results component. (e.g., analysis of variance, t test, etc.). The description of the statistical techniques or the rationale for their use should be presented in the data analysis element of the Method component.

THE RESEARCH REPORT **24**

SPECIFYING LEVEL OF SIGNIFICANCE AND/OR DEGREE OF RELATIONSHIP

Results of tests of significance must also be included in the Results component. This is usually done by presenting the numerical values of the statistics along with a statement of the probability of statistical significance. This information can be presented in narrative form, (e.g., "The obtained value of t was 3.56 which is significant beyond the .01 level") or in abbreviated form, (e.g., $t = 3.56$, $p < .01$). Either form is acceptable.

In general, the .01 or .05 levels of significance are used in educational research. If another level of significance is used, the researcher should present the rationale for its selection. In the report it is not sufficient merely to indicate that the significance test of the relationship between two or more variables is greater than chance; the *degree* of the relationship (e.g., correlation coefficient, F-value, etc.) must also be shown.

PREPARING TABLES

One of the tasks that may be troublesome to the researcher who is generating his first report is that of preparing the data tables and deciding where in the text they should be placed. Following are a few guidelines that, if followed, should simplify the task.

CONTENTS OF THE TABLE   The table should stand alone without the support of the text. Do not use incomplete titles such as "Correlation Matrix," or "Standard Deviations and Means," but rather provide enough information in the heading to identify the contents of the table (e.g., "Correlation Matrix for Reading Achievement, Spelling Achievement, and IQ" or "Raw Score Means and Standard Deviations on Concept Mastery Test by Feedback Groups").

There are three basic items of information that should be included in the title of a table: (1) the variable(s) for which data are being presented; (2) the groups and subgroups on whom data were collected; and (3) the names of the statistics included in the table. This information should be presented clearly in telegraphic style. An example of a table title that meets these criteria is "Means and Standard Deviations for Reading Pretest Scores of Third-Grade Remediation Group."

As a general rule, the data tables should include descriptive as well as inferential statistics. For example, results of an analysis of variance or correlation should be accompanied by a tabular presentation of the number of subjects and information on the central tendencies and dispersions of the sample measures.

TEXTUAL REFERENCE
AND PLACEMENT OF THE TABLE   The table should be presented after it is initially referenced in the text. Avoid providing only perfunctory references such as "Table 1 presents the results of an analysis of variance performed on recall scores." To do so is to impose upon the reader the task of determining why the data is presented and what it means. A more effective textual reference to a table is:

> Table 1 presents the results of an analyses of variance performed on recall scores. These results clearly indicate significant differences in performance between grades with fourth-grade pupils showing greater average recall scores than third-grade pupils.

The above explanation is clear and sufficiently complete to enable the reader to grasp the main ideas without having to examine the table.

Draft copies of tables are usually typed on separate pages so that they will not have to be redone each time the report is revised. After the final draft has been generated, the tables can be inserted in the appropriate places in the manuscript. Instructions for table placement should appear in the draft copy at the desired location of the table. If, for example, we wanted a table to appear at this point in the report, we would indicate it with an instruction to that effect, set off by lines above and below as follows:

— —

INSERT TABLE 00 APPROXIMATELY HERE

— —

PLACEMENT OF TABLE NUMBER AND TITLE   Tables are numbered consecutively in Arabic (not Roman) from the beginning to the end of the report. Typically the word "table," accompanied by its number, is centered and placed on the first line. The title appears beneath it and is also centered. If the title should exceed one line in length, make the succeeding lines narrower than the first line (resulting in an inverted pyramid format). An example of placement of a table number and title is shown in Table 1.

TABLE 1
SUMMARY OF THE RANDOMIZED BLOCKS
ANALYSIS OF VARIANCE FOR THE
READING ACHIEVEMENT TEST

Source of Variation	df	MS	F
MA	1	248.52	11.15**
Response Mode	1	3.62	——
Interaction	1	108.10	4.85*
Blocks	39	40.22	
Within	37	22.28	
Total	79	422.74	

Note: ___N = 80
*p ≤ .05
**p ≤ .01

TABLE HEADINGS AND LABELS   The row and column captions or headings of tables should be brief without sacrificing accuracy or completeness. The test of the adequacy of the headings is whether the reader can easily identify the meaning of each data entry in the table.

Table 2 on page 28 provides an example of row and column headings of a relatively complex table.

The overall heading in Table 2 labeled "Group" indicates that the rows will identify the specific grouping used in the study. Subsumed under this caption are the labels that define the specific subgroups. They indicate to the reader that the groups related to different IQ levels (above and below median IQ) and types of response mode (overt and covert).

The columns have three levels of headings: The first indicates the nature of the data (i.e., posttest); the second heading identifies the specific test on which data was obtained (i.e., criterion and one-year retention); and the third defines the specific types of data presented (i.e., N = number of subjects, M = mean, and SD = standard deviation).

A test of the adequacy of the labels is to take any number within

TABLE 2
RAW SCORE MEANS AND STANDARD
DEVIATIONS ON POSTTEST, BY
RESPONSE MODE AND IQ

| Group | Posttest | | | | | |
| | Criterion Test | | | 1-Year Retention Test | | |
	N	M	SD	N	M	SD
Above Median IQ						
Overt	40	27.80	5.08	42	26.88	4.86
Covert	40	29.70	4.65	42	26.05	4.05
Below Median IQ						
Overt	41	26.60	5.88	39	24.17	6.23
Covert	41	23.85	6.13	39	24.25	5.86

Note: Possible score was 40.

the body of the table and determine its meaning, using only the information provided at the top of the columns and at the side of the table.

SIZE AND SHAPE   An ideal table is rectangular and strikes a balance between the horizontal and vertical dimensions involved. Avoid pencil-like or ribbon-like tables in which only one or two columns or rows of data are presented. As a rule, tables should cover no more than the page size of the manuscript. Fold-out pages, although occasionally used, provide both the reader and the printer with unnecessary work.

FOOTNOTES   As shown in Table 2 above, footnotes of a table are typed directly below the body. There are three types of footnotes: general, specific, and probability level. Explanations for their use are described in the various style manuals, e.g., *American Psychological Association Publication Manual.*

CRITERIA OF A WELL-CONSTRUCTED RESULTS COMPONENT

Two criteria may be used to evaluate the presentation of findings contained in the Results component. They include:

1. The completeness of the data

2. The objectivity of the presentation

COMPLETENESS OF DATA   A basic criterion of a good Results component is that all of the data analyses related to the hypotheses or research questions are presented. Occasionally research results are reported in which some of the important data appear to be missing. An example was found in which a series of tests was administered to five hundred subjects but the results were reported for only four hundred subjects. One had no way of telling from the Results component whether or not the data for these subjects had been lost, deliberately omitted, or invalidated in some way. As a general rule, all of the relevant data should be presented. If there are valid reasons for omitting data, the report should identify the omitted data, indicate why it was not included in the report, and discuss what, if any, implications it has for the interpretation of the data.

Completeness of data presentation does not mean that the researcher should present voluminous tables of data which are either redundant or unrelated to the hypothesis. For example, even if a researcher has access to his subject's histories, socioeconomic background, aptitude and intelligence test scores, etc., there would be little point in providing all of this information in the Results component if it were not directly related to the experimental hypothesis. Thus the researcher must be certain that all relevant data are presented and, at the same time, verify that no unnecessary data are included.

To prevent the Results component from being padded with non-essential data, the researcher should inspect each data item and ask himself, "What effect would the omission of this piece of data have on the reader's understanding of the study?" If the honest answer is, "none" then it should be omitted. It is best to apply this rule early in the data compilation and analysis process. To apply it after many hours have been spent preparing tables often leads to a reluctance to discard data presentations.

OBJECTIVITY OF PRESENTATION   Exposition rather than interpretation of the data is the purpose of the Results component. Ordinarily, this is accomplished by using tables, graphs, and figures along with whatever narrative is required to explain the data. Data should be objectively and accurately presented including evidence that does not support the stated hypothesis. The researcher must be careful in preparing the Results component that he does not ignore, minimize or distort evidence that does not support his hypothesis. Also, data interpretations and inferences should be reserved for inclusion in the Discussion component.

EXERCISE 5

ANALYSIS OF RESULTS COMPONENT

Identify, by circling the letter, any missing elements that are not adequately presented in the following Results component of a research report: Look for the following:

1. Substantive Content
   a. Statement of the research hypothesis and/or problem
   b. Name of the statistical technique(s) used
   c. Specification of the level of significance
   d. Complete presentation of the data
   e. Objective presentation of the data (exposition without interpretation)

2. Tabular Presentation of the Data
   a. A table title indicating variables, groups, and statistics used in study
   b. A textual reference identifying the table number, content, and main ideas
   c. Placement of the table closely following the text reference
   d. An Arabic table number
   e. Appropriate placement of the table number and title
   f. Clear table headings and labels, easily identifying the meaning of each data entry in table
   g. A table shape within acceptable visual limits (not pencil-like or ribbon-like) and not exceeding the size of the manuscript page
   h. Placement of table footnotes immediately below the table

TITLE: Effects of Immediate and Delayed Feedback on the Multiplication Performance of Third-Grade Pupils

EXCERPT: The experimental hypothesis was that immediate feedback in multiplication exercises will result in shorter completion times and lower error rates than does delayed feedback.

Table 3 presents the means, standard deviations, and number of subjects for the treatment groups. A one-tailed t test was used to test the differences in treatment means. In both cases, for time ($t = 6.04, p < .01$) and program error rate ($t = 3.59$, $p < .01$), hypothesized differences favoring the immediate feedback condition were found.

TABLE III
TIME TO COMPLETE PROGRAM AND
ERRORS ON PROGRAM FOR IMMEDIATE AND
DELAYED FEEDBACK GROUPS

Groups	Measure				
	Time (Minutes)		Program Errors		
	M	SD	M	SD	Error Rate
Immediate Feedback	64.8	13.0	12.4	7.2	.09
Delayed Feedback	80.3	15.2	29.5	11.8	.22

Note: Comparison of immediate and delayed feedback mean time: $t = 6.04, p < .01$
Comparison of immediate and delayed feedback mean errors: $t = 3.59, p < .01$

The results of this study are consistent with the studies of Wilbur (1968) and Frank (1964) and suggest that immediate feedback may be superior to delayed in almost all mathematical learning tasks.

The above example specifies: (1) the research hypothesis, (2) the statistical technique used, and (3) the level of significance. It appears complete (at least for a highly condensed presentation format) and is expository except for the last sentence. The last sentence is interpretative and belongs in the Discussion component. Thus, item 1e should be circled. Inspecting the table, its title identifies the variables and treatment groups but does not specify the statistics. Item 2a should be circled.

The text's reference to the table is minimally adequate and would be better had it identified the treatment groups in the first sentence (i.e., *immediate and delayed feedback* treatment groups). The table, table number, and title are correctly placed; however the second line of the title should have been made narrower than the first (see Placement of Table Number and Title). Thus, item 2e should be circled. The title number should also have been written in Arabic rather than Roman (item 2d).

The table captions are clear and all data entries are easy to identify. The size and shape of the table are within acceptable limits and the footnotes are correctly placed.

Discussion

After the major findings of the research study are presented in the Results component, the researcher must explain what implications the findings have for educational theory, research, or practice. Basically, the information in this component should: (1) provide all evidence related to the research hypothesis and competing hypotheses; (2) establish the relationships of these findings to results obtained in earlier studies; and (3) define the limitations of the research study and the findings.

Every effort must be made to provide a discussion of results that is objective, accurate, and avoids incorrect interpretation or misrepresentation. As a safeguard, the Discussion component should be read, reread, and revised by the researcher:

To avoid false inferences and interpretations that go beyond the data.

To make certain that all reasonable inferences are noted. (Occasionally a researcher will be overcautious in reporting the results and will fail to see relevant points or inferences that may quite reasonably be drawn from the data.)

To be sure that previous concepts do not bias the inferences that are drawn from the data.

To be sure that results reported are relevant to the research hypothesis.

Some cautions to be observed in interpreting the results of research in the Discussion component are:

Guard against erroneous interpretations due to pre-conceived ideas, biases, and prejudices.

Be careful not to omit evidence or inferences that are contrary to your hypothesis or to your own opinion.

Scrupulously avoid statements that are dependent upon subjective judgment.

Do not try to draw conclusions from results provided by inaccurate instruments of measurement (or instruments the accuracy of which is not known).

Be careful not to generalize from a single or limited number of cases. (Do not generalize from insufficient data.)

In associational studies, be certain you do not mistake correlation for causation. (A common causal factor may be accounting for the correlation.)

The above "cautions" do not mean that the researcher may never speculate or make interpretations that go beyond the data. It is permissible to do so, provided the researcher clearly indicates in the report that the interpretation is only speculative.

EVIDENCE RELATED TO THE HYPOTHESIS

This element of the Discussion component usually begins with the major findings of the Results component and places them in a framework in which the research hypothesis can be evaluated.

Too often, particularly if the researcher has attained statistically significant results, there is a tendency to gloss over both the competing hypotheses and limitations of the study. This probably stems from a feeling that the hypothesis was sound and that the "truth" was able to shine through despite minor experimental frailties. Whatever the basis, the effect is to obscure relevant and sometimes critical aspects of the study. A basic requirement of the Discussion component is that it present an honest account of possible alternative hypotheses and interpretations of the obtained results. Competing hypotheses should be fairly described and this presentation followed by a discussion of why they were rejected in favor of the stated hypothesis. Findings that are both consistent and inconsistent with the results of earlier studies should be noted.

Occasionally a researcher may reject his experiment outright rather than abandon his hypothesis. This typically happens when the researcher has a strong commitment to some pet theory or method. Rejection of the experiment, after the fact, is not acceptable researcher behavior. If the experiment was poorly conceived or lacking in controls, it should not have been done. If the researcher changed his mind during the research and began to question its utility, he should have stopped the experiment before reporting the results. It should be remembered that the Discussion component is intended only to discuss the data as they came out. If they do not support the research hypothesis, then it is the researcher's obligation to discuss the implications of these findings reflected on the present relevant body of knowledge. Unfortunately, too many educational research projects are still positive-results oriented (i.e., the researcher is prepared to interpret positive results only). A well-conceived and conducted research project, however, will yield useful information irrespective of whether the results are positive or negative.

RELATIONSHIP TO PREVIOUS RESEARCH

After presenting evidence related to the hypothesis or research question, the researcher should discuss the relationship of the findings to previous research. Aspects of the findings that are either consistent or inconsistent with the results of earlier studies should be pointed out and their research and theoretical implications discussed. Subsequent to analyzing the implications of the findings to educational practice, it may be appropriate to: (1) discuss actions that should be taken based on the findings and/or (2) suggest future avenues of research that will provide better data relevant to the problem.

LIMITATIONS OF THE STUDY

The limitations and weaknesses of the study should also be discussed in the Discussion component. This can be overdone, undoubtedly, as all research studies have some inadequacies and many pages can be written belaboring a study's limitations. The objective here is not to "put down" the study or to make a great show of humility. It is only necessary to indicate the limitations of the study to help the reader judge the validity of the conclusions drawn from the data. Frequently, a novice researcher will list uncontrolled factors without carefully considering how they might have affected the results. Thus, he might list as weaknesses of the study his inability to control for such factors as pupil illnesses, outside traffic noise, etc. It is wise to consider carefully all the variables that may be related to a given experimental situation. The researcher should acknowledge an uncontrolled variable, but not as a weakness of the study — unless there exists some basis for assuming its relevance to the outcome of the experiment.

SUMMARY OF DISCUSSION COMPONENT

To review, the Discussion component should present the research hypothesis, major findings, competing hypotheses, and discussion of the relationship of the results to previous research. Finally, the researcher should summarize the limitations of the findings that are presented (for example, sampling problems, possible irrelevant factors, and the like). Having done so, he will have provided the reader with all the critical information needed to evaluate his study.

EXERCISE 6

ANALYSIS OF DISCUSSION COMPONENT

Identify each of the six elements of all Discussion components if they are present in the following Discussion (Sassenrath & Garverick, 1965). Circle the passage containing each element that you can find, and label it in the margin. Look for these six elements:

1. A statement of the research hypothesis
2. A statement of all major findings related to the research hypothesis

3. A discussion of competing hypotheses and interpretations of results
4. A rationale for the rejection of competing hypotheses (if positive results were obtained)
5. A discussion of the relationship of the present findings to earlier studies (If negative findings were obtained, discussion should attempt to reconcile or integrate results with previous research.)
6. Description of any limitations or weaknesses of the present study

DISCUSSION

This experiment tested the general hypothesis that, with an increase in amount of information from feedback on examinations, there would be an increase in the retention and the transfer scores on a final examination. It was assumed that the group receiving no feedback would have the least amount of information, the group which checked its answers from the correct ones on the blackboard would have slightly more information, the group which had the questions discussed by the instructor would have even more information, and the group which reread the material covering questions they missed would get the most amount of information.

Analyses of the results in general showed that on both the retention and transfer tests the group which had the questions discussed in class and the group which checked their answers from the correct ones on the blackboard were better than the control-no feedback group and the group that reread material on items they got incorrect on the three midsemester examinations. These results particularly support the old study by Curtis and Wood (1929) with high school subjects showing that methods of feedback that provide for discussion are best. One can only speculate on the reasons why the group that reread material they missed did not do as well as expected. One reason is that subjects in this group focused only upon questions they got right; some of which they may have gotten correct primarily by chance. Consequently, they may not have actually received as much feedback information as initially assumed. Also a few subjects in this group forgot to bring their textbook to class the day of the feedback treatment and had to borrow the use of a book from another student: again cutting into the amount of relevant feedback information they may have received. Thus had this group, as a whole, received the amount of information they should have, perhaps they would have performed as well or better than the groups which received discussion or checked over their answers from the correct ones on the board.

Another methodological weakness of this experiment is that subjects were not assigned to treatment conditions at random. This procedure was precluded by subjects having class schedules which would have posed a conflict in the majority of cases. However, an analysis of the scores on the first examination indicated that there was no sampling bias between the treatment groups in initial performance in educational psychology.

One could also raise the question that a Hawthorne effect may explain the results of this study. However, it was not emphasized in classes that an experiment was underway, and also the treatments were not unusual but similar to those used by many instructors.

A further argument can be raised that the results are due to instructor effects, since it was not possible to perfectly counterbalance nor analyze for this variable. However, the five different instructors each taught two of the four different feedback treatments in an effort, at least, to partially control for instructor effects. Therefore, it seems most plausible to conclude that advising teachers to discuss examination questions with students or letting students check over their examinations is no idle suggestion. However, the type of feedback appears to be less important than the fact that they get it. Students receiving any of the three feedback conditions employed in this experiment did better than those receiving no feedback, as the absolute difference among the three experimental groups is not large.

Here too, all essential elements are present. A clear statement of the research hypothesis is presented in the first labeled paragraph. It is followed by a statement about assumptions related to the treatment condition. The second labeled paragraph contains a brief statement of the major findings of the study, after which the relationship of the findings to previous research is mentioned. This is followed by a full description of problems and limitations noted in the study. The last two labeled paragraphs discuss the competing hypotheses along with the rationale for their rejection.

> RESEARCH
> HYPOTHESIS: *This experiment tested the general hypothesis that, with an increase in amount of information from feedback on exminations, there would be an increase in the retention and the transfer scores on a final exmination.*

It was assumed that the group receiving no feedback would have the least amount of information, the group which checked its answers from the correct ones on the blackboard would have slightly more information, the group which had the questions discussed by the instructor would have even more information, and the group which reread the material covering questions they missed would get the most amount of information.

Analyses of the results in general showed that on both the retention and transfer tests the group which had the questions discussed in class and the group which checked their answers from the correct ones on the blackboard were better than the control-no feedback group and the group that reread material on items they got incorrect on the three mid-semester examinations.

RELATIONSHIP
TO PREVIOUS
RESEARCH: *These results particularly support the old study by Curtis and Wood (1929) with high school subjects showing that methods of feedback that provide for discussion are best. One can only speculate on the reasons why the group that reread material they missed did not do as well as expected.*

LIMITATIONS: *One reason is that subjects in this group focused only upon questions they got right; some of which they may not have actually received as much feedback information as initially assumed. Also a few subjects in their group forgot to bring their textbook to class the day of the feedback treatment and had to borrow the use of a book from another student: again cutting into the amount of relevant feedback information they may have received. Thus had this group, as a whole, received the amount of information they should have, perhaps they would have performed as well or better than the groups which received discussion or checked over their answers from the correct ones on the board.*

Another methodological weakness of this experiment is that subjects were not assigned to treatment conditions at random. This procedure was precluded by subjects having class schedules which would have posed a conflict in the majority of cases. However, an analysis of the scores on the first examination indicated that there was no sampling bias between the treatment groups in initial performance in educational psychology.

DISCUSSION OF
COMPETITING
HYPOTHESES
AND
RATIONALE FOR
THEIR REJECTION:
One could also raise the question that a Hawthorne effect may explain the results of this study. However, it was not emphasized in classes that an experiment was underway, and also the treatments were not unusual but similar to those used by many instructors.

A further argument can be raised that the results are due to instructor effects, since it was not possible to perfectly counterbalance nor analyze for this variable. However, the five different instructors each taught two of the four different feedback treatments in an effort, at least, to partially control for instructor effects. Therefore, it seems most plausible to conclude that advising teachers to discuss examination questions with students or letting students check over their examinations is no idle suggestion. However, the type of feedback appears to be less important than the fact that they get it.

Students receiving any of the three feedback conditions employed in this experiment did better than those receiving no feedback, as the absolute difference among the three experimental groups is not large.

Conclusions

When a report requires that a Conclusions component follow the Discussion component, it is usually best to limit its content to succinct statements based on the findings and consistent with the discussion. Since the Discussion component amplifies the implications of the findings for theory and practice, the Conclusions component should present clear and concise statements with limited elaboration. Ordinarily the Discussion component will have to be modified to ensure minimum redundancy and protect the Conclusions component from being gratuitous.

Irrespective of where the conclusions are presented, there are some common pitfalls to avoid. Frequently, especially when some kind of statistical significance has been achieved, a researcher may ignore questions of limited practical or theoretical significance and improperly use the Conclusions component to turn supportive findings into hard proof of great generalizability. This, of course, carries the researcher well beyond his data and threatens the utility of the study.

An example of stating a supported hypothesis as a proven fact is shown below. The stated hypothesis was:

> Self-organization of biology instructional materials will improve both rate of learning and the amount learned by ninth-grade students.

But the following statement was made in the report:

> The major conclusion is that student control over the organization of instructional materials and methods used in learning produces higher learning performance than does instructor control of materials and methods.

Even if we assume that the Conclusions component from which the above statement was drawn will contain additional qualifying information, the conclusion stated above goes well beyond the data in several respects. A more appropriate statement of a major conclusion might be:

> Results of this study suggest that procedures for involving ninth-grade students in the organization of their own instructional materials in biological science warrant further study. Particular attention should be given to the value of such procedures as they interact with type of learning task, specified performance criteria, and with age level of students.

EXERCISE 7

STATEMENT OF MAJOR CONCLUSION

Identify the major conclusion warranted from the following paragraphs.

A study was performed to test the following hypothesis: Providing immediate feedback will result in fewer pronunciation errors in learning French than delayed feedback.

College freshmen students were randomly assigned to either of two treatment groups. Both groups were presented with single recorded

French words which they were to say back. One group was provided with an immediate playback of each response and stimulus word. The other group did not receive immediate feedback but were provided with a playback of all their responses and stimulus words at the end of the session.

The group receiving the immediate feedback had statistically significantly fewer pronunciation errors than the other group.

MAJOR CONCLUSION: _____

_____

_____

_____

_____

_____

Your statement of the major conclusion in the above study should be something to the effect of: The results of the study suggest that, for college freshmen, instructional procedures which include immediate feedback are beneficial in learning to reproduce French words orally. The utility of immediate feedback with language acquisition and other learning tasks warrants further study.

Summary and Abstract

The summary or abstract of a research report should be constructed only after the previous components have been developed. Both the summary and abstract represent a condensation of the study; their specific differences are defined below.

SUMMARY

Many research report formats require that a summary of the study be included as a component of the report or as an addendum. Although usually it is the final section of the report, some agencies require that it be presented as the initial section of the report. Wherever it is placed its function remains the same. The summary is intended to provide a highly condensed account of the study and its findings for those who do not have time to read the complete text. It is, therefore, primarily a synoptic rerun of all the critical elements of the report.

The information contained in this component usually includes a very brief presentation of:

Research questions or hypotheses and rationale for the study

Target population and method of sampling

Outline description of treatment conditions and design

Types of statistical analyses performed

Major findings obtained (no tables should be presented)

Discussion of (1) whether evidence supports or fails to support the hypothesis and (2) competing hypotheses that may account for the results

Limitations of study

Implications of the findings and recommendations for future research or other action

ABSTRACT

An abstract is an even more highly condensed summary of the report (150 to 200 words) that contains the following items of information:

Variables studied

Number and type of subjects

Description of procedures

Synopsis of major findings

THE RESEARCH REPORT **42**

The function of the abstract is to tell the reader something about the Method, Results, and Discussion components. The results are generally given the greatest emphasis in the abstract. In many journals, the abstract precedes the report and provides the reader with:

1. Enough information to decide whether or not he is interested in the article

2. A synoptic preview of what he is about to read

IDENTIFYING PARTS OF AN ABSTRACT

Identify any missing elements in the following Abstracts component of a research report (Caro, 1962). Look for these four elements:

1. Names of the variables
2. Number and type of subjects
3. Description of design and procedures
4. Synoptic statements of major findings

The effects of attending class and of structuring an introductory psychology course with respect to time and content were studied, using 335 undergraduates in an introductory psychology course in a 2 × 3 factorial design. Time structuring was accomplished through schedules of testing. Using end-of-course achievement test scores as the criterion, F ratios for neither the class attendance variable, the time structure variable, nor the treatment interaction were significant at the .01 level. It was concluded that students performed as well through independent study as in the conventional class situation, and time structured content was ineffective as a determiner of student achievement. Student dropouts and the number of students seeking individual assistance were unrelated to the experimental treatments.[3]

MISSING ELEMENTS: _____ _____

The example is well organized and contains most of the information required of an abstract. It names the variables (class attendance, course structure, and final exam scores) and provides information on the number and type of subject (335 undergraduates in psychology course). The treatment conditions are not clearly specified in the abstract; but, type of design is indicated. It also includes a statement of the major findings.

In this sequence the functions of the essential components of the research report have been identified and labeled within a commonly used format. As has been indicated this format is not always used and both the labels and the configuration of the components may change. But once the function and content of the components are known, it is easy to comply with the specifications.

Whether you are preparing a final report for an agency, an article for submission to a journal, or a dissertation for a university department, it is *critical* that you follow precisely the prescribed format. Deviations from the accepted format, in the case of an agency report or dissertation, may require complete retyping of the draft. In the case of a submitted article, it may reduce the probability of its acceptance. Remember, the reviewers of the research report are accustomed to locating information under certain headings. If you deviate from the specified format, they may overlook an important piece of information because it is not located in the conventional section of the document. Special formats are easily accommodated once the basic reporting information is well conceived and precisely stated.

As you develop your report, the following Component Checklist may help you to identify any omissions or deficiencies in the draft of your report.

REPORT COMPONENT CHECKLIST

Component	Conditions	Conditions Met — Yes	Conditions Met — No	Comments
1. *Title*	Specifies variables, relationship, and target population; not longer than 15-20 substantive words.			In published research articles it is acceptable to omit the identification of target population in title.
2. *Problem* Background of the Problem	Presents synopsis of related studies, identifies relevant variables, and discusses those selected for the study.			May be very abbreviated in published articles.
Problem Statement	States research problem and indicates its educational significance.			
Hypothesis	Specific, testable and, if possible, related to theory.			
Research Plan	Identifies research plan/treatments.			Optional
3. *Method* Target Population and Sampling	Indicates number of subjects, rationale for selection, and representativeness of sample to target population.			May be very abbreviated in published articles.
Stimulus Materials and Measurement Instruments	Gives complete information (see pages 19 and 20) on characteristics of materials.			May be very abbreviated in published articles.
Design	Identifies relationship of design to hypothesis and shows how			

Component	Conditions	Conditions Met Yes	Conditions Met No	Comments
	design controls confounding variables.			
Data Collection Methods	Provides complete description of what was done in conducting experiment.			May be very abbreviated in published articles.
Data Analyses	Describes analyses performed, statistical procedures used, and the rationale for their use.			
4. *Results* Substantive Content	1) States research hypothesis/problem. 2) Describes statistical techniques used. 3) Presents level of significance. 4) Provides complete and objective presentation of data (no interpretation).			
Tabular Presentation of Data	1) Title indicate variables, groups, and statistics used. 2) Headings and labels are clear. 3) Shape of table within acceptable limits. 4) Titles correctly placed. 5) Text reference gives table number, content, and main ideas.			
5. *Discussion*	Presents: 1) Research hypothesis/problem. 2) Major findings. 3) Limitations of the study.			

Component	Conditions	Conditions Met Yes	Conditions Met No	Comments
	4) Competing hypotheses. 5) Relationship of results to previous research.			
6. *Conclusions*	1) Reviews most significant findings. 2) States major conclusions. 3) Discusses implications of findings for educational action or research.			Sometimes Conclusions component is included in the Discussion component.
7. *Summary*	Presents a synopsis of the critical ingredients in each of the above components.			Often omitted in published research articles.
8. *Abstract*	Usually not over 200 words in length. States: 1) Variables studied. 2) Number and type of subjects. 3) Description of procedures. 4) Synopsis of major findings.			

SUMMATIVE EXERCISE

EXERCISE 9

EVALUATION OF A RESEARCH REPORT

Read the following research report (Sullivan, Baker, and Schutz, 1967) and indicate whether the conditions for each component have been met. Checklists have been provided to make your evaluation more systematic, and the paragraphs in the report have been numbered to facilitate later discussion. Complete all the checklists before you verify the answer.

EFFECT OF INTRINSIC AND EXTRINSIC REINFORCEMENT CONTINGENCIES ON LEARNER PERFORMANCE[1]

76 Air Force ROTC cadets participated in an investigation of the effects on learner performance of variations in (a) knowledge of results for responses to mastery items inserted in instructional material and (b) reinforcement contingencies for performance on a 100-item final criterion test over the material. Ss receiving no knowledge of results for mastery-item responses scored significantly higher (p < .001) on the 11 mastery tests than did Ss receiving immediate feedback through chemically treated answer sheets. However, the 2 groups did not differ significantly in criterion-test performance. 1/2 of the Ss could earn $4 for a criterion-test score of 80% or higher, while the remaining Ss earned $2.50 irrespective of criterion-test performance. No significant differences in test scores were associated with these reinforcement conditions. The data suggest that Ss receiving immediate feedback employ a markedly different strategy from "no feedback" Ss in learning instructional material.

ABSTRACT CHECKLIST

Indicate whether the following conditions have been met:

Component	Conditions	Conditions Met Yes	Conditions Met No	Comments
Abstract	Usually not over 200 words in length. States: 1) Variables studied. 2) Number and type of subjects. 3) Description of procedures. 4) Synopsis of major findings.			

(*1*) The facilitating effect of reinforcement on student learning is well recognized. Yet in studies of applied learning the term "reinforcement" frequently has been used to describe a variety of stimulus conditions without specifying the possible differential effects related to these diverse conditions. For example, in many studies knowledge of results for student responses to en route test items over the instructional materials has been treated as reinforcement. Reinforcement in these studies is a condition that is intrinsic to (i.e., built into) the learning materials. In other studies reinforcement is a stimulus condition ex-

[1] This research was supported under Contract AF 33 (615) 1507 with the Aerospace Medical Research Laboratories, Air Force Systems Command, Wright-Patterson Air Force Base, Ohio.

trinsic to the learning materials. Here, the presentation of reinforcement is contingent upon level of performance on the instructional material, but the reinforcement is not a condition built directly into the material. Gold stars, course grades, and special awards for performance serve as examples of extrinsic reinforcement.

(2) The present study sought to investigate the effects of both intrinsic and extrinsic reinforcement on student performance when both conditions were employed in the same instructional program. The intrinsic reinforcement condition included variations in the knowledge of results provided for student responses to sets of mastery items inserted at various points in the instructional material. The extrinsic reinforcement condition consisted of variations in the amount of money that could be earned by subjects (Ss) for acceptable performance on a final criterion test over the material.

TITLE AND PROBLEM CHECKLIST

Indicate whether the following conditions have been met:

Component	Conditions	Conditions Met Yes	No	Comments
Title	Specifies variables, relationship, and target population; not longer than 15-20 substantive words.			In published research articles it is acceptable to omit the identification of target population in title.
Problem Background of the Problem	Presents synopsis of related studies, identifies relevant variables, and discusses those selected for the study.			May be very abbreviated in published articles.
Problem Statement	States research problem and indicates its educational significance.			
Hypothesis	Specific, testable and, if possible, related to theory.			
Research Plan	Identifies research plan/treatments.			Optional

METHOD

Subjects

(3) The *S*s were 76 Air Force Reserve Officers Training Corps cadets who were second semester freshmen enrolled in the AFROTC program at Arizona State University. The *S*s were selected at random from among approximately 100 cadets who volunteered to participate in the experiment during the time when they normally attended AFROTC classes and drill periods.

Design

(4) The study employed a 2 × 2 factorial design. The variations in intrinsic reinforcement conditions served as one factor in the design. The variations in extrinsic conditions served as the second factor.

Procedures

(5) The *S*s attended four 50-minute class periods on a twice-a-week basis to read the instructional material and answer the mastery items. Each *S* was randomly assigned either to a room in which knowledge of results was provided or to a room in which no knowledge of results was provided. The extrinsic reinforcement conditions were randomized within both the "feedback" and "no feedback" rooms. Printed instructions explaining the appropriate extrinsic reinforcement contingency and specifying the time schedule for the experiment were given to each *S* at the beginning of the first class meeting. The final criterion test was administered to all *S*s at a fifth session 2 days after the final instructional period.

(6) The *S*s read the instructional material and responded to the mastery tests at their own pace. The "feedback" group received immediate feedback on their responses to each mastery item as a function of chemically treated answer blanks. Individuals in this group used special pens to mark their responses to the mastery items. When *S* marked the correct response blank, the blank turned red; when he marked an incorrect blank, it turned yellow. The *S*s in this group were told that if their first response to an item was incorrect, they were to continue responding to the item until they answered it correctly. The "no feedback" group received no knowledge of results on their responses to the mastery items.

(7) Two levels of extrinsic reinforcement were included in the study. Instructions for *S*s under the Contingent Reinforcement condition stated that *S* would be paid $4.00 if he scored 80% or higher on the final test over the instructional material, $2.00 if he scored from 50% to 79%, and nothing if he scored below 50%. Individuals in the Assured Reinforcement group were told that they would be paid $2.50 if they attended all five scheduled sessions. Instructions to the Assured Reinforcement group stated that there would be a final test over the instructional material, but the instructions did not relate the test to the $2.50 in any way. Thus, no extrinsic reinforcement based upon level of performance on the criterion test was available to the Assured Reinforcement group.

Materials

(8) The textual material used in the experiment was a revised edition of the Air Force manual, *The Military Justice System* (United States Air Force Reserve Officers Training Corps, 1962). This text was originally selected for revision because it included sufficient concept complexity and developmental continuity directly applicable to Air Force and ROTC curriculum. After subjecting the original version of the text to a logical analysis of objectives, a final list of 69 specific behavioral objectives was complied. The Instructional Specification strategy (Schutz, Baker, & Gerlach, 1964; Schutz, Baker, & Sullivan, 1966) was then employed to specify the stimulus conditions required for the attainment of these objectives. The materials were revised on the basis of these specified conditions, item analyses of the performance of cadets from earlier studies on the final criterion test, analyses of interview data from individual cadets who had read the materials, and application of the gap and mastery principles of programmed instruction (Silberman, Coulson, Melaragno, & Newmark, 1964).

(9) A set of 131 mastery items was developed pertaining to the behavioral objectives specified for the instructional materials. These items were grouped into 11 unit-mastery tests and inserted at appropriate points in the 60-page revised text. Each mastery test contained items covering only the material from the section of the text immediately preceding the test. Determination of the place in the text where each mastery test was inserted was a function of optimum length or logical determination of appropriate homogeneous blocks of content.

(10) A final criterion test of 100 three- and four-choice multiple-choice items was developed from an original pool of 200 items. Only items with a difficulty index of .75 or lower for a sample of 50 Ss who had read the original text were included in the final 100-item test. The reliability coefficient for the criterion test, computed by the KR-20 formula on a sample of 76 Ss who had read the revised text, was .86.

METHOD CHECKLIST
Indicate whether the following conditions have been met:

Component	Conditions	Conditions Met		Comments
		Yes	No	
Method Target Population and Sampling	Indicates number of subjects, rationale for selection, and representativeness of sample to target population.			May be very abbreviated in published articles.

Component	Conditions	Conditions Met Yes	No	Comments
Stimulus Materials and Measurement Instruments	Gives complete information (see pages 19 and 20) on characteristics of materials.			May be very abbreviated in published articles.
Design	Identifies relationship of design to hypothesis and shows how design controls confounding variables.			
Data Collection Methods	Provides complete description of what was done in conducting experiment.			May be very abbreviated in published articles.
Data Analyses	Describes analyses performed, statistical procedures used, and the rationale for their use.			

RESULTS

(11) The mean score for each group on the 100-item criterion test is shown in Table 1. It is apparent from the table that the Contingent Reinforcement group scored approximately three points higher than the Assured Reinforcement group, and the "no feedback" group scored slightly more than one point higher than the "feedback" group. These differences were tested for significance using a two-way analysis of variance. Neither the main effects nor the interaction was statistically significant.

(12) Analyses of performance on the mastery test, however, did reveal important differences between the treatment groups. Only three of the 38 Ss in the "feedback" group failed to complete all 11 mastery tests during the four periods of the instructional program. In the "no feedback" treatment, however, 15 of the 38 individuals completed only 10 or fewer tests and failed to reach the final mastery test. Clearly, the "no feedback" group was spending more time studying either the textual material or the mastery items than was the "feedback" group.

(13) Descriptive statistics relating to the mean standard score on unit-mastery tests completed by each S are shown in Table 2. Since data on mastery-test scores were not available on four Ss from the contingent-reinforcement-plus-feedback cell when the statistical analyses were performed, these Ss were assigned the computed mean standard score for their cell on mastery-test performance. This accounts for the slight variation of the grand mean score (49.85) from a grand mean of 50.00.

TABLE 1
CRITERION TEST MEAN SCORES

Extrinsic reinforcement	Intrinsic reinforcement				Totals	
	Feedback		No feedback			
	N	Score	N	Score	N	Score
Contingent ($4–$2–0)	19	61.37	19	61.32	38	61.35
Assured ($2.50)	19	57.00	19	59.63	38	58.32
Totals	38	59.18	38	60.47	76	59.83

TABLE 2
MASTERY TEST MEAN STANDARD SCORES

Extrinsic reinforcement	Intrinsic reinforcement				Totals	
	Feedback		No feedback			
	N	Standard score	N	Standard score	N	Score
Contingent	19	47.10	19	53.24	38	50.17
Assured	19	47.07	19	51.97	38	49.52
Totals	38	47.09	38	52.61	76	49.85

(*14*) The data in Table 2 reveal that the "no feedback" Ss performed considerably better on the mastery items than did the "feedback" Ss. The mean standard score for mastery-test performance is 5.52 standard score points higher for the "no feedback" group. A two-way analysis of variance of mastery-test scores revealed that this difference is significant at the .001 level ($F = 22.08$). Neither the extrinsic reinforcement contingency effect nor the interaction between intrinsic and extrinsic reinforcement approached statistical significance.

RESULTS CHECKLIST
Indicate whether the following conditions have been met:

Component	Conditions	Conditions Met		Comments
		Yes	No	
Results Substantive Content	1) States research hypothesis/problem. 2) Describes statistical techniques used. 3) Presents level of significance. 4) Provides complete and objective presentation of data (no interpretation).			
Tabular Presentation of Data	1) Title indicate variables, groups, and statistics used. 2) Headings and labels are clear. 3) Shape of table within acceptable limits. 4) Titles correctly placed. 5) Text reference gives table number, content, and main ideas.			

DISCUSSION

(15) The results of the study suggest that there were important differences between the "feedback" and "no feedback" treatment groups in the strategies that they employed to learn the instructional material. The better performance of the "no feedback" group on the mastery tests and the failure of 15 *Ss* from this group to finish the instructional program indicate that the "no feedback" *Ss* expended more time and effort attempting to learn from the prose textual material. For these individuals, of course, this is the only instructional material

286 |

in the text. The "feedback" Ss, on the other hand, apparently neglected the textual material to some degree and used the instructional value of the immediate feedback to their mastery-item responses. Such a procedure would account for their greater speed in working through the textual material and their inferior performance on the mastery items. That the "feedback" Ss were successful in learning from the immediate feedback to their mastery-test responses is demonstrated by their subsequent performance on the criterion test. Their criterion-test performance was comparable to that of the "no feedback" group, even though their mastery-test performance was significantly inferior.

(16)   An interesting phenomenon to note here is the apparent sensitivity of the learner to subtle procedural cues implicit in the instructional material. For example, one might predict that both the "feedback" and "no feedback" groups would study equally hard on the textual material and that no difference would occur in mastery-test performance between the two groups. Since feedback is not received until after the learner responds to a mastery item, one would expect that on subsequent items over the same material (e.g., the criterion test) the feedback would result in an advantage for the individuals receiving it. However, it appears that "feedback" Ss quickly observe that they need not labor over the textual materials to learn the material to be covered on the criterion test. Where individuals in the "no feedback" group may choose to look on the preceding pages for the correct answer to a puzzling mastery item, an S in the "feedback" group can employ the easier and simpler expedient of marking in succession his highest-order response choice until the feedback indicates a correct response.

(17)   How can one capitalize upon the advantages of the intrinsic reinforcement involved in the immediate feedback procedure on the mastery items while at the same time maintaining the control of the textual material over the reader's learning? One possible procedure would be to provide the learner with extrinsic reinforcement for acceptable performance on the mastery items, as well as for acceptable performance on the criterion test. Thus, performance of the "feedback" Ss on the mastery test should be improved because of the extrinsic reinforcement associated with good mastery performance. The immediate feedback on these items should still serve to facilitate subsequent performance on the criterion test.

(18)   A final word should be said concerning the effect of extrinsic reinforcement in using instructional materials. The differences in the levels of the monetary reinforcement contingency employed in the present study were not of sufficient strength to significantly affect student performance. However, there is little doubt that extrinsic reinforcement is required in the learning task to maintain control of the instructional material over student responses. In the classroom setting such teacher strategies as the use of appropriate verbal statements (praise, encouragement, exhortation, etc.), assignment of perseverant students to preferred activities, and the permission of free choice of student activity upon completion of assigned work may be employed to develop and maintain desired learner responses to learning materials. The use of these strategies and other effective procedures by the classroom teacher is an essential technique for maximizing the effectiveness of instructional materials. No matter how excellent the quality of the material, the student will not learn it well unless he is provided with an incentive for doing so.

DISCUSSION AND CONCLUSIONS CHECKLIST

Indicate whether the following conditions have been met:

Component	Conditions	Conditions Met Yes	Conditions Met No	Comments
Discussion	Presents: 1) Research hypothesis/problem. 2) Major findings. 3) Limitations of the study. 4) Competing hypotheses. 5) Relationship of results to previous research.			
Conclusions	1) Reviews most significant findings. 2) States major conclusions. 3) Discusses implications of findings for educational action or research.			Sometimes Conclusions component is included in the Discussion component.

Now compare your completed checklist with the one provided below. Note that in addition to indicating whether the conditions have been met, the Comments section of the checklist includes notes justifying the check mark and referenced to specific paragraphs in the report.

Component	Conditions	Conditions Met Yes	Conditions Met No	Comments
1. *Title*	Specifies variables, relationship, and target population; not longer than 15-20 substantive words.		X	Independent variable = type of reinforcement contingencies; dependent variable = learner performance (could have been more precisely stated as

Component	Conditions	Conditions Met Yes	Conditions Met No	Comments
				Military Justice Course Test Scores); target population is not specified.
2. Problem Background of the Problem	Presents synopsis of related studies, identifies relevant variables and discusses those selected for the study.	X		Extremely brief— found in paragraph one.
Problem Statement	States research problem and indicates its educational significance.		X	Paragraph two has an approximation of problem statement but it is stated as an interrogative sentence.
Hypothesis	Specific, testable and, if possible, related to theory.		X	No hypothesis is presented.
Research Plan	Identifies research plan/treatments.	X		Paragraph two identifies the treatment condition.
3. Method Target Population and Sampling	Indicates number of subjects, rationale for selection, and representativeness of sample to target population.	X		Described in paragraph three.
Stimulus Materials and Measurement Instruments	Gives complete information (see pages 19 and 20) on characteristics of materials.	X		Described in paragraphs eight to ten.
Design	Identifies relationship of design to hypothesis and shows	X		Described in paragraph four.

Component	Conditions	Conditions Met		Comments
		Yes	No	
	how design controls confounding variables.			
Data Collection Methods	Provides complete description of what was done in conducting experiment.	X		Brief description of experiment procedures and data collection methods is presented in paragraphs five to seven.
Data Analyses	Describes analyses performed, statistical procedures used, and the rationale for their use.		X	Statistical techniques used are presented in Results component.
4. *Results* Substantive Content	1) States research hypothesis/problem. 2) Describes statistical techniques used. 3) Presents level of significance. 4) Provides complete and objective presentation of data (no interpretation).	X X X	X	Identifies statistical techniques used (paragraphs eleven to fourteen) and level of significance (.001); no unnecessary data are presented; and results are presented objectively.
Tabular Presentation of Data	1) Title indicates variables, groups, and statistics used. 2) Headings and labels are clear. 3) Shape of table within acceptable limits. 4) Titles correctly placed. 5) Text reference gives table number, content, and main ideas.	X X X X	X	Table could have been made more specific; in the present form, they could only be fully understood if the text is read.

Component	Conditions	Conditions Met		Comments
		Yes	No	
5. *Discussion*	Presents: 1) Research hypothesis/problem. 2) Major findings. 3) Limitations of the study. 4) Competing hypotheses. 5) Relationship of results to previous research.	X	X X X X	Discussion carefully defines and interprets major findings of the study. It does not, however, indicate what, if any, limitations there may be to the study, nor does it relate results to previous research.
6. *Conclusions*	1) Reviews most significant findings. 2) States major conclusions. 3) Discusses implications of findings for educational action or research.	X X X		In this report, the Conclusions component was incorporated into the Discussion component. All conditions are met for this component.
7. *Summary*	Presents a synopsis of the critical ingredients in each of the above components.		X	No summary is provided in this report.
8. *Abstract*	Usually not over 200 words in length. States: 1) Variables studied. 2) Number and type of subjects. 3) Description of procedures. 4) Synopsis of major findings.	X X X X	 X	Abstract is presented immediately preceding the article. All conditions are met except for procedures synopsis. This was omitted to restrict the abstract length to approximately 150 words.

REFERENCES

Caro, P. W., Jr. "The Effect of Class Attendance and 'Time Structured' Content on Achievement in General Psychology," *Journal of Educational Psychology*, 53(1962), 76-80.

Cook, D. R. *A Guide to Educational Research*. Boston: Allyn and Bacon, Inc., 1965.

Fox, D. J. *The Research Process in Education*. New York: Holt, Rinehart and Winston, Inc., 1969.

Krathwohl, D. R. *How to Prepare a Research Proposal*. Syracuse, N. Y.: Syracuse University Bookstore, 1965.

Muehl, S. "The Effects of Visual Discrimination Pretraining on Learning to Read a Vocabulary List in Kindergarten Children," *Journal of Educational Psychology*, 51(1960), 217-221.

Sassenrath, J. M., and Garverick, C. M. "Effects of Differential Feedback from Examinations on Retention of Transfer," *Journal of Educational Psychology*, 56(1965), 259-263.

Sax, G. *Empirical Foundations of Educational Research*. Englewood Cliffs, N. J.: Prentice-Hall, Inc., 1968.

Sullivan, H. J., Baker, R. L., and Schutz, R. E. "Effect of Intrinsic and Extrinsic Reinforcement Contingencies on Learner Performance," *Journal of Educational Psychology*, 58(1967), 165-169.

Van De Riet, H. "Effects of Praise and Reproof on Paired-Associate Learning in Educationally Retarded Children," *Journal of Educational Psychology*, 55(1964), 139-143.

NOTES

NOTES

NOTES

NOTES

REFERENCES ON INSTRUCTIONAL
PRODUCT RESEARCH

Anderson, T. W. *An Introduction to Multivariate Statistics.* New York: John Wiley & Sons, Inc., 1958.

Baker, R. L. and Schutz, R. E. (eds.) *Instructional Product Development.* New York: American Book Company and Van Nostrand Reinhold Company, 1971.

Barch, A. M., Trumbo, D., and Nangle, J. "Social Setting and Conformity to a Legal Requirement," *Journal of Abnormal Social Psychology*, 55(1957), 396-397.

Barg, W. R. *Educational Research: An Introduction.* New York: David McKay Company, Inc., 1963.

Box, G. E., and Draper, N. R. *Evolutionary Operation.* New York: John Wiley & Sons, Inc., 1969.

Campbell, D. T., and Stanley, J. C. "Experimental and Quasi-Experimental Designs for Research on Teaching," in N. L. Gage (ed.), *Handbook of Research on Teaching.* Chicago: Rand McNally & Company, 1963, chap. 5.

Caro, P. W., Jr. "The Effect of Class Attendance and 'Time Structured' Content on Achievement in General Psychology," *Journal of Educational Psychology*, 53(1962), 76-80.

Chapin, F. S. *Experimental Designs in Sociological Research.* New York: Harper & Row, Publishers, Incorporated, 1947; revised edition, 1955.

Cochran, W. G. "The Design of Experiments," in *International Encyclopedia of the Social Sciences.* New York: The Macmillan Company, 1968, vol. 5, 245-254.

Cook, D. R. *A Guide to Educational Research.* Boston: Allyn and Bacon, Inc., 1965.

Cox, D. R. *The Planning of Experiments.* New York: John Wiley & Sons, Inc., 1958.

Davitz, J. R., and Davitz, L. J. *Guide for Evaluating Research Plans in Education and Psychology.* New York: Columbia University, Teachers College, 1967.

Dial, O. E. *Computer Programming and Statistics for Basic Research.* New York: Van Nostrand Reinhold Co., 1968.

Dubois, P. H. *Multivariate Correlation Analysis.* New York: Harper & Row, Publishers, Incorporated, 1957.

Dunnette, M. D. "Fads, Fashions, and Folderol in Psychology," *American Psychologist*, 21(1966).

Eisenhart, C., et al. *Selected Techniques of Statistical Analysis.* New York: Dover Publications, Inc., 1970.

Educational Resources Information Center. *How to Use ERIC.* Washington, D. C.: U. S. Office of Education, National Center for Educational Communication, 1970.

Edwards, A. L. *Experimental Design in Psychological Research.* 3rd edition. New York: Holt, Rinehart and Winston, 1968.

Feldt, L. S., and Mahmoud; M. W. "Power Function Charts for Specification of Sample Size in Analysis of Variance," *Psychometrika*, 23(1958), 201-205.

Fellin, P., Tripodi, T., and Meyer, H. J. *Exemplars of Social Research.* Itasca, Ill.: F. E. Peacock Publishers, Inc., 1969.

Finan, J. L. "The System Concept as a Principle of Methodological Design," in R. M. Gagne (ed.), *Psychological Principles in System Development.* New York: Holt, Rinehart and Winston, Inc., 1962.

Fox, D. J. *The Research Process in Education.* New York: Holt, Rinehart and Winston, Inc., 1969.

Fry, E. "A Classification of Variables in a Programmed Learning Situation," in J. P. De Cecco (ed.), *Educational Technology.* New York: Holt, Rinehart and Winston, Inc., 1964.

Gage, N. T. *Handbook of Research on Teaching.* Chicago: Rand McNally & Company, 1963.

Gilbert, T. F. "A Structure for a Coordinated Research and Development Laboratory," in J. P. De Cecco (ed.), *Educational Technology.* New York: Holt, Rinehart and Winston, Inc., 1964.

Glennan, T. K., Jr. "Issues in the choice of development policies," in T. Marschak, T. K. Glennan, Jr., and R. Summers, *Strategies for R and D.* New York: Springer-Verlag, 1967, Chapter 2.

Good, C. V. *Introduction to Educational Research.* New York: Appleton-Century-Crofts, Inc., 1954.

Goode, W. J., and Hatt, P. K. *Methods in Social Research.* New York: McGraw-Hill Book Company, 1952.

Greenwood, E. *Experimental Sociology: A Study in Method.* New York: King's Crown Press, 1945.

Guba, E. G. "Guides for the Writing of Proposals," in J. A. Culbertson and S. P. Hencley (eds.), *Educational Research: New Perspectives.* Danville, Ill.: The Interstate Printers & Publishers, Inc., 1963.

Guilford, J. P. *Fundamental Statistics in Psychology and Education.* 4th edition. New York: McGraw-Hill Book Company, 1965.

Gwynn, J. M., and Chase, J. B. *Curriculum Principles and Social Trends.* New York: The Macmillan Company, 1969.

Harmon, H. *Modern Factor Analysis.* Chicago: University of Chicago Press, 1960.

Hill, J. E., and Kerber, A. *Models, Methods, and Analytical Procedures in Educational Research.* Detroit: Wayne State University Press, 1967.

Hillway, T. *Handbook of Education Research.* Boston: Houghton Mifflin Company, 1969.

Hyman, R., and Anderson, B. "Solving Problems," *International Science and Technology*, September, 1965, 36–41.

Kaplan, A. *The Conduct of Inquiry.* San Francisco: Chandler Publishing Company, 1964.

Kerr, W. A. "Experiments on the Effect of Music upon Factory Production," *Applied Psychology Monograph*, No. 5, 1945.

Kerlinger, F. N. *Foundations of Behavioral Research.* New York: Holt, Rinehart and Winston, Inc., 1964.

Krathwohl, D. R. *How to Prepare a Research Proposal.* Syracuse, N. Y.: Syracuse University Bookstore, 1965.

Levine, S., and Elzey, F. F. *A Programmed Introduction to Research.* Belmont, Calif.: Wadsworth Publishing Company, Inc., 1968.

Lindquist, E. F. *Design and Analysis of Experiments in Psychology and Education.* Boston: Houghton Mifflin Company, 1953.

Lindvall, C. M. *Defining Educational Objectives.* Pittsburgh: University of Pittsburgh Press, 1964.

Lohnes, P. R., and Cooley, W. W. *Introductory Statistical Procedures: With Computer Exercises.* New York: John Wiley & Sons, Inc., 1968.

McCullough, J. D. *Cost Analysis for Planning—Programming —Budgeting Cost—Benefit Studies.* RAND Corporation, Paper P-3479, 1966, p. 18.

Muehl, S. "The Effects of Visual Discrimination Pretraining on Learning to Read a Vocabulary List in Kindergarten Children," *Journal of Educational Psychology,* 51(1960), 217-221.

National Science Foundation. *Federal Funds for Research, Development, and Other Scientific Activities,* NSF 65-19, 1965.

Nelson, R. R., Peck, J., and Kalachek, E. D. *Technology, Economic Growth, and Public Policy.* Washington, D.C.: The Brookings Institution, 1967.

Popham, J. W. *Educational Statistics: Use and Interpretation.* New York: Harper & Row, Publishers, Incorporated, 1967.

Popham, W. J. and Baker, E. L. "Rules for the development of instructional products," in R. Baker and R. Schutz (eds.), *Instructional Product Development.* New York: American Book Company and Van Nostrand Reinhold Company, 1971, pp. 129-168.

Ray, W. S. *An Introduction to Experimental Design.* New York: The Macmillan Company, 1960.

Rundquist, W. N., and Spence, K. W. "Performance in Eyelid Conditioning as a Function of UCA Duration," *Journal of Experimental Psychology,* LVII (1959), 249-252.

Sanford, F. H., and Hemphill, J. K. "An Evaluation of a Brief Course in Psychology at the U. S. Naval Academy," *Educational and Psychological Measurement,* 12(1952), 194-216.

Sassenrath, J. M., and Garverick, C. M. "Effects of Differential Feedback from Examinations on Retention of Transfer," *Journal of Educational Psychology,* 56(1965), 259-263.

Sax, G. *Empirical Foundations of Educational Research.* Englewood Cliffs, N. J.: Prentice-Hall, Inc., 1968.

Schutz, R. E. "Research, development, and improvement in education," *Psychology in the Schools,* 5(1968), 303-309.

————. "The nature of educational development," *Journal of Research and Development in Education,* 3(1970), 39-64.

Schutz, R. E., Page, E. B., and Stanley, J. C. "Experimental Design in Educational Media Research," in *Curriculum Guide for a Course in Educational Media Research*. Washington, D. C.: U. S. Office of Education, NDEA Title VII Project B-236, 1962.

Selltiz, C., Johoda, M., Deutsch, M., and Cook, S. W. *Research Methods in Social Relations*. New York: Henry Holt and Company, Inc., 1951.

Sidman, M. *Tactics of Scientific Research*. New York: Basic Books, Inc., 1960.

Siegel, L., and Siegel, L. C. "A Multivariate Paradigm for Educational Research," *Psychological Bulletin*, 65(1967), 306-326.

Siegel, S. *Nonparametric Statistics for the Behavioral Sciences*. New York: McGraw-Hill Book Company, 1956.

Smith, G. R. "A Critique of Proposals Submitted to the Cooperative Research Program," in J. A. Culbertson and S. P. Hencley (eds.), *Educational Research: New Perspectives*. Danville, Ill.: The Interstate Printers & Publishers, Inc., 1963.

————. "How to Write a Project Proposal," *Nation's Schools*, 76(August 1965), 33-35, 57.

Stanley, J. C. *The Improvement of Educational Experimentation*. Madison, Wisc.: University of Wisconsin, Laboratory of Experimental Design, 1965.

———— (ed.) "Improving Experimental Design and Statistical Analysis," *Proceedings of the Seventh Annual Phi Delta Kappa Symposium of Educational Research*. Chicago: Rand McNally & Company, 1967.

Sterling, T. D., and Pollack, S. V. *Introduction to Statistical Data Processing*. Englewood Cliffs, N. J.: Prentice-Hall, Inc., 1968.

Sullivan, H. J., Baker, R. L., and Schutz, R. E. "Effect of Intrinsic and Extrinsic Reinforcement Contingencies on Learner Performance," *Journal of Educational Psychology*, 58(1967), 165-169.

Symonds, P. M. "A Research Checklist in Educational Psychology," *Journal of Educational Psychology*, XLVI (1956), 101-109.

Tatsuoka, M. M., and Tiedeman, D. V. "Statistics as an Aspect of Scientific Method in Research on Teaching," in N. L.

Gage (ed.), *Handbook of Research on Teaching.* Chicago: Rand McNally & Company, 1963.

Tripodi, T., Fellin, P., and Meyer, H. J. *The Assessment of Social Research.* Itasca, Ill.: F. E. Peacock Publishers, Inc., 1969.

U. S. War Department Information and Education Division. "Opinions about Negro Infantry Platoons in White Companies of Seven Divisions," in T. M. Newcomb and E. L. Hartley (eds.), *Readings in Social Psychology.* New York: Henry Holt and Company, Inc., 1947.

Van Dalen, D. B., and Meyer, W. J. *Understanding Educational Research.* New York: McGraw-Hill Book Company, 1966.

Van De Riet, H. "Effects of Praise and Reproof on Paired-Associate Learning in Educationally Retarded Children," *Journal of Educational Psychology,* 55(1964), 139-143.

Veldman, D. J. *FORTRAN Programming for the Behavioral Sciences.* New York: Holt, Rinehart and Winston, Inc., 1967.

Weiss, Eric (ed.) *Computer Usage Fundamentals.* New York: McGraw-Hill Book Company, 1969.

Wiersma, W. *Research Methods in Education: An Introduction.* Philadelphia: J. B. Lippincott Company, 1969.

Wiesner, J. B. "Technology and innovation," in D. Morse and A. W. Warner (eds.), *Technological Innovation and Society.* New York: Columbia University Press, 1966, pp. 11-26.

Willower, D. J. "Concept Development and Research," in J. A. Culbertson and S. P. Hencley (eds.), *Educational Research: New Perspectives.* Danville, Ill.: The Interstate Printers & Publishers, Inc., 1963.

Winer, B. J. *Statistical Principles in Experimental Design.* New York: McGraw-Hill Book Company, 1962.

GLOSSARY OF TERMS

Italicized words in the definitions are themselves defined elsewhere in the Glossary.

Affective behavior	*Behavior* characterized by an emotional response usually differentiated from *cognitive behavior.*
Alternative hypothesis	See *substantive hypothesis.*
Analogous practice	An activity similar but not identical to the *terminal behavior.*
Appropriate practice	An activity identical to that specified or implied by the *behavioral objective.*
Associational study	A study in which the *variate* is potentially manipulable, but is not manipulated.
Behavior	Individual performance which is directly or indirectly observable.
Behavior mode	The physical characteristics of the learner's response, e.g., written, oral, pointing.
Behavioral contract	An explicit agreement, usually between teacher and learner, stating that if under specified conditions the learner does certain things, then a specified consequence will occur.
Behavioral objective	The planned result or specified outcome of instruction as it relates to pupil behavior or product.
Causal relationship	See *statement of causality.*
Cognitive behavior	Behavior characterized by a verbal response. Usually differentiated from *affective* and psychomotor *behavior.*
Computer program	A set of instructions to a computer to perform a specified operation.
Construct	One of five general verb classes used in stating a *behavioral objective* in which the

	learner generates a product (e.g., a drawing, map essay, article of clothing, etc.).
Contingency	The relationship between a specified consequent event and a specified learner *behavior*.
Contingency management	The arrangement of circumstances so that specified consequent events may be made dependent upon the completion of specified learner *behaviors*.
Control card	A *punched card* which specifies basic information required for the operation of a *computer program*.
Control group	A comparison group included in an experiment to assess the effects of environmental *treatment*.
Correlational study	A study which yields *statements of* relationships or *association*, not *statements of causality*. This category includes both status and *associational studies*.
Criterion measure	An instrument or test designed to measure specified outcomes referenced to predetermined objectives and instruction. It is often used as a "posttest."
Cue	A verbal statement providing the minimum information required by the learner to perform the desired *behavior*. A component of an *instructional specification*.
Data card	See *punched card*.
Dependent variable	The *variable* examined in an experiment to determine how it is affected by manipulation of the *independent variable*.
Design	See *research design*.
Describe	One of the five general verb classes used

in stating *behavioral objectives* in which the learner generates and reports the necessary categories of object properties, events, event properties and/or relationships relevant to a designated referent.

Educational outcome	See *behavioral objective*.
Elicitor	Verbal statement used to elicit or bring out the desired response from the learner.
En-route behavior	A *behavior* component not normally expressed in the objective statement but found to facilitate the attainment of the *terminal behavior*.
End-of-file card	The last card of every set of *punched cards*. It signals that all input has been entered into the computer.
Entry skills	The skills and/or operations a learner must possess prior to receiving instruction for a given *behavioral objective*. Also a component of an *instructional specification*.
Environmental conditions	The givens (in testing or instruction) to which the learner must attend in some specified way.
Equivalent practice	Activity in which the learner responds in a manner identical to the *terminal behavior* defined.
Execute card	A card which informs the computer that the end of the *program deck* has been reached and that what is to follow is the information (the data) for a particular job.
Experimental study	Any research study in which a *manipulable variable* is actually manipulated and the defined experimental units are assigned randomly to the *treatments*.

Field	The number of columns in a *punched card* allotted to a particular *variable* score or code.
Finish card	A *punched card* which indicates the end of a data group.
Formulation	The initial stage in the *product development* cycle that leads to the preparation of *instructional specifications*.
Hypothesis	An assertive statement of a tentative relationship between two or more *variables*.
Identify	One of the five verb classes used in stating *behavioral objectives* in which the learner indicates membership or non-membership of specified objectives or events when the name of the class is given.
Independent variable	The *variable* that is manipulated in an *experimental study*.
Instructional objective	See *behavioral objective*.
Instructional outcome	See *behavioral objective*.
Instructional specification	A written guide to the development of effective instruction for a given instructional objective which includes essential instructional and assessment content.
Interval scale	The assignment of numerals to subjects or objects based on equated units of measurement which will permit both statements of order and the amount of difference between categories.
Level of significance	The statistical probability that chance factors alone produced the observed results.
Limits	Descriptions of the characteristics of correct and plausible but incorrect re-

sponses or response choices for the desired *behavior* as essential information for preparing *instructional specifications*.

Manipulable variable

A *variable* having different properties or values to which subjects can be randomly assigned.

Mastery items

Items used to provide the learner practice of the desired *behavior* and assess learner ability to perform the *behavior*. Also a component of an *instructional specification*.

Name

One of five general verb classes used in stating *behavioral objectives* in which the learner supplies the correct verbal label for a referent or set of referents when the label for the referent is not given.

Negative consequence

The presentation of an undesirable condition which increases the probability that the preceding behavior will not occur again under similar conditions.

Nominal scale

The assignment of numerals, letters, or symbols as an identifying label to each subject or object with no ordering of the various categories intended.

Non-manipulable variable

See *non-manipulable variate*.

Non-manipulable variate

A *variable* having properties or values to which subjects cannot be randomly assigned.

Null hypothesis

A statistical statement that there is no relationship between the *variables*.

Operations analysis

The stage in the *product development* cycle in which the adequacy of the procedures which were employed in preparing the product are appraised.

Order

One of five general verb classes used in stating *behavioral objective* in which the learner is given specified instructions

	for arranging two or more class members which are given or must be recalled.
Ordinal scale	The assignment of numerals to subjects or objects which are used to rank order the various categories with respect to some characteristic and the amount of differences between and among categories disregarded.
Population	That portion of a defined universe to which a researcher has access, e.g., all second-grade learners who cannot read beginning word elements.
Positive consequence	The presentation of a condition which increases the probability that the preceding behavior will occur again under similar conditions.
Premack principle	An assertion that of any two activities in which a person is freely engaged, the one in which he is involved more frequently can function as a *positive consequence* for the other one.
Product development	The stage of the *product development* cycle in which the instructional materials are prepared according to *prototype* specifications.
Product revision	The stage of the *product development* cycle in which the results of field tryouts are used to improve the product.
Product tryout	The stage of the *product development* cycle in which the instructional materials are used extensively with appropriate groups of learners to determine product efficacy.
Program deck	A set of *punched cards* containing the *computer program*.
Prototype	The original mock-up or model from which the final product is developed.

Prototype item tryout	The stage in the *product development* cycle in which *prototype* test items are administered to a small number of learners in the *target population*.
Punched card	A rectangular card on which information is stored in the form of specifically located holes.
Randomization	The process of selecting a portion of a *population* in which all members of the population have equal probabilities of being included in the *sample*.
Reactive measures	A measurement procedure which by its use alone, may produce a change in the learner's *behavior*.
Reinforcement	An event which increases the probability that the *behavior* which just occurred will reoccur under similar conditions.
Reliability	The consistency and/or stability of measurement by a test.
Research design	The overall plan or strategy for the conduct of a study. In the statistical sense, it details the *population* specification, *sampling plan*, and data collection procedures.
Sample	A portion (usually a small fraction) of the *population* which has the same distribution of essential characteristics as the *population*.
Sampling plan	A statement which specifies the number of subjects selected, basis for selection, and controls used.
Standards	A statement of the quality or quantity of learner *behavior* in a *behavioral objective*.
Statement of association	An indication of the extent of relationship between the *variate* and the criterion variable.

Statement of causality	An indication of the effect of induced change in the *variate* on the *dependent variable.*
Status study	A research study in which the *variate* is non-manipulable.
Stimulus	A specified environmental event.
Substantive hypothesis	An "if—then" proposition which posits what is likely to occur if various conditions are evoked.
Target population	A group to whom the results of research and development activities are directed.
Terminal behavior	The desired learner *behavior* or end product for any one unit of *behavior* or instruction.
Title card	A *punched card* which instructs the computer to print an appropriate label along with the results of the analysis.
Treatment	A manipulated *variable* in an experiment.
Unobtrusive measure	Criterion data which does not require the cooperation of the respondent.
Validity	An index of the utility of a measuring device.
Variable	Any factor having two or more mutually exclusive properties or values.
Variable format card	A *punched card* that indicates to the program the *field* format.
Variate	Any common characteristic or experience of the subjects that serves as the basis for combining them to form the group or groups being studied, e.g., high school graduation, sex, text assigned, curriculum configuration, etc.

INDEX

INSTRUCTIONAL PRODUCT RESEARCH